JAPAN TODAY

Reluctant Ally

JAPAN TODAY

Reluctant Ally

JAMES CARY

FREDERICK A. PRAEGER
Publisher • New York

BOOKS THAT MATTER

Published in the United States of America in 1962 by
Frederick A. Praeger, Inc., Publisher
64 University Place, New York 3, N.Y.

Library of Congress Catalog Card Number: 62-13744

Printed in the United States of America

For NORMA

Special Acknowledgment

When the riots over the new Security Treaty between the United States and Japan erupted in the spring of 1960, it was part of my job as news editor of the Associated Press Bureau in Tokyo to assign members of the staff to the various aspects of coverage. Consequently, I became acutely aware of the hardships imposed on them as the riots grew in intensity and violence.

All the members of the Tokyo AP staff were pressed into service. At times, they were compelled by the scope and significance of the story to work almost round the clock, frequently in cold, driving rainstorms and under threat of injury from flying stones and the agitated crowds of students who were apt, when excited, to stampede into battle with the police. It was sometimes difficult to keep from getting caught in the middle.

Naturally, in the latter stages of the anti-Treaty campaign, many members of the staff who had worked without let-up for almost a month were nearing a state of exhaustion. They were going mainly on nerve and their determination to do a job that had to be done. The excellence of their performance—imperfect though an operation under such circumstances must always be—is perhaps even more noteworthy because the events were reported by a joint force of both American and Japanese newsmen, every one a seasoned veteran, every one a credit to his nation and profession. In considering the breadth and depth of coverage, I cannot help but feel a deep sense of pride in having been associated with them in their unrelenting efforts to get at the facts and present them in a manner that would have meaning in the context of world events.

This book is largely an outgrowth of that period of turmoil, although the interpretations and conclusions reflect my own thinking. Nevertheless, I shall always be in the debt of these men of the AP staff in Tokyo: John Randolph, general executive for Asia, who, although on home leave at the time of the riots, was responsible for organizing and training the personnel of his bureau; Nathan Polowetzky, then assistant chief of bureau in Tokyo, who guided the entire coverage operation; René-Georges Inagaki, Hiroshi (Day) Inoshita, Kenneth (Kenichi) Ishii, Eugene Kramer, John Roderick, Kay Kanemitsu Tateishi, Takaaki Ishii, Masao (Vic) Takahashi, Torao Tominaga, Yasutaro (Bob) Uchima, Kazuyoshi Francis Ichigaya, Masao (Don) Sawato, Peter Shinobu Higashi, Michio Yoshida, Tadashi Wada, Harold (Hal) Buell, George Imai, Yuichi Ishizaki, Mitsunori Chigita, Makoto Saito, Akio Murakami, Nobuyuki Masaki, Mineo Mizukami, Masashi Kuramitsu, Bunji Watanabe, Reiji Takita, Yoshiaki Jinguji, and Hideyuki Mihashi.

I am also particularly indebted to Itaru Tanaka and Fred Saito of the Japan Broadcasting Corporation, and to Tadashi Wada of the AP staff for assistance in research.

J. C.

Preface

THE MASS OF Communist Asia lies like a dark cloud on the western rim of the Pacific. Along the periphery of the cloud are outposts of the anti-Communist alliance—Japan, South Korea, the Ryukyu Islands, Nationalist China's Taiwan, the Philippines, and South Vietnam. On the lush, tropical island of Guam, 1,300 miles to the east of this forward screen of air, ground, and radar bases, the great war birds of America's Strategic Air Command are based. The powerful Seventh Fleet of the United States, capable of fighting either a conventional or nuclear war, patrols and dominates the area in between.

These are the boundaries of the Cold War in the Far East. Japan is the most vital link and the keystone—the only modern industrial economy in Asia.

Japan's rebirth since the end of World War II is one of the wonders of our age, for it is more prosperous today than it has ever been in its history. Yet, strangely, it is a deeply troubled land. It suffers from an internal form of the ideological madness that has split the world into Communist, anti-Communist, and neutralist camps. But unlike other nations, its allegiance does not lie wholly with any one of the three. Instead, the forces of the Cold War have collided within its borders and left the Japanese people violently divided over which road they should follow to achieve peace and progress.

Although the root of this dilemma reaches far into the past, it has been nurtured and shaped by forces of recent origin. This book attempts to dig out and examine some of the more obvious sources of trouble and show how they produced the explosive anti-Security Treaty riots of 1960—an uprising that is a forewarning of much more turmoil ahead.

Contents

Part Three: The Battle Begins

Part Four: Conflict on the Periphery

Part Five: Japan's Tomorrow

Part One

BACKDROP TO TURMOIL

1. Past to Present

JAPAN'S DIET BUILDING loomed eerily in the darkness over the scene of battle. Nearby, at one of the gates into the Diet grounds, disheveled, near-hysterical students, some of them sobbing and bleeding, their clothes plastered to their bodies by the driving rain, were massing again for a new assault on blue-helmeted police blocking their way.

"Murderers! Kishi's dogs!" they screamed.

It was June 15, 1960. Japan was in turmoil, caught up in a Cold War storm over whether it should remain aligned with the West or adopt a new policy of neutrality.

Wreckage was strewn everywhere. Floodlights erected by television cameramen revealed the charred, overturned hulks of police trucks burned earlier in the evening. Torn, discarded placards proclaiming "Down with the Security Treaty" and "Kishi, Resign" littered the pavement. Remnants of red flags, tires ripped from cars, and lost shoes were scattered through the broad streets leading from the Imperial Palace Moat to the besieged Diet—Japan's capitol and symbol of government. Despite the rain, gasoline spilled from overturned vehicles burned in small rivers of fire; black smoke and the stench of burning rubber filled the air. Ambulance sirens wailed through the darkness; and above it all rose the savage rumble of the mob, mounting to a thunderous roar and subsiding to a beastlike, babbling sound compounded of thousands of voices and the struggles of human bodies.

Before that night was over, the mob had stormed into the Diet grounds twice, sacked a two-story annex that housed the secretariat and a guardhouse, engaged in two bloody fights with massed policemen, burned twenty vehicles, and left nearly 1,000 people injured after a final charge and tear-gas attack by the police. Miraculously, only one person was killed.

To many, Japan seemed perilously close to revolution. For almost a month, marching, chanting leftist columns, sometimes up to 300,000 strong, had roamed the streets of the major cities at will. The police either were unable to control them or never got orders from their superiors to try. The government of Prime Minister Nobusuke Kishi backed away from what seemed the logical solution: calling up Self-Defense Forces under antiriot laws to meet force with force. So the mobs held sway whenever they desired.

The spark that touched off this explosion was a revision and renewal of a treaty originally passed in 1951. The revision authorized the United States to maintain troops and military bases in Japan for at least another ten years, just as it had been doing since the end of World War II. It was this provision, popularly known as the United States–Japanese Security Pact—and the swiftness with which Kishi's forces, without prior notice, pushed its ratification through the lower house of the Diet in a dramatic, postmidnight session on May 20, 1960—that led to the most turbulent period in Japan's postwar history. To Japan's neutrality-demanding, militant left wing—Socialists, Communists, Marxists of many shades, as well as many others imbued with pacifism—this was tantamount to setting Japan on the road to war. To them, admittedly with some justification, the American military bases provided an open invitation to nuclear destruction by the Communist world, and they instigated a series of violent demonstrations aimed at blocking the Treaty's final validation. In the absence of upper-house action, this would have come automatically thirty days after the lower house's approval, and an exchange of ratification documents with the United States.

The upheaval caught most of the Western democracies completely by surprise. Until then, Japan had seemed a stable, northern anchor in Asia for their world-wide, anti-Communist alliance. Now it had suddenly turned into a mad dog seized with an inner frenzy that seemed to defy analysis. What kind of nation was it? Was it on the road to Communism? Would it ever menace the world again as it had in World War II? Had the Communists created this crisis, or did it have deeper, more subtle roots in Japanese psychology?

Any tourist stepping into Japan's raucous, teeming capital, Tokyo, just before or after the riots would have found little indication of social unrest. Tokyo's business districts are jammed daily with milling throngs eager to spend money. Cars glut the streets, and elevated trains rattle by overhead. Policemen's whistles, honking horns, and loudspeakers blaring advertisements fill the air. Skeletons of new buildings rearing against the sky, huge glass-fronted stores, beer halls, bars, glittering cabarets, and lusty night clubs; secluded Japanese inns up a shadowy walkway, fine restaurants, geisha parties, and gawking tourists—all are part of the new Japan, a nation vibrant with the greatest prosperity in its history, a nation busy with myriad tasks. How, then, had it arrived at such a paradox of obvious industry and prosperity on the one hand, and violence and bloodshed on the other?

Modern Japan has been shaped by many forces that have left it a mosaic of paradoxes, of past and present, East and West. Its unique geography and history are among the most important.

From the snow-tipped pinnacle of Mount Fuji on the main island of Honshu, Japan stretches like a rumpled green carpet to the sea. To the north, it emerges as the semiarctic land of bears, forests, and snow that is Hokkaido. To the south, across the picturesque, winding Inland Sea, lies Shikoku, its villages, seaports, and people almost untouched by time. And farther south and east is Kyushu, a curious composite of smoke-belching industries and wind-rippled fields of rice. Four islands—Honshu, Hokkaido, Shikoku, and Kyushu—dropped in a giant festoon off the coast of Asia; four islands caught between two cultures, the Orient and the Occident, between the two great forces dividing the world today, Communism and Western democracy.

The origin of this ancient land of the Mikados is lost in time. Mythology says one of the gods of the universe dipped his spear into the sea and the water dripping off hardened into the first Japanese island. Gods descended to create more islands and to people their shores with a chosen race, the Japanese.

Geological studies, however, indicate quite different origins. The entire Japanese archipelago was torn from the mainland in a great mountain-making cataclysm of the past. For a time, the land lay deep in the sea. Then mountains were formed as the earth's crust buckled and bent, and repeated volcanic explosions hurled debris, hissing and steaming, up through the boiling waves. Higher and higher they thrust until the Japanese island chain was complete, and only the rumbling volcanoes remained to tell of the violent birth. Life-giving rains borne by the winter and summer monsoons bathed the new land and sent short, swift rivers rushing to the sea. Soon the mountains were clothed in pine, fir, cedar, and cyprus, and the plains and harbors were formed.

Until about 2000 B.C., the islands were uninhabited. Then a new Stone-Age Caucasoid people, the Ainus (or their ancestors), appeared, presumably after a migration into Japan from Asia. In the first millennium before Christ, Chinese, Mongols, and Koreans followed. And finally from the south came others, most certainly Malayans, and perhaps even those great voyagers from the South Seas, the Polynesians, to lend a touch of soft, sensuous grace to later generations of Japanese women.

This blend, called by the Japanese the Yamato race, grew rice on the land and hauled great harvests of fish from the sea. It organized tightly knit tribes or clans, concentrated mainly at the eastern end of the Inland Sea, a curving waterway lying between Honshu, Shikoku, and Kyushu. At the head of each tribe was a leader who was supposed to have descended from the heavens, an origin that made him both chief and priest—a dual role still preserved in the Japanese Emperor today. The top clansmen were supposed to be related to the chief by blood and formed, in effect, an aristocracy. Beneath them were workers and slaves, many of them captured members of other clans, who provided the main economic support. These tribal groupings clashed in battle after battle until, by the middle of the fourth century A.D., one clan, the Yamato, from which the Japanese race took its name, emerged supreme. Its leaders became the Imperial family, already enfolded in the myth of descent from the sun goddess, Amaterasu.

In the sixth century, Buddhist priests bore the great culture of ancient China into Japan through Korea. The priests built pagodas and temples with massive bells, whose mellow, booming tones echoed across the countryside at dawn. They brought improved forms of architecture, fine paintings, and sculptures, and they taught compassion for all living things.

In the middle of the seventh century, a centralized government was created, using China as a model, and a capital was erected among the pines at Nara, still a city of shadowy, lichen-encrusted temples, redolent with age. The privileged aristocracy of the clans more and more centered their activities upon the Imperial court. There they grew rapidly in power, for they formed the only group from which the new centralized government bureaucracy could be drawn. In 793 A.D., the capital was moved to nearby Kyoto, where by the ninth century one court group, the Fujiwara family or clan, became dominant. It exercised influence over the Imperial family by furnishing all the Imperial brides and concubines and by encouraging the Emperors to become more and more engrossed in cultural activities—for this was the Heian period, one of Japan's greatest in literature, art, music, and calligraphy—while the Fujiwaras ran the government. Eventually, the Fujiwaras even encouraged Emperors to abdicate and then ruled through the infant Emperors they placed on the throne.

By this time a manor system had been established in the countryside, not unlike that of feudal Europe. Under the reforms that created the centralized government, the Emperor was supposed to assume title to all land and give much of it to the people. Actually, however, the former clan aristocracy received the largest share because it was running the governmental bureaucracy. This led to the rise of a new, powerful class—the warriors or samurai. While the nobles concerned themselves with the soft, almost feminine life at court, the samurai, whose traditions of combat had been forged in campaigns against the barbarian Ainus, administered the estates and became increasingly aware of their own power. An extended period of conflict began, at first involving clashes of rival court groups, in which the samurai fought for their own particular nobles, and then conflicts between warrior groups, which fought more for their own personal interests. Two great warrior families emerged—the Taira and Minamoto. The Minamoto finally defeated the Taira in a great battle at Shimonoseki in 1185, and their leader, Yoritomo, became Japan's first shogun or military dictator.

Thus began seven centuries of military rule in Japan—a rule that was finally ended in 1868 when Emperor Meiji took control of the government from the hands of the tottering Tokugawa shogunate after the reopening of Japan by America's Commodore Matthew C. Perry. Yoritomo, however, moved his capital to Kamakura, near present-day Tokyo, away from the intrigues of the court at Kyoto and onto the Kanto plain, where his power was centered. Then another family, the Hojos, gradually gained control of the shogunate, just as the Fujiwaras had of the Imperial court; they ruled from far behind the scenes, exercising authority largely by naming new shoguns. They carried the concept of indirect rule—a principle still maintained in the influence business interests have over Japan's present government—to great lengths: Eventually there was a puppet Emperor who had delegated a puppet shogun to run the government; but he, in turn, was responsible to a minor member of the Minamoto family who was controlled by an adult member of the Hojo family.

Despite this awkward arrangement, the shogun's armies were strong enough to beat off attempted invasions of Japan by Kublai Khan's golden hordes, first in 1274 and then again in 1281, when the Mongols actually succeeded in establishing a beachhead on northern Kyushu. Japanese forces rushed in from all parts of the country and, with the help of a kamikaze (divine wind) or typhoon, drove the invaders back into the sea. A new threat then arose to the Hojo power: An adult Emperor, Go Daigo, ascended the throne and with the aid of Ashikaga Takauji, who once had been allied with the Hojo forces, defeated the Hojo armies in 1333. But no sooner had Go Daigo gained control of the government than Ashikaga in turn deposed him and placed another member of the Imperial family, whom Ashikaga could control, on the throne. A series of civil wars followed, and Japan fell into serious economic difficulties. Yet even in these dark days the forces of change were at work, for a merchant class, built upon an expanding maritime trade with

China and Southeast Asia, was evolving. It would one day be the most powerful in Japan.

When its first real contact with the West began, Japan was still seriously torn by internal strife. In 1543, three Portuguese sailors were shipwrecked on an island north of Kyushu, bringing with them the first firearms the Japanese had ever seen. In 1549, the Jesuit priest St. Francis Xavier arrived; more Christian missionaries followed, and the faith spread rapidly among the Japanese. By 1600, however, the leaders of Japan decided that the missionaries had taken sides in Japan's internal political troubles and that their insistence on a higher loyalty to God might undermine the feudal loyalties of the manor system. A fierce persecution of Christians followed, and thousands were slaughtered.

While the troubles over Christianity were slowly rising, three great military leaders had marched on stage to bring about the political unification of Japan. First came Oda Nobunaga, a soldier who broke the power of the great Buddhist monasteries and won control of the area between Tokyo, Kyoto, and Osaka. Although he ended the Ashikaga family's hold on the office of shogun, he was quickly succeeded by Toyotomi Hideyoshi, the only commoner ever to become a political leader until then. He attempted to conquer Korea and had dreams of invading China too, but he failed in the former and never attempted the latter. In his declining years, he made strong efforts to ensure that his son Hideyori would succeed him, but after Hideyoshi's death, in 1598, Tokugawa Iyeyasu won control. He decisively defeated Hideyori in 1600 at the battle of Sekigahara and finally broke the last of Hideyori's forces at the battles of Osaka in 1614 and 1615.

Iyeyasu set out to create a system so stable that it would remain unchanged down through the years. He divided the feudal warrior lords into traditional lords (fudai), those who had been allied with him, and outside lords (tozama), those who had either fought against him or remained neutral. He gave the traditional lords most of the more important offices, but all were forced to spend part of the year in his capital, Yedo, the present-day Tokyo, and leave their families behind as hostages when they departed elsewhere.

In the late 1630's, the decision was finally made to shut Japan off from the world in order to protect its new-found political stability. Only a restricted number of Chinese, Korean, and Dutch traders were permitted to remain, but they were kept virtual prisoners at Nagasaki. So Japan's great sleep—a period of more than 200 years—began. It was not interrupted until the industrial revolution in the West had produced the steamship and caused many nations to search for new markets and coaling stations around the globe. This brought Commodore Perry's black ships to Japan and led to the reopening of its ports to trade.

Swift rebirth followed. Japan, fully aware of the superior power of the West after its long isolation, set out to rebuild its society along more modern lines. The Tokugawa shogunate collapsed; the monarchy was restored, and Emperor Meiji ascended the throne to rule in his own right. Obsessed with the fear that, like China, it might suffer the ills of foreign exploitation, Japan quickly learned Western industrial techniques and methods of warfare. In 1894, it startled the world by defeating China in a swift war; in 1905, it emerged as a world power after an amazing victory over Czarist Russia, and both times it added to its empire—from China, Taiwan and the Pescadores; from Russia, South Sakhalin and rights that led to the annexation of Korea.

World War I brought more spoils—the German holdings in China and, under a League of Nations mandate, the Mariana, Marshall, and Caroline islands, scattered like broken strands of pearls across the Pacific. Thereafter, industries mushroomed, pouring out a torrent of cheap export goods that stirred angry charges of "dumping" in major markets of the world. A new exploitation of China began, and the military class, inheritors of the samurai tradition, gained tight control over the government. Then came more agression in China, the annexation of Manchuria as a puppet state, and the eventual extension of the war into China proper.

After World War II began, Japan's militarists seized the opportunity to hurl their armies southward and capture a new empire, which, China included, they had come to call the East Asia Co-Prosperity Sphere. The Philippines, Indochina, Indonesia, Burma, and Thailand were conquered by Japanese armies that surged to the gates of India before the tide was halted. But then a slow rollback began. The island campaigns brought defeat after defeat under the increasing weight of American power. Saipan, Iwo Jima, and Okinawa fell. Bombs rained on Japanese cities, and atom bombs tore asunder Hiroshima and Nagasaki. Defeat, surrender, and finally peace settled over a broken empire. Japan was stripped of all its outlying territories—South Sakhalin, the Kuriles, all holdings on the Asian continent, and the Marianas, Marshalls, and Carolines.

The new Japan that has since emerged, however, is potentially far more powerful than the old. It has a democratic Constitution that begins, "We, the Japanese people . . ." It is gripped by an industrial revolution that is producing vacuum cleaners, washing machines, automobiles, and refrigerators, instead of guns and bullets. In an economic sense, Japan is once again a major power, and national income is at an all-time high. In 1959, for example, it produced 18.3 million tons of steel and in 1960, recording the highest rate of increase in the world, jumped to 24.4 million tons. This amount is more than France produced and much more than Communist China, and it establishes Japan as the dominant economy in Asia for many years to come.

This growing industrial strength has made Japan a priority target of the Communist world. Since World War II, Red propaganda has had but one aim: to separate Japan from America, neutralize it in the Cold War, and eventually bring it into the Communist fold. Then the rest of Asia will be easy prey. A series of conservative postwar Japanese governments has, however, remained unswervingly aligned with the United States and the Western anti-Communist alliance, but a large segment of Japan's population seriously questions the wisdom of this course. Many advocate some form of neutrality or closer ties with Communist nations, particularly with the People's Republic of China. Even in the hearts of the stanchest advocates of the United States alliance, there is the easily detectable fear, born largely of the horrors suffered in World War II, of being caught in the middle of an East-West war.

The Communists have been most skillful in exploiting this fear, for they have constantly bombarded Japan with warnings of eventual atomic destruction unless it casts out the Americans. Japanese students, teachers, workers, and intellectuals, most of whom are not Communists, not only have taken up Communist arguments for neutrality but have repeated them daily until they have created an appearance far out of proportion to the facts.

Thus, the battle is joined both in the realm of international affairs and in the minds of the Japanese people. It is an issue that could yet tear Japan's new democracy apart and will at best have to be endured for many years to come. The basic question is whether Japan should align itself with the West, assume a policy of neutrality, or find a position nearer the Communist powers.

Japan's past has ill-prepared it for the struggle. Since clan loyalties are still strong, Japanese politics are subject to extreme factionalism. There is no tradition of true parliamentary government, which makes the process of debating and enacting new laws very difficult. The ghosts of the old methods of ruling Japan from behind the scenes, as the shoguns did through the Emperor and as some future group could do through the Prime Minister, linger on. Widespread pacifism, especially among women and Socialists; a sense of a deep-rooted affinity for China as the fountain of Japanese culture; a strong fear of foreign intervention; and the always-present Oriental distrust of Caucasians—these have made many Japanese reluctant, if not halfhearted or actually hostile, allies of the United States.

Today 94 million Japanese are crammed into the four home islands, an area the size of Montana, and a million more are being added every year. They are a tough, virile, intelligent people, highly energetic, frequently emotional, self-pitying, illogical, and subject to tormenting feelings of inferiority. But they are brilliant in their ability to organize and produce. They are, without question, one of the most resolute, dynamic, and perhaps potentially great people in the world today, rushing down a road whose direction no one can foresee.

2. Pacifism, Democracy, and Prosperity

LET US BEGIN our story of the new Japan at that tragic moment in history when its cities were burning and the structure of the old militaristic totalitarianism was crumbling in the flames. For it was then that the first of three forces affecting the destiny of Japan was born. It was pacifism—soon to be followed by democracy and prosperity. Pacifism emerged from the fire bombings of World War II. Democracy followed during the Occupation period, when the United States imposed sweeping reforms upon Japanese society. Prosperity was added later by opening American markets to Japanese goods in a deliberate move to tie Japan to the West in the Cold War. Each of the three has played a major role in creating the psychological and ideological ferment that has left Japan such a divided nation today. Each will perhaps play an even more important role in setting Japan's future course.

Japan was in ruins when pacifism arose. Tokyo and sixty-five other cities were choked with rubble. Entire districts were a gray-black wasteland of broken tiles, bricks, charred timbers, tangles of wire, twisted iron, and sifting ashes. Here and there, the scorched husk of a concrete building rose above the wreckage. This was the harvest of a disastrous war, the almost total devastation left by repeated assaults from armadas of B-29's, carrier- and land-based fighter planes, and massed naval gunfire.

The war that had started with such sweeping victories for Emperor Hirohito's forces underwent a slow reversal after the Battle of Midway in June, 1942. And when Saipan, Tinian, and Guam in the Marianas fell to the U.S. Marines in the spring of 1944, the fighting entered a critical stage for Japan. The home islands were now within range of America's giant Superfortress bombers; the raids that followed were to be the softening-up process for full invasion.

Japan was almost helpless to resist the aerial attacks. Throughout the nation, about 2 million people, perhaps 3 million, had lost their lives in the war, and those spared were hungry and in tatters. The Japanese Army was reeling in defeat, most of the Imperial Fleet was at the bottom of the sea, and the merchant marine had dwindled from 6 million gross tons to less than 2 million. The effective fighting forces Japan still had were being hoarded to meet the American landings, expected soon.

Against this background, the B-29's began the final stage of destruction. They turned Tokyo's Broadway, the Ginza, into a flattened ruin; the heart of the capital into a burned-out wilderness. The rich, the very young, and the old moved to the country, and many of those left behind were forced to live in dugouts and caves. "Have you been burned out yet?" became a standard greeting, and people slept in their clothes so that they could make a hasty dash for safety. In all, 178 square miles of the most densely populated areas in Japan's six major and sixty secondary cities were laid waste. More than 300,000 persons were killed, almost equal to America's total combat deaths in World War II; hundreds of thousands more were injured, and millions were left homeless. Only the sparsely populated countryside, the temple cities of Kyoto, Nara, and Nikko, and the smaller communities were spared.

The U.S. Navy played a major role in the devastation, too. On February 16, 1945, Admiral Halsey's carrier aircraft swooped down to attack Tokyo for the first time. On February 25, they struck again. Then they pulled back to participate in the American landings on Okinawa, but on July 10 planes from a fast carrier task force again began hammering Japan, smashing industries and airfields in the Tokyo area. Next, the task force steamed north to pound northern Honshu and southern Hokkaido on July 14 and

15. Heavy fleet units moved in to shell key industrial targets up and down the Japanese coast. On July 17, the Third Fleet cut south to join units of the British Pacific Fleet in lashing Japanese airfields. Battleships shelled the coast northeast of Tokyo again. On July 18, British and American carrier planes discovered concealed Japanese fleet units at the Yokosuka naval base south of Tokyo and damaged many ships. On July 24 and 25, they found other naval ships at the big Kure base in the Inland Sea. They again hit Kure the next day, and on July 30 they turned their fury on Tokyo as battleships shelled the port of Hamamatsu in southeast Honshu.

But it was the B-29's that brought Japan to its knees in one of the great cataclysms of modern history. It had all begun on a clear, brilliant November afternoon in 1944, when the war seemed far away. Although the Japanese people knew that there had been reverses in the island fighting to the south, they lived under a controlled press and had no idea how swiftly the war was closing in on them. Then, as if painted by a giant, invisible hand, a white vapor trail seemed to etch itself slowly across the Tokyo sky. It was made by a lone plane, sailing serenely above the black bursts of antiaircraft fire. People on the sidewalks stopped to stare; others in cars, seeing everyone gazing at the heavens, stopped to look too, and streetcars, buses, and trucks also halted. An eerie silence gripped the capital as the unspoken message of this first American aerial reconnaissance flight from new bases on the Marianas struck home. Other flights followed, and a few weeks later the raids began.

At first, the attacks were not very successful. American losses were heavy and results doubtful. The Superforts were trying to hit strategic targets with the same high-level precision bombing, from 20,000 feet and higher, that the American Air Force used in Europe, but Japan's heavy cloud cover made it difficult to achieve accuracy. Then, on the night of March 9–10, 1945, General Curtis LeMay, chief of the XXI Bomber Command, experimented with new tactics. He stripped the B-29's of armament, loaded them with all the incendiary bombs they could carry, and sent them over Tokyo at night in a long, steady stream at low altitudes—4,900–9,200 feet. Japan's agony had begun.

Although there were many other such raids, that first one and two others on May 23 and May 25 were militarily, at least, the greatest successes. Initial fires spread swiftly before a stiffening wind; when the B-29's spread out to touch off new fires, they merged to form great conflagrations, and heat waves bounced the B-29 crews around the skies as they circled more widely for targets. Tail gunners on their way home reported that they could see the glow of the flames for 150 miles.

During that first March 9–10 raid alone, the 334 attacking bombers burned out 15.8 square miles or four whole wards—Sumida, Koto, Asakusa, and Nihonbashi. They destroyed 22 industrial targets, 267,171 buildings (comprising about one-fourth of those in Tokyo), killed 83,793 persons—more than died in the later atomic blast at Hiroshima—wounded another 40,918, and left more than 1 million homeless. The May 23 and May 25 raids did not kill as many people, but they burned out 5.3 and 16.8 square miles of Tokyo, respectively. By the end of the war, 50.8 per cent (56.3 square miles) of Tokyo had been destroyed. And the five other major industrial areas of Japan—Yokohama, Nagoya, Osaka, Kobe, and Kawasaki—suffered a similar fate. The Japanese who endured the agony of either the March 10 or May 23 and May 25 raids survived a more devastating catastrophe than Nero's burning of Rome, the Chicago fire of 1871, or San Francisco's earthquake and fire in 1906. Of history's great conflagrations, only Japan's 1923 earthquake and the fires it touched off constituted a greater disaster.

The March 10 raid was so successful that the tactics were repeated on other Japanese cities. Although they didn't achieve such spectacular results, they steadily weakened Japan's ability and will to resist. General LeMay's bombers began to raid both night and day and met little resistance; but since they also scattered leaflets that gave advance warning of targets, many Japanese were enabled to reach safety. By May 23, thousands of Japanese had left the capital for the countryside. But Tokyo's fire departments were no better equipped to handle the situation than they had been on March 10. That night, 520 B-29's came in low, and two nights later, while the capital was still smoldering, 502 more were back. Two gigantic bonfires finally merged into one conflagration that swept through the city; the Imperial Palace was damaged, and much of the downtown area was wiped out.

Kimpei Shiba, now editor of Tokyo's English-language daily, *The Asahi Evening News,* was a reporter when the bombers struck. Unable to find a streetcar operating on the morning of March 26, he tried to walk to his office. This is his description of the panorama that confronted him:

> As I reached an elevation, I beheld as far as the eye could see a stretch of ruins. Here and there were a few small, white fireproof warehouses and, in the distance, what appeared to be mist but was actually smoke. The nearer I came to the city proper, the more people I encountered walking in the opposite direction. Halfway downtown in Shibuya, I began hearing disquieting stories.
>
> "Thousands were burned alive in Aoyama," a man told a group of refugees. "It was horrible—like the great earthquake of 1923," someone else added. [Aoyama is only a few blocks from Shibuya, and one of the best-known streets in Tokyo leads from the Aoyama streetcar line to Meiji Shrine. This broad thoroughfare, Yoyogi Street, was built after the 1923 earthquake, partly as a firebreak; during the war years, it was considered an ideal place for residents of congested Aoyama to seek refuge from fire.]
>
> As the B-29's dropped their incendiaries . . . Aoyama was enveloped in flames, and thousands rushed to the wide avenue. The place was soon packed. What I saw when I came upon it shocked me. I could hardly believe my eyes. The entrance to the broad thoroughfare was a sea of corpses. Hundreds had died in what was regarded as a haven of refuge. Leaning against a telephone pole was a dead man, still partly standing. Holding onto the back of a baggage van was another image: There was the figure of a woman kneeling; her face was turned toward Meiji Shrine, and she was bowing—doubtless praying for divine mercy when death overtook her. I turned from this scene, slightly nauseated, and walked north trying to find a friend's house. There was no trace of him. I asked a sentry what had happened.
>
> "Columns of black smoke rose east of Aoyama as soon as the B-29's unloaded their incendiaries," he explained. "We gave the alarm to seek refuge in Meiji Shrine compound, and in no time thousands assembled in the darkness. Many reached the shrine grounds and were saved, but when the bombers dropped incendiaries on the apartment houses on one side of the avenue, the strong

westerly wind blew the flames eastward so that the thoroughfare soon became impassable. Hundreds were trapped and were either burned to death or asphyxiated."

Shiba's journey through the ruins of Tokyo could have been repeated in almost any city of Japan. By the final month of the war, August, 1945, the largest cities were considered destroyed as far as major military targets were concerned. The smaller cities were crumbling fast. The destruction seemed complete.

Soon the Potsdam Declaration was issued, calling upon Japan to surrender; but Japan's militarists refused, despite increasing pressure from Emperor Hirohito. Then the terrible atomic suns burst over Hiroshima and Nagasaki, and Japan's agony was over. On August 15, 1945 (August 14 in the western hemisphere), the Emperor broadcast a message of surrender to his people. In a high-pitched, quavering voice, he read this Imperial Rescript:

> To our good and loyal subjects:
>
> After pondering deeply the general trends of the world and the actual conditions obtaining in our empire, we have decided to effect a settlement of the present situation by resorting to an extraordinary measure.
>
> We have ordered our government to communicate to the governments of the United States, Great Britain, China, and the Soviet Union that our empire accepts the provisions of their joint declaration. . . .
>
> The war has lasted nearly four years. Despite the best that has been done by everyone—the gallant fighting of military and naval forces, the diligence and assiduity . . . the war situation has developed not necessarily to Japan's advantage. . . . Should we continue the fight, it would not only result in the ultimate collapse and obliteration of the Japanese nation, but also lead to the total extinction of human civilization. . . .
>
> We have resolved to pave the way for a grand peace for all the generations to come by enduring the unendurable and suffering the insufferable. . . .

Thus the war ended and Japan endured the unendurable, suffered the insufferable and converted its yearning for a grand peace for all the generations to come into a burning national obsession.

Revulsion against war—pacifism—became almost a national characteristic, seared on the Japanese mind. The Japanese people could not then foresee that a cataclysm of perhaps even greater import than the burning of their cities was awaiting them. Their society was to be made over by a deluge of new democratic concepts and principles. A new voice was to be heard in their land, a voice that spoke in ringing phrases but was completely alien to the Japanese ear.

"We, the Japanese people . . . do proclaim that sovereign power resides with the people. . . ."

This is not the voice of Japan.

"We . . . desire peace for all time . . . the banishment of tyranny and slavery, oppression and intolerance. . . . We recognize that all peoples . . . have the right to live in peace, free from fear and want."

This is not the voice of Japan.

". . . the Japanese people forever renounce war as a sovereign right of the nation and the threat or use of force . . . land, sea, and air forces . . . will never be maintained.

"All of the people shall be respected as individuals. Their right to life, liberty, and the pursuit of happiness shall . . . be the supreme consideration. . . . All of the people are equal. . . . Universal adult suffrage is guaranteed. . . . Every person shall have the right of peaceful petition for the redress of damage. . . . No person shall be held in bondage. . . . Involuntary servitude . . . is prohibited. Freedom of thought and conscience shall not be violated. Freedom of religion is guaranteed to all. . . . Freedom of assembly and association as well as speech, press, and all other forms of expression are guaranteed."

This, too, is not the voice of Japan.

It is that of the American Constitution, the American Bill of Rights, the Declaration of Independence, the Virginia Declaration of Rights, the French Declaration of the Rights of Man. It is Franklin D. Roosevelt's freedom from want and fear. It is Plato and Locke and all the Western philosophers who have contributed to the emergence of the concept of the democratic state. Yet all the quotations are from Japan's post-World War II Constitution, a foreign document imposed on Japan by the American Occupation.

Historically, Japan has been a nation with strong authoritarian traditions—the strict stratification of society, an inferior position for women, an aristocracy that could never accept the premise that every person is equal in the eyes of the law and has the right to say what he pleases. Japan's prewar militarists and police would have rejected any suggestion of renouncing force as an instrument of policy, in either domestic or international affairs. Yet the new Japanese Constitution is a cornerstone of the Japanese state today, even though it may have been laid in sand.

Japan's cities were still in ruins from the fires left by the B-29's when the Constitution was promulgated on November 3, 1946. In the years since, it has taken its place alongside pacifism as one of the major forces influencing postwar Japanese thinking; it represents a set of progressive ideas that Japan has been forced to accept and live by in its continuing search for a better life for its people. It was only one of the many changes the Occupation attempted to introduce after the Pacific war ended on August 15, 1945. In the fields of government, labor, land reform, education, and religion, the Occupation tried to create in America's own image a new nation with the shape and form, if not the traditions, of a democracy. It gave Japan a government freely elected by the entire adult citizenry; it freed the forces of organized labor to seek a greater share of social and economic justice; and it fulfilled the age-old yearning of Japan's tenant farmers to own their own land. It ripped the poisonous nationalistic hatred from textbooks that had long imprisoned the Japanese mind, and it permitted the press to print news as it saw fit, without dictate from the government.

Long before General Douglas MacArthur's plane landed at Atsugi Air Base, near Tokyo, to begin the Occupation, plans for this great experiment in democracy had been under study. Research on the United States postsurrender policy began in 1942; the goals were laid down in the Potsdam Declaration of July 26, 1945, and crystallized in President Truman's policy statement of September 6, 1945.

Briefly, they were as follows: disarm and demilitarize Japan to make certain that she never menaced the world again; break up the economic concentrations of power that provided the basis for Japan's war machine and throttled competing business enterprises; mete out stern justice to war criminals; strip Japan of all territory but the four main islands and such minor outlying islands as might be determined; create a peaceful, responsible government; encourage development of individual liberties and respect for human rights, particularly the freedoms of religion, assembly, speech, and press; eliminate ultranationalists and militarists from public life and from the school system; reorganize education to eliminate nationalistic bias and encourage students to explore new ideas; encourage the formation of democratic political parties and labor unions; and destroy the tenancy system of Japanese agriculture.

These goals were fulfilled in whole or in part. But how well the reforms succeeded, or the extent to which they failed, is a matter for appraisal later; yet the tremendous scope of what was attempted can easily be illustrated here.

Except for its major and secondary cities, Japan is blanketed with tiny farms. Intensely cultivated, they are green carpets of rice seedlings in the spring and summer; golden fields of ripened grain in the fall, placid and picturesque to the eye. But, historically, they were the cause of tension in prewar Japan.

No man knows their history better than Wolf Ladejinsky, the American specialist who has studied the Orient's land problems for years and who engineered much of the land reform during the Occupation. "A tenant farmer paid roughly 50 per cent of his crop in rent," he recalled in an interview long after Japan had regained her independence. "He had to pay for fertilizer and other things, too. He could keep no more than 25 to 30 per cent of his crop. Consequently, the Japanese village was full of unrest. Under the influence of Communist propaganda, it could have been a very serious political situation during the aftermath of the war."

Serious it was indeed. An estimated 40 per cent of Japan's population was then bottled up on farms, working an average tract of 2.7 acres, one-third of the holdings being less than 1.2 acres. Of the approximately 2.8 million farm operators, 2 million were tenants who year after year, just for the privilege of working the land, had to turn over half or more of what they raised to the owners of the land. By the time a tenant had paid as well for the materials he needed to raise his crops, he had been forced to the very brink of starvation.

Such exploitation made at least 47 per cent of the farm population a floating, restless surplus. These people served as a source of cheap labor for factories, and from the Meiji period on, as the main source of manpower for Japan's militarists. The young farmer, indeed, made an excellent soldier for Imperial Japan's purposes; he was physically strong, subservient to authority, and had far less reason than most soldiers to be concerned with the means he and Japan used to better their lots.

This situation was one the American Occupation tried to change. It ordered the Japanese Government to buy up farm land from the landlords at prices fixed by the Occupation authorities. Absentee landlords were required to sell all their land; noncultivating landlords living in local communities near their land had to sell all but one small holding. The land acquired—27 million plots comprising 4.6 million acres—was turned over to the tenant farmers, who were given up to thirty years to pay for it. In addition, rent ceilings were imposed on land not redistributed; farm cooperatives were encouraged to help farmers buy the fertilizer and other supplies they needed; and a system of farm credit on reasonable terms was established. The result was a reform that gained overwhelming support from most of the Japanese population and laid at least one firm footing for Japan's postwar climb out of the old feudal-fascist-militarist state toward the goals of democracy that beckoned ahead.

In education, too, a massive enterprise was launched—the rewriting of textbooks. "From primary grades on, the Japanese taught nationalism and hatred of white people," Miss Helen Heffernan, who served for fourteen months with the Occupation in Tokyo, pointed out. "Even in arithmetic problems, you had such examples as this: 'If you can kill x number of white people with one grenade, how many can you kill with 10?' When you took out the propaganda, you didn't have much but the back cover left."

The power to control the contents of texts was taken away from the Education Ministry and vested in education committees established in each of the forty-six prefectures and five major cities. Some Communists and ultranationalists were thrown out of the school system; nine years of free education became compulsory; schools were made coeducational; curriculums were standardized and revised to include many more social and cultural studies. "Morals" courses, which had been one of the militarists' principal means of molding the Japanese mind, were banned, and the number of high schools, colleges, and universities was greatly increased.

One educational goal was dropped: the effort to convert Japanese script from Oriental characters to a romanized form. It was, admittedly, a complex problem, one of far-reaching importance to Japan's future generations, and there was strong resistance to the proposed change. Had it succeeded, however, Japanese students might have been freed of years of drudgery—years that could have profitably been used in acquiring other disciplines of knowledge.

The attempt to break up Japan's Zaibatsu, the great industrial combines, was probably the most complicated of all the reforms undertaken. The Occupation approached the problem cautiously and without sufficient knowledge of the extensions of these huge complexes into many, many fields of industrial enterprise. But by the end of 1949, the eighty-three holding companies through which the Zaibatsu had exercised much of their power had been dissolved, and fifty-six Zaibatsu family members were excluded from positions of responsibility. Eleven of the largest firms were ordered to divide into separate smaller concerns; six other companies were directed to make structural changes or to stop certain activities that restrained trade. The government took over 216 million shares of salable stock and sold more than 120 million shares, one-quarter of it to former employees of the companies involved. Japan's nine major electric-power companies were placed under governmental regulation, and another 1,200 concerns were deprived of their intercorporate holdings.

The other Occupation changes are well known. The major war criminals were hanged or imprisoned. Japan was completely disarmed until the Korean War broke out, and only small Self-Defense forces have been created since. Its empire was cut back to the four main islands, a few coastal islands, and the Amami Oshima islands of the Ryukyus, which were returned later. A vigorous party system and labor movement were launched. Political prisoners, including 150 Communists, were freed. The state and the Shinto religion were separated. Basic civil rights and a democratic form of government were outlined in the new constitution.

At first glance, it would seem that any program of such a sweeping, revolutionary nature was bound to fail before it started. It is most certainly true that imposing democracy from the top down, rather than letting it rise from the bottom up—that is, from long years of yearning and agitation by the people themselves—is not the best way of building a viable political system. There is ample evidence, of course, that much of what was attempted has failed; the riots of 1960, the distorted view of parliamentary government held by Japanese intellectuals, and some of the strange concepts voiced by teachers and even university presidents attest to this. But the Occupation reforms loosed tremendous torrents of change in Japan and their ultimate effect cannot be foretold. Japan was shaken up and stimulated, and the native democratic feeling that did exist was given an opportunity to grow. Japan came face to face with a vast array of new ideas and is still struggling to absorb, understand, and use them. And while it struggled with these problems of the mind, it was busy rebuilding its economy with a dash and brilliance that has startled the world.

The story of a city, Yawata, in northern Kyushu, testifies to that economic rebirth. Ugly and bleak, Yawata squats along the slopes of Mount Sarakura and spills across the flat valley below. Monotonous concrete apartment buildings line scores of its streets. Heavily loaded freight trains rattle continuously into this sprawling metropolis of 300,000, and big iron-ore carriers from mines in Malaya, the Philippines, Goa, and Canada unload at the modern docks of the nearby port of Tobata. In the distance are the dirty waters of Bokkai Bay. At night, the flares of blast furnaces redden the sky. In the daytime, a heavy pall of smoke, emitted by 600 stacks, hangs over the city. Pittsburgh, Detroit, Manchester, Magnitogorsk, the Ruhr—these are the cities and areas the scene immediately evokes. For Yawata is a steel town, the heart of Japan's resurgent economy, home of the Yawata Iron and Steel Company—the largest in Japan and one of the largest in the world.

In the final months of World War II, B-29's devastated the Yawata works, leaving behind twisted wreckage, gutted buildings, shattered factories. So effective was the bombing there and at other plants that Japan's steel production dropped from a wartime peak of nearly 8 million metric tons of crude steel in 1943 to less than 2 million tons at the time of the surrender in 1945. Then began the slow climb back with the help of the Occupation. In 1951, Yawata, like many other plants, started a modernization program, scheduled to run for five years. In 1956, a second modernization and expansion plan was launched, and by 1961, Japan had outstripped both France and Great Britain to become the fourth largest steel producer in the world.

In 1961, Japan poured 31 million tons of steel from its open hearths and blast furnaces, an increase of more than 550 per cent over the 4.8 million tons produced in 1950. And plans were mapped for turning out 38–40 million tons by 1970. Today, Japan is topped in this widely accepted measure of a nation's economic strength only by the United States (99–117 million tons), the Soviet Union (72 million), and West Germany (37.6 million). And tomorrow—1970—Japan could even nudge aside Germany in its thrust toward a level of production and consumption never before dreamed of in a teeming, formerly feudal land opened to trade with the world only a little more than a century ago. This, in effect, could mean that Japan had attained the third most powerful economy in the world.

Japan's economic accomplishments are particularly remarkable because it has so few natural resources upon which to build heavy industry. It has low-grade coal in abundance, and some iron-bearing sands and pyrites. But it has to import at least 58 per cent of its iron ore, 48 per cent of its coking coal, and most of its scrap. Even 20 per cent of its food and virtually all of its oil, cotton, and wool must be brought in at heavy cost. Foodstuffs and raw materials alone account for 85 per cent of its imports.

Japan, truly, has only one great source of wealth—its people—and it has exploited them to the fullest. From the earliest times, Japan's farmers have been among the most industrious and successful in Asia. According to one theory, Japan's capital accumulation, which distinguishes it from other Asian nations today, began with its farmers. Long before Commodore Perry forced the Tokugawa shogunate to open Japan to trade in 1853, Japanese farmers were working in their tiny fields with characteristic industry to produce two crops of rice a year, while farmers elsewhere in the Orient were reaping only one under similar circumstances. This led to a rice surplus in those early days before Japan's population explosion. And a rice surplus meant a negotiable commodity —purchasing power—that could be used to obtain other goods and thereby increase the wealth of the nation.

After Perry's arrival, the same energy was quickly applied in other fields to train the technicians needed by modern industry. The fate suffered by a backward China at the hands of European powers in the nineteenth century served as a goad, for Japan realized that it had to hasten modernization or risk the danger of being similarly exploited. By 1882, the first blast furnaces were constructed, and by World War II Japan had become a modern power in every sense of the word. But what has happened since the war far outstrips all Japan's economic accomplishments of the past.

If you could stand at the pinnacle of Mount Fuji and look with telescopic vision across the land, you would see belching smokestacks of fifteen more steel companies and the massive factories of electronics, chemical, textile, and machine-tool industries. You would see huge cranes gliding over the unfinished hulls of new ships at Kure and Inoshima; endless miles of cotton fabrics rolling through washing, bleaching, printing, dyeing, shrinking, starching, and pressing machines at Osaka; red-hot billets sliding, hissing, and steaming through wire-rod works at Kobe; the slow pouring of optical glass at Tokyo; thousands of fishing boats dotting the sea, and trains endlessly clattering to ports crammed with the commerce of the world.

In the few short years since Japan surrendered in 1945, it has grown these economic muscles: It leads the world in shipbuilding and fishing haul; it is third in textile production; its foreign-exchange reserves have stood for several years comfortably over $1 billion and in 1960 reached a record-shattering $1.82 billion; industrial production is more than double that of the prewar boom period of 1934–36, and 1960 exports soared to a postwar high of

$4 billion—17.3 per cent higher than in 1959. This included $1.5 billion worth of goods sold to America.

How did it happen? How could any nation so broken and prostrate as Japan was in 1945 recover so quickly? Even the Japanese are not certain. The Economic Planning Board attributes the swift recovery partially to "A desire to lift ourselves from the depths of poverty . . . a serious but not total war damage to production facilities . . . United States aid [$2 billion in postwar assistance and more than $4 billion in special-contract and U.S.-troop yen purchases receipts] and strong efforts to curb inflation. . . ."

The general prosperity that buoyed world economies after World War II, the stimulus of Korean War orders, and Japan's organization of society from top to bottom to promote production also certainly played a part. Anyone who studies Japanese public affairs soon realizes that the nation's economic impetus often begins with the government, for it is directly involved or closely associated in all production. Sometimes, this takes the form of subsidies to put an industry on its feet; sometimes, there is partial or total ownership of company stock (in 1959, the government had investments valued at $2 billion in fifty-nine corporate organizations); and frequently there is at least close liaison to make certain that raw materials are made available.

Unlike the practice in the United States, where production is normally conducted without government involvement, in Japan almost no major phase of economic activity—particularly in the production of goods for export—is free of government participation—at least as a silent associate. This is one of the key differences between Japan and the other nations of Asia—its total organization for production. From the Prime Minister on down, every person gainfully employed in Japan has a contribution to make toward keeping exports streaming out of Japan's ports and the necessities of life streaming in. Despite this, probably the biggest reason for Japan's recovery has been the opening of the American market to Japanese products. The $1.5 billion Japan exported to the United States in 1960 was more than five times as much as it sent to any other nation, an astonishing record considering the resistance provided by American enterprise.

Japan's postwar industries began recovering rapidly under the stimulus of the Korean War and the industrial contracts it brought with it in 1950. It averaged an 11 per cent increase in production annually between 1950 and 1959, when the curve soared to 16 per cent. In the fiscal year 1961, while the government was heavily braking the demand on foreign exchange reserves, the gross national product still soared to $40.4 billion, a 13.4 per cent jump over the previous fiscal year.

By 1955, the torrent of products gushing from Japanese factories was overflowing home shores and bringing screams of anguish from some sectors of the American economy. The states of South Carolina and Alabama, for example, passed laws requiring merchants to display signs stating, "Japanese textiles sold here"—obviously with the intent of discouraging sales of the Japanese products. U.S. textile-industry representatives complained that their cotton blouse sales dropped 30 per cent, gingham 47 per cent, and velveteen 71 per cent under the Japanese "hit and run tactics" of concentrating on a few key markets. They reported the curtailment or cancellation of expansion in seven mills in South Carolina, Virginia, and Massachusetts, and the abandonment of plans for a new plant in Texas. Japan, fearing reprisals, cut back annual cotton-blouse exports through a self-imposed quota system, and the crisis subsided. One incongruity was that some of the Southern American states whose textile industries complained most were at the same time benefiting greatly because Japan was buying American cotton, grown in their states, with which to make the goods. An almost equally serious situation developed in umbrella frames, tuna-fish exports, pottery and porcelainware, plywood, photographic equipment, high-fidelity speakers, stainless-steel tableware, and ready-made clothing. Some American restrictions were eventually imposed.

But both America and Japan handled the situation with considerable wisdom. The U.S. State and Commerce Departments suggested that such crises could be avoided by diversifying Japanese exports, by placing more emphasis on quality rather than on cheap goods. Japan took the advice, imposed strict disciplines on its own industries, particularly in those sensitive fields that had been hit too hard in the American market, and reluctantly turned to more expensive lines, although obviously harboring great doubts that much good could come of it. But $2 billion in exports in 1959 and 1960 stand as proof that the effort was successful, and the final limits are not in sight. Japan's orderly exploitation of the American market seems virtually unlimited.

But America, too, has profited. Japan spent $1.11 billion on American purchases in 1959 and $1.3 billion in 1960, making it, next to Canada, the United States' best customer. This means that if those advocating high tariffs to keep out Japanese products ever seriously threaten again, they may find themselves opposed by an equally strong economic bloc supporting the trade.

While this revolution in Pacific trade was under way, Japan's own internal economy was undergoing equally startling changes. Vacuum cleaners, washing machines, dishwashers, electric refrigerators, television sets, and automobiles poured onto the market from its own factories. At first, they were only dream products for the rich to enjoy; then they slowly came within reach of those groups bordering on the wealthy, and now they have invaded middle-income families to the point where they are desired by almost every Japanese, not only because they are useful and provide comfort but because they are symbols of success, of the better life. Now one of every four Japanese families has a television set. This "keep-up-with-the-Suzukis" psychology has brought with it another familiar feature of American life—installment buying. Nearly 10 per cent of the refrigerators, washing machines, and television sets purchased is by deferred payments, a process enhanced by high-pressure advertising tactics such as the filmed advertisements presented in virtually all motion-picture theaters.

Thus, prosperity has spread throughout Japan. Per capita income has jumped from $130 annually in 1953 to $433.12 in fiscal 1961—still very low by Western standards but bolstered in Japan by additional benefits in many occupations. National income soared to more than $25.5 billion and industrial production jumped 78 per cent over 1955. Millions of farmers, fishermen, factory workers, and housewives for the first time in their lives found they had surplus cash to invest. Investment trusts, created in 1951, gave them an easy access to the stock market; since then, the trusts have acquired more than 200 billion yen ($555 million) of stocks or about one-tenth of the 601 issues on the Tokyo Exchange.

"The Japanese stock market has been transformed from an area for speculators into a gigantic pool of millions of invisible investors," one financial expert said. Konosuke Koike, Oxford-educated chairman of the board of Yamaichi Shoken, Japan's biggest securities company, agrees. "A new era has opened," he said.

More than 9 million Japanese—one out of every nine—have entered the market in this manner and sent Japan's average of 225 active issues rocketing upward from 167.80 yen (46.6 cents) to more than 1,350 yen ($3.75) over a period of ten years. But, despite this increased activity, investment capital remains one of the great limitations in Japan's economy today. Anyone or any institution with money to lend can command interest rates ranging from 12 per cent to more than 20 per cent. It is in this field that the banks remain supreme and exert tremendous influence over Japan's business life. Without credit, even the biggest industrialists cannot expand. Therefore, it has been said that those who control Japan's banks—and through the banks the right to decide which enterprises are worthy of financial support and should have access to the limited capital at Japan's disposal—are the men who truly rule Japan. Whether or not this is entirely true, those who control the extension of credit do have within their hands, in an economic sense, the power of life and death over one of the most volatile and powerful economies in the world.

At the heart of the economy is the Bank of Japan, a government-controlled and 80 per cent government-owned institution, which discounts all the negotiable paper of the other major banks. The demand for credit is so great, and the supply so limited, that banks in Japan have frequently operated without reserves, keeping their cash constantly in circulation and relying on the Bank of Japan for what further backing is needed. This hunger for investment capital has been insatiable; as long as it continues, and capital continues to be pumped in as fast as possible, Japan's economy will continue to expand.

The towering heights that could be scaled in the future are already visible. The Japanese Economic Council, an advisory organ to the Prime Minister, has made these predictions:

Exports will rocket to $8.4 billion by 1970 and $11.1 by 1980.

Gross national product will advance from $27.04 billion of 1956 to $65.22 in 1970 and to $106.24 by 1980.

Mining and manufacturing will increase 6.5 times over 1956–58 levels.

Per capita income will rise to $794 by 1980.

The economy will grow 7 per cent a year until 1970 and 5 per cent annually from 1971 to 1980, a total advance of 120 per cent, or double the present level, plus 20 per cent more.

This expansion, launched while Japan was paying off more than $1 billion in war reparations, contrasts sharply with the expansion taking place in nearby Communist China, the former fashioned by a free-enterprise economy, the latter by a controlled economy. Increased production in any given field of a free economy actually represents a much broader and greater accomplishment because it requires increases in other fields to make it possible. Tsutomu Kawasaki, Research and Statistical Chief of the Japanese Iron and Steel Federation, once put it this way, in commenting on boosting the output of steel: "It is not easy to produce steel. You have to produce technicians, increase power and transportation, obtain more water, and provide industries to consume the steel after it is made."

Douglas MacArthur II, then U.S. Ambassador to Japan, spoke in a similar vein at the Japanese International Trade Fair at Osaka in 1959:

> Now there is no doubt that a totalitarian government can effectively mobilize people and resources for particular goals, such as building heavy industry. A Communist regime has two advantages in this respect. It can force individuals to work where the regime wishes them to work and . . . it can deny to its people many of the basic requirements of everyday life, so that the state can have a command of more goods and services. . . . But even at the cost of liberty and human dignity, does it follow that the Communists do, in fact, have a superior system for expediting economic development? It seems to me that the Japanese people, of all people, have made clear to the world that the answer is no.

It is of course part of an ambassador's job to say nice things about the nation in which he is stationed. But even if what MacArthur said is not entirely true, in the long run the basic premise is. Japan cannot move people and capital around with the abandon of Communist planners. If large amounts of its investment capital are to be used to increase steel production, there must be an adequate indication that the markets for Japanese steel can use the increased output and pay for it. This means that more automobiles, refrigerators, ferro-concrete buildings, ships, and other steel-consuming products must be built and sold. And more steel must be exported to obtain the foreign exchange with which to purchase the raw materials needed for the expansion. Thus, in one sense, the leap in Japanese steel output from a low of about 500,000 tons in 1946 to a projected 38–40 million tons by 1970 represents an equivalent percentage of increase in a wide segment of Japan's entire economy.

The prosperity that has resulted from the continual economic expansion has most certainly started to build a better life for millions of Japanese and has given the nation the beginnings of a middle class. The better organized labor groups, for example, have done quite well. In five major industries, wages average the equivalent of $62 a month, in addition to a wide range of fringe benefits, often including housing, medical care, transportation, and the chance to purchase many necessities at special prices. This form of patronage is common in Japanese industry.

But in addition to these well-treated working groups, there is a vast sea of people who work from dawn until dusk over wheels, lathes, and other small equipment set up in their homes to turn out components of a larger product assembled at nearby factories. These are the cottage industries that have accounted for a large part of Japan's ability to produce in the past, but the income from such work is often negligible and just enough to keep a family alive.

Still, there are others much worse off. Some live in giant ragpickers' villages in the slums of Tokyo and other major cities; some have settled down as squatters in Tokyo's famous Ueno Park, and thousands live in shantytowns scattered throughout the nation. Those who cannot find work in the cities often drift back to the farms from which they came, an excess labor force whose potential can be only partially used in rural areas and whose income remains pitifully low. There they remain, dammed up, a great reserve of manpower that could send Japan's production soaring to undreamed-of pinnacles if ever tapped and properly channeled. Those who do not have a farm to return to are the true unemployed in Japan. How many there are is difficult to say because Japan classifies anyone who works one hour a week as gainfully employed. Some sources have estimated that Japan's unemployment by Western measurements ranges from 5 to 10 million—far, far too many in a nation enjoying the greatest prosperity in its history.

But, despite this poverty, Japan has indeed been reborn and the resurgence of its industries is a testimonial to the ability of its people and Japan's potential as a nation. At the same time, it was partly this growing economic power that set the stage for an international tug of war over Japan's allegiance in the East-West fight for dominance in the world.

3. Outline for Conflict

As the gigantic outline of the new Japan emerged, its rebuilt industries, skilled people, and strategic geographical location off the coast of the largely Communist Far East made it a prize in the Cold War struggle.

To the Communist world and its planners in Moscow and Peiping, Japan presented a paradox. On the one hand, a Japan aligned with the Western democracies would be a powerful enemy to be feared, subverted, sabotaged, and yet, if possible, lured into a friendlier attitude. On the other hand, a Japan brought into the Communist fold could be a rich industrial source, whose modern methods and factories could supply the means to alleviate the poverty of the peoples under Communist control.

Important as Japan was to the Communists, it was even more important to the United States. For Japan would be the logical U.S. ally in the Pacific, analogous to the British in the Atlantic—the foundation for a great bridge stretching from London, through Washington, to Tokyo, spanning the world's two major oceans, and dominating the areas on their periphery.

But to millions of Japanese, despite an apparently widespread desire to remain loosely aligned with the Western democracies, the new power of their economy meant something entirely different. It represented a hope of gaining a more independent role, of achieving a position between the two contending giants of the world, the Soviet Union and the United States. In this way, Japan could free itself from obligation to both and perhaps escape the obliteration it felt was inevitable in a nuclear war.

Thus, at a critical period of history, three contending ambitions springing from three different sources collided in Japan. They resulted in a titanic struggle for Asia's only modern industrial power. The stakes were very high: Whichever of the two great power blocs controlled Japan would dominate the western Pacific, and the one dominating the western Pacific would be in a position to control vast, undeveloped resources and millions of people.

The Communists could not at first even hope to bring Japan under their domination, let alone into full membership as a satellite within the Communist fold, for America, by right of conquest, was already deeply entrenched in Japan. But if the Communists could only maneuver Japan into a position of neutrality, this in itself would deny the West the use of Japan's economic might and would be a step toward eventual domination.

So Japan was the key in a struggle of much broader implications than was apparent at first: The entire postwar balance of power in Asia was involved. For example, Yokosuka Naval Base near Yokohama was particularly important to America. Since the end of World War II, it had been the Far East pivot of the U.S. Seventh Fleet, and it had the only facilities in Asia capable of drydocking aircraft carriers. If the base and its 10,000 Japanese technicians were ever denied to American arms, the Seventh Fleet would have to shift repair operations thousands of miles across the Pacific to Pearl Harbor. Sasebo, another base used by the U.S. Navy, was of almost equal importance, and other good harbors were available, if needed, at Tokyo, Nagoya, Hakodate, and Kure.

Geographically, too, Japan was significant. Situated directly on the Far East's Cold War frontier, its four main islands extended southward from a point off the Soviet maritime territory more than one-third of the way down the remainder of Asia's coast. This 1,200-mile segment, lying astride almost the same temperate-zone latitudes as the American East Coast from Maine to the northern border of Florida, was laced with air bases that could be used either for offensive or defensive purposes. It was also shielded by a fine radar net to help guard against surprise attack. In effect, then, Japan was a gigantic, unsinkable aircraft carrier poised only 200–500 miles off Communist Asia, and if lost, the world's anti-Communist defenses would be breached from the Aleutians to the Ryukyus. For these reasons, it was one of the most coveted geographical-industrial complexes in the world, second perhaps only to West Germany.

The United States recognized Japan's strategic importance very early and attempted to do something about it. During the Occupation, as we noted, the United States set out to lay the foundations of a healthy, democratic society aligned with the West and responsive to the needs and aspirations of its people. It prevented the Soviet Union from taking over the northern main island of Hokkaido after the Japanese surrender; it provided at San Francisco, in 1951, a peace treaty called by the Japanese themselves "a treaty of reconciliation"; it linked American military might to the future of Japan with an accompanying security treaty that provided for American military bases to remain in Japan indefinitely. (This was the predecessor of the treaty that touched off the 1960 riots.) Finally, it waived any claim to reparations, and it opened its markets to a flood of Japanese goods—such a flood, in fact, that a nation which had been considered simply the "Workshop of Asia" emerged as a commercial giant stumping five continents in search of raw materials and markets.

But even while this apparent American-Japanese partnership was being forged, multiple fears and pressures, which under more normal circumstances would have made Japan seek neutrality, were at work. They created deep tensions even among those who felt with their minds, but not with their emotions, that this new role was in Japan's own best interest. The most imperative of these pressures was Japan's long-range problem of making a living. True, the new torrent of trade with America had brought unprecedented prosperity, but many Japanese felt it was bound to be transitory. In the postwar years, Japan had had a deficit of $500 million or more annually in its international balance of trade; that is, it was spending that much more in purchases abroad than it was earning through sales of its own products. This gap was covered through indirect earnings from the United States, particularly yen purchases by American troops and offshore contracts let by the American military forces, both of which served, in effect, as temporary subsidies.

The only logical solution, it seemed, was for Japan to seek markets wherever it could, including markets in the Communist world—a plan that was strongly advocated by left-wing forces, which sought to break the growing ties with the United States. Japan particularly wanted to trade with Communist China, since it was a market of great future potential, and it did so on a limited and private basis until 1958. But then, after a dispute about its right to fly the Red Chinese flag over a proposed trade mission in Tokyo, China angrily closed its doors to all further commerce with Japan. China has demanded full diplomatic recognition as the price for reopening its markets, a concession virtually impossible for Japan to give because of its commitments to the United States. This dispute has placed the American alliance in direct conflict with Japan's deep affinity for China, the source of its culture, and provided good emotional fuel for the leftist campaign to push Japan toward neutrality.

Another pressure has been the deeply rooted fear of foreign exploitation. The entire Meiji period (1867–1912) serves as a prime example of such a phobia. Since Japan had seen Western colonialism in nineteenth-century China, the appearance of Commodore Perry's black ships in 1853 had reawakened fears of similar exploitation. And little more than a century later, the post-World War II alliance with America evoked stirrings of the same emotions.

But the strongest of all the reasons for seeking neutrality was Japan's vulnerable geographic position between the Communist and anti-Communist worlds. With memories of World War II bombing still fresh in mind—particularly the horrors of the atomic holocausts at Hiroshima and Nagasaki—the Japanese understandably disliked becoming a priority target for the nuclear rockets of either side.

And finally, since the Soviet Union kept tight control over some of Japan's choice fishing waters in the north Pacific (off Sakhalin, the Kurile Islands, and the Siberian coast), it was in a position to bring pressure upon Japan whenever it desired simply by restricting access to these waters and thus cutting down on a prime source of

Japanese food. It has done exactly that every year when the annual authorized quotas are negotiated with Japan; as a result, Japan's permitted catch has dropped from 120,000 tons in 1957 to 67,500 tons in 1960, and the areas from which its fishing fleets have been excluded have been steadily expanded.

Thus, by 1960, a great postwar struggle for the allegiance of the Japanese was well under way. The Communist world, attempting to deny its enemies access to Japan's industrial wealth, and to divert that wealth into Communist channels, confronted America and the Western alliance, which had equally compelling reasons for retaining and strengthening their bonds with Japan—to maintain firm control of the West Pacific and anchor down their holding action against Communism in Asia.

In the middle were the Japanese people. They needed the aid and financial assistance of America and its Western philosophy of democratic liberty to continue their efforts to erect a new nation with far more ambitious social and economic goals than Asia had ever known before. But they were reluctant to accept the risks that went with this role.

The result was a psychological rebellion among at least a highly vocal minority against the strange new course their nation was pursuing—alignment with a Caucasian nation; an alignment that was sweeping Japan along a path running directly counter to multiple pressures to seek neutrality; an alignment that was destroying old familiar patterns and replacing them with the new, untried, and unfamiliar.

The ingredients of the struggle, then, were powerful forces pulling from the East, powerful forces pulling from the West, and psychological unrest—a volatile and dangerous mixture.

The development that brought these ingredients into their first explosive contact was the proposed revision in 1958 of the U.S.–Japanese Security Treaty. In particular, Japan wanted to substitute for the provision permitting America to maintain military bases in Japan indefinitely, an authorization that could be terminated after ten years, upon a one year's notification by either side. But although the new Security Treaty contained many more favorable provisions than the old, it represented to many neutrality-minded Japanese a reaffirmation by a now-independent Japan of an alignment they felt had been forced upon a weak and subservient nation at the signing of the San Francisco Peace Treaty. The reaffirmation also appeared to provide a direct challenge to the Communist aim of driving Japan into neutrality and an opportunity for Japan's left wing to destroy the concept of alignment with America. Furthermore, it was a challenge to Japan's deeply embedded fear of war, and it provided Japan's restless, divided, and repeatedly defeated Socialist Party with an issue it hoped would rebuild its political fortunes.

Japan, therefore, was soon torn into two warring camps. On the left were the anti-Treaty forces, centered around the Japanese Socialist Party and including the giant Communist-influenced 3.6-million-member labor federation Sohyo, the Japanese Communist Party, the radical student federation Zengakuren, and a wide array of Communist propaganda fronts. On the right and in the center were those favoring the Treaty, who worked largely through Prime Minister Kishi's Liberal-Democratic Party. They included the pre-World War II Zaibatsu industrial combines, which were slowly re-forming; some of the leaders of prewar Imperial Japan; nearly all of Japan's organized business interests; many conservative Japanese citizens who believed that the Treaty, although it made them uneasy, offered the best course for the country; and the new rightist groups, who became more active as the Japanese Communists stepped up opposition to the Treaty.

The Liberal-Democrats charged that those fighting revision of the Security Treaty were the handmaidens of international Communism, and the Socialists fired back with accusations that the Liberal-Democrats represented the forces of reaction that wanted Japan, with American help, to revert to a warlike, militaristic nation. A verbal battle raged for months, and, as a result, thousands of Japanese students, intellectuals, workers, and even many conservatives came to identify the Treaty with war. The Soviet Union encouraged this view with repeated warnings that American bases placed Japan in great danger of becoming involved in an East-West war, and it threatened that if the bases were ever used against a Communist nation, nuclear annihilation would follow. To underscore the point, the U.S.S.R. periodically launched giant rockets over Japan into the central Pacific.

So Japan was caught between East and West. Culturally, it stood with one foot in the Oriental past and one in the largely Western present. Geographically, it lay between a Communist-dominated mainland and an American-dominated Pacific. Politically, it was divided between forces of the left, deeply influenced by the teachings of Karl Marx, and conservatives of the right, many of whom only a few years before had been leaders in prewar, fascist Japan. Strategically, it was an industrial prize coveted by both sides, and ideologically, it was a battleground for the conflicting concepts of each, with the forces of the left leaning more and more toward acceptance of Communist views and the forces of the right casting their lot with the Western anti-Communist alliance.

Out of these swirling crosscurrents Japan emerged as a largely pacifist nation, deeply afraid of the horrors of modern warfare, but with more democratic freedoms and prosperity than it had ever known before. The far left played upon Japan's pacifist feelings to undermine the alliance with the United States. The democratic society provided the freedom of action the far left needed to create unrest and confusion—one of the goals of the Communist Party—and the prosperity reinforced the convictions of Japan's powerful conservative leaders that they must fight off the assault from the left and maintain the alignment with America, whose trade had made the economic progress possible.

This was the pattern of conflict and division that the Japanese Communist Party, with the assistance of Moscow and Peiping, set out to exploit prior to and during the 1960 riots over the Security Treaty. It was one of the most influential of all the groups lining up to battle for the allegiance of Japan in the coming Treaty crisis, and obviously its preparations had been under way for many years.

Part Two

THE STRUGGLE FOR JAPAN

4. Communism

AT FIRST IT WAS only a spark brought into Japan with other Western ideas of the Meiji period. From this insignificant beginning, about 1889, the influx of left-wing political thought into Japan grew stronger and stronger over the years and eventually became a small but persistent fire of two flames—one, revolutionary socialism or Communism; the other, nonrevolutionary socialism, varying in character from the moderate, parliamentary traditions of the Social Democrats in Europe to a pure Marxism that differed very little from Communism. To Japan's authoritarian government, each represented an equally dangerous challenge to the privileges of a class society; increasingly severe methods were employed to stamp out these flames. In the years immediately preceding World War II, the repression appeared to have succeeded completely. But the fire continued to smolder within Japan, while outside the nation it was kept alive by political exiles and the international Communist movement. When the war ended, the embers were quickly fanned back into life.

The progress of the two flames, which until the end of World War II seemed almost to have merged into one, can be traced by listing events that took place along the way: the formation of Japan's first labor union at about the turn of the century; the organization in 1901 of a Social Democratic Party that was dissolved the same day by the government; the founding of the Japanese Socialist Party in 1906 and the Japanese Communist Party on July 5, 1922; the government's counterattack with passage of the notorious Peace Preservation Law in April, 1925—a statute with provisions broad enough to stamp out any heretical new thinking; the severe crackdown on leftists in 1928, 1929, and 1933, when thousands were thrown into jail; the militarists' rise to power from 1931 to 1937; the establishment, after World War II, of a democratic society that permitted the Socialists and Communists to operate openly with few restraints; the cleavage of Japan into two bitterly opposed groups divided along roughly the same lines as those dividing the world in the Cold War; the formation of the People's Council Against the Security Pact—the Japanese Communists' first truly successful popular front—in an attempt to crush the alliance with the United States; and, finally, the riots of 1960 that followed ratification of the Treaty in the Diet.

These were the high points in the development of Japan's proletarian movement, but the story is far more than a recitation of such dates and happenings. It is made up of the material of living history, of people and feelings, their aspirations for a better life, and particularly their efforts to find a creed that offered more hope of attaining such a goal than had the unyielding dogmas of the past.

In the beginning, the movement included many people concerned with the well-being of their fellow men. There were Japanese Christians, whose faith had survived the brutal persecutions of the 1600's, teachers, professors, intellectuals, and many others of strong, humanitarian persuasion. At secret meetings, they discussed the new ideas, and then began operating more openly, giving lectures and conducting small gatherings. Many of the disciples, pushing handcarts piled with literature provided by foreign sources, carried their message into the most remote corners of the nation. This agitation led to formation of the first Japanese Socialist Party, an organization destined to survive only two years. In 1908, to dramatize their cause, the Socialists marched into downtown Tokyo, waving red banners and singing revolutionary songs. Police descended on the column. They surrounded and arrested the marchers, and ultimately the twelve leaders were executed.

Under such crushing retaliation, Japan's tiny group of Socialists and budding Communists was silenced, but constant efforts to rekindle the fire continued abroad. When the first congress of Communist organizations of the East convened in Moscow, in November, 1918, a resolution was adopted that set up an international propaganda department with one division assigned solely to dealing with Japan. In 1921, Grigori Zinoviev, President of the Comintern—the international arm of Communism—told the Third Comintern Congress in Moscow that the Communists "must secure a foothold" in Japan.

History helped him to reach his goal. The period following World War I was one of greatly increased liberalization in Japan, and the leftist fires were soon burning again. A Japanese delegation, including Mosaburo Suzuki, later Chairman of the Japanese Socialist Party, attended the First Congress of the Toilers of the Far East, held in Moscow in January, 1922. Again Zinoviev spoke, and this time he virtually prophesied both the fight international Communism would wage in the succeeding years for control of Japan, and the important bearing this would have on Communist success elsewhere in Asia:

> The Japanese proletariat holds in its hands the key to the solution of the Far Eastern question. . . . The presence at this Congress of the representatives of the Japanese workers is our only serious guarantee that we are at least starting on our way to a true solution of the problem. . . . The only thing that can really solve the Far Eastern question is . . . the final victory of the revolution in Japan.

With this recognition, the Communists made 1922 one of their most successful years in Japan. On July 5, 1922, the Japanese Communist Party was founded, followed in November by the organization of a student federation that spawned the first Communist cells in Japanese universities. It is not surprising that many intellectuals were among the initial Party members, and to this day, the intellectual has been the prime Communist target in Japan. This is not to say that all professors, teachers, scientists, and writers who joined in the Communist movement even at its very beginning were professional revolutionaries, but some were and most became quick and willing converts to the Marxism that was then gaining ground in Japan, and was to produce manifold difficulties later.

The first student cells included the New Man Society at Tokyo Imperial University (renamed Tokyo University after World War II) and the Cultural Association at Waseda. The New Man Society quickly fell under the domination of Yoshio Shiga, a brilliant student of political economy and an ardent Marxist who later became a Communist Party leader. During this same period, Communists infiltrated the scholastic system of Japan so successfully that Marxian economics, interpretations of world affairs, and concepts of class warfare soon became standard fare in the curriculums of most schools; and Marxism's ready-made answers for perplexing problems have had a strong appeal to the Japanese mind ever since. This, in turn, has made it possible for the Communists to find a particularly receptive audience in groups dedicated to intellectual activities. The Communists soon discovered that by boring into such organizations they could maneuver a large segment of the articulate members of Japanese society over to their side in many international disputes. To exploit this potential to the fullest, an entire section of the Party was assigned to infiltrating what the Communists called "cultural front organizations."

Soon young Japanese intellectuals were going to Moscow for training and study, and Communist cells were planted in farming communities, factories, government agencies, and the armed forces. The flames lighted by that tiny spark more than three decades before reached such threatening size that the government took countermeasures. The Peace Preservation Law was enacted and a roundup of radicals begun. In 1928, the crackdown became severe. More than 2,000 people were arrested for Communist activities that year, and all left-wing student organizations were dissolved. Among those taken into custody was Dr. Hajime Kawakami, Chairman of the Economics Department of Kyoto Imperial University and Japan's leading authority on Marxist theory. More arrests in 1929 and again in 1933, when 15,000 people were picked up, virtually extinguished the Communist-Socialist fires for all practical purposes, and they remained so until after World War II. The Communist leaders jailed included Yoshio Shiga, who in the early days had been the leader of the New Man Society, Kenji

Miyamoto, Kiuchi Tokuda, and Sanzo Nozaka. Unlike Tokuda and Shiga, Nozaka was released in 1931, after two years' imprisonment, and made his way to Moscow. Meanwhile the militarists headed Japan down the road to totalitarianism. In 1931, without the sanction of the Japanese Government, the militarists launched a war of conquest in Manchuria. Six years of assassination, intimidation, and coercion ensued in Japan, and by 1937, the militarists were in complete control of the Japanese state.

At this time, the fate of Japanese Communism was largely in the hands of one man—Nozaka—a brilliant and dedicated disciple of Marx and Lenin, whose life had equipped him well for the job. Nozaka was born into a poor family on March 30, 1892, in Hagi, on the north shore of the Japan Sea directly across from Korea. At fourteen, he became an orphan and went to live with an elder brother who operated a lumberyard in Kobe. In high school, he developed such an interest in socialism that when he entered Tokyo's Keio University at eighteen, he neglected his studies to devour Japanese and foreign books on socialism. Nevertheless, he graduated second in his class. In 1919, he went to Britain to study in the London School of Economics under a dour little man named Clement Attlee, later a Prime Minister of Great Britain. Nozaka's political orientation soon moved far to the left, and he became a charter member of the British Communist Party. He spoke frequently at Communist meetings—an activity ended abruptly by Scotland Yard in 1921. He was summoned, charged with radicalism, and ordered to leave the country within seventy-two hours. Nozaka visited France, Switzerland, Germany, and Russia before returning to Japan, in the spring of 1922. There he joined the Japanese Communist Party, founded that year.

Nozaka's subsequent flight to Moscow put him in position to make the next major move to aid Japanese Communism when the opportunity presented itself, in 1940. He had come to know the Soviet leaders well, including Premier Stalin, and convinced them he should go to Yenan, the cave capital of Red Chinese leader Mao Tse-tung and headquarters for his Eighth Route Army. There, in a whitewashed cave, Nozaka began the labor of making over the minds of captured Japanese prisoners. He started with a class of ten but thousands more were subjected to his indoctrination sessions.

"What causes war?" he asked as they sat in a circle around him. "What future do you have as workers in Japan?"

Slowly the seeds were planted. The prisoners were given a cause they thought would bring them a better life; they were given symbols to hate and blame for all their ills—capitalism and imperialism; they were given a sense of belonging, of being part of a larger team; and, most of all, they were given a philosophy that provided answers to banish all uncertainty. Life was fixed. There was only one course to follow, and the rewards of peace and plenty lay at the end of the road.

Armed with this religion, cadres from the school in Yenan began infiltrating Japanese lines in China, singing nostalgic songs of home, scattering leaflets, and carrying messages to undermine Japanese fighting spirit. In 1943, Nozaka predicted the coming defeat of Japan and issued an "appeal to the Japanese people" to rise up and establish a "people's government." When Japan surrendered, in August, 1945, he ordered all his agents, cadres, and students into Japan and prepared to follow himself.

Recalling his parting from Mao Tse-tung, who has since climbed almost to the pinnacle in the Communist hierarchy, Nozaka related: "Mao clutched my hand. 'Do your best to create a new Japan,' he said. I promised to meet him again when this task was done."

Nozaka walked, rode horseback, traveled by oxcart, and even hitched a ride on an American military plane to reach Japan on January 10, 1946. With the backing of Japan's Communist chiefs, Tokuda, Shiga, Miyamoto, and others, who had been freed by an American Occupation directive of October 4, 1945, Nozaka immediately proclaimed what has come to be called a "lovable" Communist Party policy for Japan. The Communists hailed the American Occupation troops as liberators and endorsed Occupation objectives, since these coincided with the first two stages of Nozaka's three-stage plan for creating a "people's government" in Japan: (1) the destruction of Japan's authoritarian, militaristic state by a democratic revolution; (2) the establishment of a Western-style capitalistic democracy; and (3) the destruction of capitalism and the establishment of a socialist (Communist) order.

The lovable policy meant that the Communist Party would be willing to remain relatively peaceful for a few years, but it did not mean that the Party would slacken its drive to win over the Japanese mind. Two tactics quickly became clear—the search for a united front that would give Communists the mass support they needed to overthrow the government, and the effort to exploit the deep, almost psychotic Japanese fears of being abused by a foreign power. Basically, these were the motives behind the verbal offensives of Communist speakers in the Diet during the early postwar period. They constantly attacked government leaders as traitors, fascists, and servants of foreign imperialism. "Foreigners are attempting to enslave Japan," they said. "The government is subjecting Japan to the complete domination of foreign monopolistic capital. This is a prelude to transforming Japan into a colony of foreign imperialists." The conservatives were always pictured as partners of the foreigners in enslaving the Japanese people. Nozaka, who was soon after elected to the Diet, became one of the most effective speakers in disseminating such themes.

This was a time for relighting the banked fires of Communism that had smoldered through the war, and in this the Communists had help from both the Soviet Union and the United States. The first of thousands of Japanese soldiers, brainwashed in Siberian prison camps, returned to Japan, many of them singing Communist songs and showing every indication of being new converts ready to march under the banner of Lenin—although it is doubtful many of them retained this orientation for long. Those who did, together with the Communists who came out of hiding, held repeated rallies in Tokyo's Hibiya Park, freely and openly conducted under the benevolent protection of U.S. Occupation forces. The Communists would march in, bearing their red flags, plant them in a semicircle around the outer edge of the crowd, and then proceed to shout demands that "capitalist imperialism be smashed" while white-helmeted U.S. military police stood impassively by, protecting this display of Japan's new freedom of speech from any form of interference.

The Communists also worked hard but not too successfully at

creating the united front they needed if they were to come to power. The Socialists were a prime target. The Socialist left wing, under Mosaburo Suzuki, who had been jailed in the 1930's for his political beliefs, was receptive, for it advocated largely the same goals as the Communists. But the right wing, under Suehiro Nishio, was strongly opposed, and middle groups, under Tetsu Katayama, who later was Prime Minister in a short-lived Socialist-coalition government, preferred more moderate company.

The Communists likewise spent considerable time trying to draw workers, farmers, intellectuals, and even small businessmen into joint efforts to achieve popular moderate objectives under their direction. They infiltrated unions, particularly those of government and public workers; they bombarded Japan's teachers, students, professors, professional writers, artists, actors, doctors, and journalists with Communist ideas. In 1948, they founded Zengakuren, the All-Japan Federation of Student Self-Government Associations, which later became the most violent of all the Communist-created arms in Japan—so violent that its extremist left wing was denounced by the Communist Party itself for refusing to accept Communist direction and control. Efforts to win over Japan's farmers, however, foundered, largely because the Occupation's land-reform program had succeeded. Some "Red" farm villages were created by 1948, but only a few; and Japan's farmers to this day have remained a firm backbone of conservatism.

Japanese Communism reached its peak in 1949: 100,000 acknowledged Party members and 35 seats in parliament. But this success was quickly reversed in 1950 by two events: a thunderbolt from the Cominform, which had replaced the Comintern as the international arm of world Communism, and the war in Korea. On January 6, 1950, an editorial in the Cominform newspaper sharply criticized Nozaka's "lovable" policy in Japan; it accused him of attempting to modify Leninism to suit Japanese conditions. The Japanese Communist Party, bowing with typical subservience to higher authorities, acknowledged "errors" and turned to more violent tactics. A short time later, four Americans were mauled and stoned by Communist demonstrators in Tokyo, and 600 Japanese staged a violent demonstration against the then Premier Shigeru Yoshida. With a storm brewing, General MacArthur, the Occupation commander, on June 6, 1950, directed the Japanese Government to remove and henceforth exclude from public service the twenty-four members of the Central Committee of the Japanese Communist Party. The next day, the order was extended to the seventeen editors of *Akahata* (*Red Flag*), the Party newspaper. Thus, the Occupation—which had released the Communist leaders from prison, legalized their party, permitted them to infiltrate Japan's new labor movement, and allowed them to publish and distribute Communist literature—finally had to step in and stamp out the fire again. But the Communist hierarchy, apparently forewarned of the coming war in Korea, began slipping into hiding or sped to China aboard high-speed, radio-equipped boats disguised as fishing vessels, which came to be called the "People's Fleet." A few days later—on June 25, 1950—North Korean tanks rumbled across the Thirty-eighth Parallel in Korea, and the war was on.

Some ensuing cases of sabotage directed at hindering the movement of American troops and equipment to Korea were traced to the Japanese Communist Party and the JCP was linked with a North Korean spy group that gained valuable information on the Inchon landing of September 15, 1950. But most members of the Party were driven underground and found it difficult to operate effectively while the Korean War lasted. Finally, with that bitter conflict approaching its prolonged but final stages, the United States and twenty-six other nations signed the San Francisco Peace Treaty that restored Japan's sovereignty as of April 28, 1952. Some Communists promptly reappeared, and on May 1, 1952, a group of the unions they controlled broke loose from a column of labor-union demonstrators and raced for the broad plaza in front of the Imperial Palace. Police had forbidden them to use this area and blocked their way. Japan's worst May Day riot was on. The rioters overturned and burned cars. Two American sailors were hurled into the Imperial Moat. Police and rioters were stoned and clubbed. Acid was thrown on several participants, and hundreds were injured. That violent outbreak hurt the Communist cause greatly in public eyes. A gradual shift in tactics followed—from the violence ordered by the Cominform in 1950 back to the more peaceful forms of infiltration and slow erosion of Japan's capitalist system advocated by Nozaka.

On August 11, 1955, Nozaka, Shigeo Shida, and Yojiro Konno, three of the Communist leaders who had fled to China in 1950, suddenly reappeared at a left-wing rally in the Aoyama district of Tokyo. Later that same night, they gave themselves up at Metropolitan Police Headquarters. A few days later, they were released on grounds that the regulation they had violated was an Occupation directive no longer in force since Japan had regained her independence.

The years they had lost had not hurt the Communist organization in Japan. Those manning the home front while Nozaka, Shida, and Konno were in China had painstakingly built up one of the best Communist propaganda networks ever established in a capitalist nation. It consisted of such front organizations as the Japanese Peace Council, a branch of the Communist-dominated World Peace Council. The Committee was a very active organization with 138 branches and 40,000 members, most of them non-Communists drawn into the Committee's program by sincere pacifism. Another component was the Japanese-Soviet Friendship Society, which was also functioning actively at that time, with 420 members. There were numerous other groups with parallel aims: the Japanese Council for Abolition of Atomic and Hydrogen Bombs, the Japan-China Cultural Exchange Association, the People's Council for Restoration of Japan-China Relations, and the China Research Institute.

Many of these groups were linked through a system of "interlocking directorates," that is, a few hard-core Communists whose names appeared on the executive boards of many other similar organizations. They spread their activities into many fields, disseminating literature, translating Communist works, bringing in cultural groups from Communist nations, sponsoring expense-paid tours of China and the Soviet Union, and even teaching workers to sing the "Internationale" in four-part harmony.

The network was used very effectively as the months slipped by, and its potential for promoting increased contact with the Communist world was greatly enhanced when Premier Ichiro Hatoyama restored diplomatic relations with the Soviet Union early in 1957. The two nations exchanged ambassadors, although they could not agree on a full peace treaty because of conflicting claims to the southern Kurile Islands.

So by late 1959 and early 1960, the period immediately preceding the outbreak of the Security Treaty riots, the Communists were ready for a new big push in Japan. They were small in numbers—perhaps no more than 50,000—and their organization had suffered some setbacks: exposure of a fund-raising group known as the "Truck Corps" in March, 1958; the arrest of ten seamen and the seizure of a 34.5-ton vessel that was a key part of the "People's Fleet" for smuggling goods, money, and people into and out of Japan; and the severe worsening of trade relations between Japan and Communist China in 1958 as a result of the trade-mission flag incident. But in spite of these disruptions, the Communists could be heartened by many things. First, their membership was probably much stronger than their admitted figures indicated. An estimated 25,000 Communists failed to reappear as Party members after the lifting of the ban imposed by the Occupation in 1950. It is likely that many of them are deep-cover members, strategically placed in labor unions, government ministries, publications, and schools. Second, Japan was tense and restless over the revised Security Treaty, which would soon come to a vote in the Diet. Thousands were convinced it would lead Japan into war. There was the continued presence of American troops in Japan, painful reminders to a proud people of their nation's defeat and surrender. And there were the obvious results of the Communists' skillful manipulation of such emotional issues as Japan's alignment with the United States and concurrent estrangement from China; the wide cleavage between rich and poor in a land that had already known too much of such economic disparity.

But perhaps the greatest of all the Communist assets in this period immediately preceding the 1960 riots was Nozaka himself, the Chairman of the Japanese Communist Party. His very effective role in Japanese affairs had been that of a predator hunting for and exploiting signs of weakness in a powerful prey—Japanese capitalism. To him, there was only one goal in life—the creation of a people's (Communist) government in Japan. Completely sincere and dedicated in pursuing this goal, he was the single most formidable opponent the forces favoring Japanese democracy and parliamentary government had to face, for Nozaka is an expert on the psychology of his people. His tactics have always demonstrated his acute awareness of their fear of foreign exploitation and a resurgence of militarism, and of their basic repugnance toward violence coupled with a strange and contradictory capacity for resorting to violence when convinced it serves a worthwhile cause. Then, too, he has long known that the Japanese Communist Party can succeed only if it can enlist other groups to fight its battles in a common front. In understanding this basic premise, Nozaka has shown far more acumen than his bosses in the Soviet Union and Communist China, whose judgment of how fast he could move in Japan has not always coincided with his. Not once has he made the mistake of deciding prematurely that the moment had arrived for the Communists to make their bid for power, although it seemed almost at hand at the peak of the 1960 riots.

Nor has Nozaka ever lost sight of the fact that the Communists' greatest gains have been scored by invading the minds of Japanese students, teachers, and intellectuals of all types, much more than those of the workers, who are often the No. 1 target of revolutionary socialism elsewhere in the world. Anyone who has seen leftist demonstrators from any of these groups storming through the streets of Tokyo cannot doubt the power of this man. Most who turn out for these protests are not Communists, but the willingness with which they carry out a program tailored precisely to Nozaka's purposes is, to a large extent, the measure of his skill. And when you talk to a typical Socialist, a typical student, a leader of the radical labor federation Sohyo, or some—though by no means all—professors or other members of the intellectual class, you soon realize how well Nozaka and his predecessors have done their jobs. For each in his own way all too often expresses beliefs that are exactly what the Communist Party will want them to believe when and if it ever attempts a coup. Should that day come, the Communists will know that the Socialists and some of their leaders will have helped prepare the way.

5. Three Men on the Left

INEJIRO ASANUMA lumbered across the stage at a political rally in Tokyo's Hibiya Hall, spread his papers on a podium in front of him, and in his gruff, rasping voice began an attack on Japan's conservative government, as he had so many times in the past. Suddenly, a youth in a Japanese black school uniform hurtled across the stage and drove a short sword into his chest. The Socialist Party Chairman staggered away from the dais, his face contorted into a mask of pain; his horn-rimmed glasses spilled down across his broad nose, and both hands came up, palms outward, as if in supplication. With a wild cry, the student again drove the blade into his victim's body, and five minutes later Asanuma was pronounced dead at the hands of seventeen-year-old Otoya Yamaguchi. Thus, at 3:10 P.M. JST, on October 12, 1960, Asanuma became a martyr to the cause to which he had dedicated his life—the Socialist Party of Japan.

Asanuma was a virtual personification of the party's most outstanding qualities—its overwhelming concern with Marxist ideology and class warfare, its contention that Japan should be neutral in the Cold War, its opposition to the alliance with the United States, and its advocacy of closer ties with Communist China. Often called dull, fat, and bumbling, he still was a man who unstintingly gave of himself to lead Japan toward a social and economic order that he felt would relieve the historic poverty of its toiling masses. Because of his beliefs, he lived all his life in meager circumstances, was arrested twenty-eight times, and was expounding the Socialist viewpoint when he was cut down at the age of sixty-one.

Asanuma, at five feet eight inches, was a mountain of a man, resembling a sumo wrestler more than an aspiring politician. He appeared to weigh far more than the 210 pounds he claimed. His rotund, short legs supported a mammoth trunk, a bulging belly, and powerful shoulders; his head was large, framed by double chins and bushy, black hair. Viewed directly from the front, he had a certain owl-like quality: small, black eyes peering from horn-rimmed spectacles; a generous mouth, black mustache, and flat nose—all of which belied the capacity for invective he could hurl at his political enemies.

A raucous, brawling orator, Asanuma liked nothing better than to mount the back of a truck to harangue leftist formations outside the Diet building, to shout for the downfall of the government. There, surrounded by friendly faces, his chest puffed out, arms flailing, eyes smoldering, and voice rolling in grandiloquent Japanese oratorical style, he had his fleeting moments of glory. But despite the cheers, despite his popular appeal, despite the crowds he drew wherever he went, Asanuma was a failure: He failed to achieve very many of the Socialist goals in a lifetime of effort. And his failure is in a sense the measure of the failure of his party to develop a leadership that could seize the great opportunities for democratic progress which existed in Japan at the end of World War II. Instead of becoming known for their efforts to benefit humanity, both he and the party became increasingly identified with violence in the Diet, riotous street demonstrations, a "neutralist" orientation in world affairs that many thought was heavily weighted toward the Communist side, and a virtually meaningless struggle over whether the party should be a strictly working-class affair or should draw support from all levels of Japanese life.

Asanuma was born in December, 1898, on the tiny Pacific Island of Miyake, one of the seven Izu islets 100 miles south of Tokyo. Miyake had been used in feudal days as a place of exile for political prisoners. Perhaps that climate of rebellion impressed Asanuma in his formative years, for early in his life he became gripped with an obsession for challenging authority and remaking Japan's authoritarian government. By selling a small, carefully hoarded herd of cattle, his father scraped together enough money to send him to Tokyo's Waseda University, but the solicitous parent discovered when he later visited the school that his son was devoting practically all his time to the Socialist movement, then popular at the school. In anger, he disowned the boy, and Asanuma had to obtain employment in a fountain-pen factory to continue his studies. He graduated in 1923, immediately joined in promoting the pre-World War II Labor Farmer Party, and in two years became its Secretary-General.

As Japan's proletarian movement gradually divided into Communist and Socialist segments, Asanuma remained with the latter, claiming that his sole purpose in life was to establish a socialist democracy that would give the Japanese people a better share of the national income and be responsive to their will. Yet when his first great opportunity came to stand up for these principles against Japan's militarists in the 1930's, he failed to put up any significant resistance. As a member of the Diet from 1936 on—eight terms in all—he eventually collaborated with Japan's warlords, unlike some of the other Socialists who went to jail for their beliefs.

After World War II, Asanuma again became prominent in the reborn Japanese Socialist Party, a political movement destined to divide twice into separate parties: Once in 1951 over whether to accept the San Francisco Peace Treaty, which restored Japan's sovereignty; again in 1959 over the violence of its radical elements. In both cases, the dominant left veered further and further toward the Communist world and the increasing use of direct action in disregard of parliamentary procedure. The right, in turn, revolted to go its own way, insisting on adherence to basic democratic and parliamentary standards. It was in this atmosphere of factional dissension that Asanuma rose to power as a compromiser.

When the Socialists split the first time, he became the Right Socialist Party's Secretary-General, and when his party and the Left Socialists were temporarily rejoined in October, 1955, he was named Secretary-General of the new combined Japanese Socialist Party. In that capacity, he soon became known as "Mah, Mah

Koji," or the "Well, Well, Man," because of his repeated use of the interjection in trying to pacify quarreling factions during intra-party discussions. It was to be expected, perhaps, that the party would turn to him as its choice to replace Chairman Mosaburo Suzuki after two of its right-wing factions again set up their own separate organization just prior to the 1960 upheaval over the Security Treaty.

But by this time a much more radical Asanuma had emerged—one who was regularly denouncing Japan's "subservience" to the United States and the need for "racial independence." Asanuma's huge figure appeared more frequently at the head of demonstrating columns of students, a broad red band stretched diagonally across his chest. He thundered with indignation over Japan's refusal to recognize Communist China; he hurled almost daily blasts at the tiny armed forces Japan maintained for its own defense; and he saw in plans to revise Japan's alliance with the United States a sinister plot to send Japanese troops abroad, revive militarism and fascism, and involve Japan in war.

On March 9, 1959, Asanuma, as chief delegate of a Socialist goodwill mission, sat down in Peiping for a conference with Chang Hsi-jo, Director of the Communist Chinese Foreign Affairs Institute. Before he finished, he declared that "American imperialism is the common enemy of China and Japan" because the United States was supporting Nationalist China on Taiwan, "which is part of China," and was occupying Okinawa, "which is part of Japan." The remark swept him into the role of the second most controversial man in Japan, right next to Prime Minister Kishi, who during the final year of his Administration was virtually everybody's favorite whipping boy. Newspapers questioned the propriety of Asanuma's remarks, Diet committees discussed them, and Kishi's Liberal-Democrats condemned him for his "utter irresponsibility" and "complete denial of Japan's present policies."

Eight months later, on November 27, 1959, a mob of radical students and labor-union members milled and shouted outside the main gate of the Diet grounds. In their front ranks, his face red with anger, was a gesticulating Asanuma. He was arguing with the police to let a delegation of twelve persons inside to present a petition against the U.S.–Japanese Security Pact. When the police opened the gates slightly to let them pass, Asanuma charged forward, the mob at his heels. Into the Diet grounds and through the broken ranks of the surprised police they poured, a screaming avalanche of red flags, black school uniforms, and white headbands. Spewing over the compound, some shouted, "Opening shot of the revolution!" as they planted their red banners on the Diet grounds, and others engaged in a mass urination upon the closed massive doors of the Diet building.

Six months later, on May 24, 1960, when the anti-Security Treaty riots were at their height, Asanuma, accompanied by other leaders of his party, again appeared in the unusual role of calling on U.S. Ambassador Douglas MacArthur II to ask that President Eisenhower's planned visit to Japan be canceled on the grounds that it would further antagonize the Japanese people. Before the heated exchange of words was completed, both men had pounded the table; Asanuma had again termed American policy "imperialistic"; and MacArthur had called upon Asanuma to retract his by then twice-repeated claim that American imperialism was Japan and China's common enemy. Asanuma angrily charged that Eisenhower's visit would cause more rioting; later MacArthur fired back in a statement that "since Mr. Asanuma had himself encouraged demonstrators, he presumably was in a position not only to predict but to organize disorders if he so chooses."

By such performances, Asanuma became the unchallenged leader of the movement to neutralize Japan in the Cold War. But from that high tide of the leftist assault against the Security Treaty—the storm center of the fight over neutrality—it was only a short distance in time to Asanuma's death. He had become the target, it seemed at the time, of rightist forces who had marked him as their principal enemy because of his sponsorship of extreme left-wing causes.

In the minds of many Western-oriented residents of Japan, Asanuma left an image of a lumbering, bombastic giant ruled by his emotions and unable to speak or think except in the ritualistic terms of Marxist dogma. But to thousands of Japanese, Asanuma was the closest approximation they had ever known of what might be called Japan's common man; to them, he was a repository of many simple virtues in a nation long afflicted with tyrannical, posturing, and arrogant leaders. For Asanuma was basically a simple, friendly, and dedicated, although very foolish, man.

For twenty-one years, he lived in the same small, cluttered apartment in the Fukugawa district of Tokyo with his wife, Kyoko, and daughter, Kinue. Asanuma rose at 5 A.M. every day to begin a whirlwind of party activities that did not end until long after dark. His first task was immediately to digest seven daily newspapers and their weekly magazines to keep himself informed on world affairs; those publications he found of interest, he saved for future reference in his party writings, and as the years passed the stocks of periodicals mounted in every corner of the home, despite the frantic protests of his wife.

To his many friends, he was usually "Numa-san," a man seldom too busy to listen to their problems. But in political parlance Asanuma was often known as "Ningen-kikansha"—the human locomotive—because of his tireless activities in pursuit of Socialist goals. By actual count he is known to have participated in 178 rallies and public discussions between April and December, 1959. Such ceaseless activity caused Mrs. Asanuma to complain one day: "It seems that this house is not his home at all, but merely a station for that locomotive." Yet it was by means of his inexhaustible energy that Asanuma tried to sell Japan on his party's long-range goals of "socializing the basic means of production and distribution" and "organizing small-scale enterprise on a cooperative basis." The party and Asanuma were consistently vague about the means for accomplishing these economic objectives, beyond nationalizing the coal, electric-power, and steel industries, if they ever won a national election. But in the field of foreign affairs they never hesitated to state what they wanted to do: abrogate the U.S.–Japanese Security Treaty; remove all American troops and bases from Japan; recognize and trade with Communist China; eliminate Japan's Self-Defense Forces; and provide for their nation's security by negotiating a four-way, Locarno-type, nonaggression pact among Communist China, the Soviet Union, Japan, and the United States.

Asanuma often gave his reasons for believing these things were necessary, not only to guarantee Japan's future prosperity but to keep it from becoming an unwilling victim of a future East-

West war. Without embellishment, the substance of one of his major efforts to explain the forces operating in Asia and Africa is as follows:

> After World War II, the formerly colonized nations of Asia and Africa were swept by a rising tide of nationalism that represented their desire for racial independence and release from colonialism. From this nationalism, Asian Socialism developed with a corresponding desire to remain aloof from the Cold War by adopting neutral foreign policies, which would help protect their recently won independence. India and Burma are in this category, and the new emerging nations of Africa will eventually be, once their economies progress beyond the agricultural level. Japan is a slightly different case, having been an independent capitalistic nation before the war and having regained independence after the war under the terms of the San Francisco Peace Treaty. But Japan's independence is not complete, due to the existence of the U.S.–Japanese Security Treaty and American military bases scattered throughout the country as well as in Okinawa, which is Japanese territory. With the United States still in the country, Japan remains under the political and economic domination of the United States in many respects. Left-wing resistance to the new Security Treaty, and an earlier campaign to block expansion of five major U.S. air bases in Japan to permit them to handle modern jets, is part of the effort of the Japanese people to free themselves from such foreign domination. The Socialist Party—not the Communists or the capitalists (meaning conservative Liberal-Democrats)—is the proper vehicle for leading this effort. It is the party of the working class. It will lead Japan to peace, neutrality, and prosperity on the basis of free will expressed through the parliamentary system and existing democratic institutions.

Although there are portions of this Socialist argument that are easily challengeable—particularly the statement that Japan is subservient to the United States and the assumption that Japan could exist as a defenseless nation so close to the Communist world—the general tenor of the party's proposal is not too difficult for many fair-minded people to accept. But the execution of that program, and particularly Asanuma's role in the execution, were a far different thing from what both had advocated. If the Socialists proved anything in the postwar years, it was that they did not believe in parliamentary government or even a government of laws and orderly procedures, at least as understood in the Western world. Whenever the party was outvoted in the Diet on a controversial issue, or threatened with being outvoted, its members attempted to block any further consideration of the matter. And when they lost a vote, instead of resorting to the only two acceptable remedies in a democracy—the courts or the election of a more sympathetic administration at the polls—they invariably attempted to force their will on the rest of the nation through violence and pressure campaigns. This is exactly what happened in the riots over expanding the U.S. air bases, which Asanuma mentioned, over Kishi's attempt to pass legislation giving the police more power, and over the Security Treaty.

If Asanuma's shadow lay heavily over the turbulent Socialist activities of 1960, the preceding decade of the party's history had been dominated by a man of distinctly different character—slender, scholarly Mosaburo Suzuki. He was little known outside Japan when the Socialist Party was created in November, 1945, only three months after the surrender. It expanded rapidly in an atmosphere of disillusionment created by the conservative forces that had led Japan to its disastrous defeat. By June 1, 1947, it was powerful enough to form a coalition government with the conservative Democratic Party and to elect veteran Socialist leader, Tetsu Katayama, Prime Minister. The coalition collapsed on February 10, 1948, and was followed by another short-lived government under Democrat Hitoshi Ashida. This, too, fell quickly, and the Socialists went down to a crushing defeat in the general election of 1949, their lower-house Diet strength dropping from 143 to 48. At the same time, the Communists reached the high tide of their popularity by electing 32 representatives and polling 10 per cent of the vote.

Suzuki was one of the causes of the Socialist wreckage. As Chairman of the Diet's lower-house Budget Committee, he seized an opportunity to gain prominence by torpedoing the coalition's budget program. This made him the recognized leader of the left-wing forces within the party which had opposed the financial plan.

Racked by dissension, the Socialists entered the troubled 1950's still technically one party, although deeply divided into left and right groupings. Suzuki was soon leading his leftists in an assault on the proposed San Francisco Peace Treaty, which the Soviet Union was refusing to sign, and against the first U.S.–Japanese Security Treaty, which was a companion document. The more conservative Socialist wing favored the Peace Treaty, although it also opposed the Security Treaty. The Socialists' battle exploded at their party convention in October, 1951: Fist fights broke out on the convention floor; chairs were thrown, and many persons were injured. The result was the formation of two separate parties, the Left Socialists, under Suzuki, and the Right Socialists, under Jotaro Kawakami. And when this breach was healed by the uneasy reunion of October, 1955, Suzuki became the new combined party's Chairman, with Asanuma as his Secretary-General.

Son of a ricksha-puller, Suzuki was born near Nagoya, in 1893, and into a life of poverty and toil. As a youth, he delivered newspapers and milk. Later, he worked as a road-construction laborer, once served as a houseboy in the home of Baron Iwasaki, and even was employed as a ricksha man himself. This harsh life whetted his appetite for better things; the eager youth worked long hours at a full-time job while attending Waseda University, and he eventually graduated with the equivalent of a master's degree in political economy. For thirteen years, he was employed as an undistinguished news reporter and even toured America in 1920 on the meager salary paid by a Japanese newspaper. Not until he gave up news work did Suzuki enter politics. Then he organized the Political Research Society. Nine years later, in 1937, he was elected to the Tokyo Municipal Assembly as a member of the now long-defunct Japanese Proletarian Party. Almost immediately, he was arrested by Japanese police for left-wing activities, languished in prison for two and one-half years, and then spent most of World War II in a protracted trial, which was finally ended by Japan's defeat and occupation.

Out of such difficulties, Suzuki, unlike Asanuma, gained tremendous stature as a man of sufficient character and integrity to stand up to the militarists without hedging on his beliefs. In the first postwar election, in 1946, he was sent to the Diet's House of Representatives and won a seat in every election after that.

When he took over as Chairman of the newly merged Japanese Socialist Party in 1955, Suzuki was sixty-two. His quiet, handsome face, enhanced by a carefully trimmed gray mustache and capped with well-groomed silver-gray hair, showed no trace of the grinding poverty in which he had spent most of his life. In appearance, he resembled a businessman far more than a left-wing political chieftain. But when he mounted a stage to address a rally, this gentility quickly slipped away in a torrent of eloquent abuse of America, capitalism, and conservatives, who he claimed were blocking Japan's full independence and leading her toward war. When he finished, the suave, quiet demeanor quickly returned. He was widely accepted as a man of integrity and honesty both by conservatives and Socialists alike, although he was widely accused of being illogically opposed to all things American and of hewing to a line almost identical with that of the Communist Party.

"This is not true," he told me emphatically one day in his Diet office. "We Socialists do want economic independence for Japan, free of commitments to America and with no bans on trade with Communist China. But we don't want violent revolution, like the Communists. We wouldn't even try to build a Socialist economy immediately if we came to power. We are for gradual democratic change. We need the cooperation of the large industrialists and economic help from the United States." Suzuki spoke with seeming sincerity, fingering a button on the vest of his worn brown suit and seldom raising his voice. Yet, like Asanuma, his deeds did not match his words, nor did those of his party.

When he spoke to Japanese audiences, his addresses were filled with Communist-styled phraseology—"racial independence," "class struggle," "oppressed masses," and "monopolistic, imperialistic capitalism." When Secretary of State John Foster Dulles—the man who framed the "treaty of reconciliation" that restored Japan's sovereignty—had to resign because of ill health, Suzuki was not above calling this "a defeat for the diplomacy of strength and an international victory for the diplomacy of negotiation." Yet Suzuki had nothing but words of praise for the Soviet Union and Communist China after his numerous postwar trips to give lectures there and improve relations.

Suzuki always seemed a cut above Asanuma both in character and intelligence, but he still spoke in the usual stereotypes of the Japanese left wing: Japan must be neutral; alliance with the United States would lead to war; Japan's economic salvation lay in trade with Communist China; armaments are unnecessary and should be abolished; the Western democracies are militaristic and the Communist nations are not; and capitalism is basically evil. The party kept drifting further and further to the left under his leadership and continued moving in that direction under his successor, Asanuma, until the shadings between it and the Communists were difficult to distinguish. This was more than many of the more moderate members could stomach and under able, handsome Suehiro Nishio they broke away to form the new Democratic Socialist Party.

The assembly hall at the Kudan Kaikan was austerely decorated. "Banzai for the organization of the Democratic Socialist Party" was emblazoned in large silver characters across the black curtain screening the stage. On the left side of the curtain was painted a large globe, decorated with ribbons. But the colorful posters, slogans, banners, and sea of red flags that characterized most Socialist gatherings were absent; instead, there was an air of relaxed gaiety in the swelling harmonies of a chorus singing spring songs and an orchestra playing Strauss waltzes. When the music faded, the eyes of all 800 in the audience fixed on the well-knit, broad-shouldered figure of Suehiro Nishio, sixty-one years old, as he moved to the center of the stage to accept the chairmanship of the newly launched party. His handsome face, etched by the trials of many political battles, was set in grim lines; the firm, well-formed mouth turned down at the corners; and deep lines arched down from the sides of his nose to frame the mouth and its wisp of a mustache. The stirring and coughing died as he began to present his thesis that the new party could succeed only by convincing the people that it would attain its objectives through parliamentary, democratic methods.

"The Socialist Party suffers from the illusion that a Marxist revolution is possible in Japan," he said. "At the same time, the Liberal-Democrats have degenerated into political agents for big business. The goal of our party is to give political expression to the aspirations of a vast segment of the nation, including impoverished farmers, fishermen, and small businessmen, whose voices have not been heeded by either the Liberal-Democrats or the Socialists."

The hall was frozen in silence, an unusual sign of attention in Japan, where audiences like to heckle or shout encouragement to any performer. "We must practice political tolerance," Nishio continued. "Totalitarianism of either the left or right stifles all opposition, and this is wrong. Our party intends to achieve Socialism through democratic methods. The essence of democracy is the belief in the value of dissension and the efforts of persuasion."

Applause swept the hall. It was a moment of personal triumph for Nishio. He was finally back in familiar and comfortable ideological waters after a painful journey that had left him stranded for four years under the control of the dominant Socialist left wing.

Although Nishio started his career as an apprentice factory hand at the age of fifteen, he became active in middle-of-the-road factions of the Socialist movement from the moment it began to flourish after World War I and particularly between 1926 and 1931. During the mid-thirties, Nishio held firmly to his beliefs, despite the rising hostility of the militarists; but he did not actively pursue them in the face of their opposition. As a consequence, he was not jailed like Suzuki, but neither did he collaborate with the militarists like Asanuma. Consistently advocating moderation, he became head of one of the party's strongest factions and Deputy Premier in the Cabinet of Democratic Party leader Hitoshi Ashida, whose brief tenure in 1948 was conditioned by support from the Socialists. From these heights, he was suddenly plunged into disgrace and seeming political oblivion by what has come to be called the "Showa Electric Works scandal." He was accused of receiving but not reporting a 500,000-yen ($1,388) contribution prior to the 1947 election campaign. He was later cleared of all charges, but admitted he had used the money only to benefit the party's right wing. For ten years, Nishio languished in the backwaters of party affairs until he began to emerge as the natural spokesman for those Socialists who felt the controlling left wing of their party was heading them more and more toward a precipice of pro-Communism and antidemocratic violence.

The climax came on October 18, 1959, when he walked out of a tumultuous Socialist Party convention that was attempting to discipline him for antileadership activities. With him went the nucleus of his new party. Although a middle-of-the-road faction headed by Jotaro Kawakami did not join in, the break seemed irrevocable. Nishio sighed with relief because the showdown had finally arrived. "I feel twenty years younger now," he admitted.

Three months later, listening to the plaudits of his confederates in the Kudan Kaikan, as the Democratic Socialist Party was officially being launched, he seemed to have taken a long stride toward the heights of public esteem needed to carry him and his beliefs to power. The Socialists were already foundering in their syndrome of increasing violence and political defeat. The Liberal-Democratic Party, which had every reason to want the Socialists weakened, welcomed the split. So did wide segments of the labor movement and the general public. Even Hayato Ikeda, soon to be Prime Minister and only one of many conservative leaders, including Kishi, on friendly terms with Nishio, seized the occasion to praise him and express the hope his new party would grow and mature.

"He is a modern, democratic politician of uncommon insight and unshakable faith," Ikeda said. "Mr. Nishio has often made it clear that he will fight to the finish against any revolutionary or class party. His separation from the left Socialists is only natural."

Ikeda continued: "Mr. Nishio has the true spirit of a laborer. He sent his son to the Sumitomo [one of Japan's largest multiple enterprise firms] trade school. This shows he is an authentic Socialist. . . . Former Prime Minister Yoshida [Shigeru Yoshida] once said he hoped Japan would one day have a grown-up Socialist Party. With the emergence of the Democratic Socialist Party, we Liberal-Democrats are now confronted with a real rival. I hope Mr. Nishio's new party will develop as a national party. I will be watching closely his future activities both as a conservative and opponent."

Thus the Democratic Socialist Party was launched under fair skies. It did, indeed, seem that Nishio and his immediate associates, particularly his Secretary-General, Eki Sone, were the custodians of concepts, beliefs, and abilities desperately needed by their nation. Both appeared far superior to any other left-of-center leaders in their understanding of world affairs, of Japan's internal problems, and of Japan's position in the Cold War. And in many ways they seemed far more convincing than the Liberal-Democrats in proclaiming their dedication to the democratic process and the improvement of general welfare. Perhaps that made the Democratic Socialists' actions—or lack of action—during the Security Treaty crisis seem an even greater failure than that of the Socialists. For the Democratic Socialists, in the trying days of May and June, 1960, virtually took no stand at all. To their credit, however, it can be stated unequivocally that they refused to participate in the Socialist violence either in the Diet or in the streets. But despite all their professions of democracy and dedication to proper parliamentary procedure, they did participate in the Socialist boycott of Diet proceedings that paralyzed government operations throughout the period. They tried to condemn both the other two major parties—the Socialists for their unlawful insurrection against the government; the Liberal-Democrats for forcing Diet ratification of the Treaty and for calling in the police to restore order the night of the Treaty passage. They also joined the Socialists in demanding new nation-wide elections as the proper remedy for the turbulence that followed.

This stand, whether the Democratic Socialists realized it or not, placed them in the position of upholding, on the one hand, the strange Socialist Party contention that it was undemocratic for the Liberal-Democrats to outvote the minority and approve the Security Treaty and, on the other, that it was proper procedure to refuse to attend parliamentary sessions. Thus, they were actually subscribing to the same formula for chaos that the Socialists were advocating, for they were in effect saying: "The majority cannot use its majority. It must consult with the minority and satisfactorily meet its wishes. If the two sides cannot agree, then they cannot act, and when such disagreements arise a new nation-wide election should be called to settle the issue." It is perhaps not unreasonable to point out that this could mean new elections every few weeks, in view of the past inability of Japan's left and right to find a common meeting ground. Under this doctrine, a government could be stalled on dead center indefinitely.

The wishy-washy attitude of the Democratic Socialists undoubtedly contributed to their debacle in the November 20, 1960, election of a new 467-seat House of Representatives, and to the substantial gains of both the Liberal-Democrats and Socialists. The line-up of party strength before and after the balloting was:

	Before	After	Change
Liberal-Democrats	283	296	+13
Socialists	122	145	+23
Democratic Socialists	40	17	−23
Communists	1	3	+ 2
Minor Parties, Vacancies and Independents	21	6	−15

Many things can be read into these results. It was a substantial victory for Prime Minister Ikeda's Liberal-Democrats, who campaigned on their approval of the Security Treaty. In Ikeda's words, it was a repudiation of Socialist neutrality; yet the greatest gains seemed to have been rolled up by the Socialists, while the Democratic Socialists, Independents, and minor parties lost. Actually, the Socialists did not gain as much as they appeared to; in fact, the entire left-of-center movement remained almost exactly where it had been before the Democratic Socialists set up their own separate party. At that time the combined Socialist Party had 165 seats and the Communists 1. After the election, the combined total of the Socialists, Democratic Socialists, and Communists was 165, or just one below the combined total for the three before the Socialist split. But there was a most distinct shift from the Democratic Socialists to the Socialists, and one clear result of the balloting was summed up by a Democratic Socialist spokesman: "We've had it. Our defeat couldn't have been worse."

The election seemed to substantiate fears that Japan was being divided into two ever-widening political camps with no middle way between. Yet despite this poor showing in its first test at the polls —and it admittedly could turn out to be a death blow—the Democratic Socialist Party could hold much of value for Japan in its future struggle for internal stability. We can argue that here was a political organization that at least in its public utterances showed some understanding of political reality; that it would have to work with a capitalistic economy if and when it came to power; and that whatever Socialist changes it desired would have to come gradually and methodically. At the same time, it demonstrated a seemingly sincere concern for more economic and social justice in a nation that has suffered from the lack of both for centuries, and it did this without either becoming the prisoner of meaningless Marxist dogma totally detached from the world of reality or sacrificing its dedication to the democratic process.

Here, possibly, was a middle road for a nation that had long been exploited by its men of property, yet in its modern period had been offered only one alternative—what appeared to be an equally bad Socialist tyranny of the left. Here, indeed, was a party with a program that promised to combine the magnificent power and ability of Japan's capitalist structure with reforms that would bring more opportunity and a badly needed and more equitable sharing of the national income. But it foundered because of its own immaturity, its lack of understanding of the responsibilities that go with democracy, and its false image of what the parliamentary process entails. Perhaps, too, it was a victim in a larger sense of the pressures of the Cold War that have tended to push all middle roaders into one camp or the other. But all this puts us a little ahead of our story. On the eve of the 1960 riots, the Democratic Socialists were still full of hope and promise. They seemed to have the potential to become a responsible, parliamentary left-wing party that could play as important a part in Japanese public affairs as the Labour Party had in Britain—a potential that still exists in an attenuated form. But as the Security Treaty storm drew closer, they were, like their more radical cousins the Socialists and Communists, a force to be reckoned with. So too were a numerically small but extremely violent band of fanatics from the other end of the political spectrum—the rightists. Signs of new life among these offspring of Japan's pre-World War II ultranationalist groupings had been apparent for some time, and as the leftists stepped up their attacks on the Treaty, the rightists became more active in opposing them. Among their leaders was a curious man named Bin Akao.

6. And One on the Right

Bin Akao sat on the straw-mat floor of his dilapidated home in the Asakusa district of Tokyo, and his bald head, ringed with a fringe of hair, glistened in the light filtering through the open shoji door.

"God has destined me to be the Hitler of Japan," he stated in his hoarse, thin voice. "I will come to power within ten years."

At sixty-three, Akao, boss of the Greater Japan Patriotic Party (Dai Nippon Aikokuto), is Japan's leading fascist, and the make-shift headquarters of his nation-wide organization were appropriately decorated with black and red swastika posters. Giant portraits of Jesus Christ, Buddha, Emperor Meiji, and Nationalist China's President Chiang Kai-shek were prominently displayed. Along one side, a Buddhist altar was draped with swastika flags, and in one corner were wooden swords and fencing masks used in the Japanese sport of kendo.

"How will you come to power?" I asked.

"The people will want me," he stated emphatically. "At some time in the future, Japan will have to go either left or right. There will be a crisis, and the nation will be divided. There will be a popular uprising, and the people will call on me to lead the fight."

Akao had said these words many times before, and he was ready to repeat them for anyone who would listen. In his opinion, he was the coming strong man who would save Japan from the multiple evils of "no faith, no God, no patriotism"; from its dedication to cabarets, gambling, horse racing, bicycle racing, jazz, mah-jongg, and dancing. These were evil, he said, because they distracted the people from facing the real danger of Communism; hence his adoption of the swastika as an anti-Communist symbol and his admiration for Hitler.

"Hitler was a strong man," Akao said. "The world needs men like Mussolini and Hitler. . . . On the whole, I think Hitler did a good job of ridding his regime of the threat of the reactionaries."

"What about the mass murders that Hitler perpetrated, his concentration camps, and gas chambers? How do you reconcile these with your professions of believing in God?" I asked.

"I am a humanist," Akao said. "I believe in humanity. Jesus Christ was a humanist. Buddha, the Emperor Meiji, Confucius . . . were all humanists. They are all the same. There is only one God."

Would Christ have approved of Hitler's mass murder of the Jews?

"I don't think so," Akao admitted, after a pause. "But Christ would have fought the Communists. If Jesus Christ were alive today, he would be leading the fight against the Reds. Hitler was quite right in exterminating those who were trying to sabotage his anti-Communist crusade." Akao said he is writing his own *Mein Kampf*, outlining how he will take over the government. And when he achieves his goal, he plans the re-emergence of Japan as a strong, military power.

What means is he willing to use to gain his ends?

"I am ready to use any means," he stated.

Bin Akao is, of course, a fanatic, with a meager following of about 15,000 throughout Japan. Although he is considered of little consequence by most Japanese, he is in much the same position as Hitler was before his rise to power in Germany and therefore represents a threat that could become dangerously real if he ever gained strong backing from well-financed conservative interests who might want to make use of his anti-Communist program. In the meantime, the main significance of this lean, tense little man with the fiery brown eyes is that he symbolizes the rebirth of the extreme right in Japan with all of its evil overtones from the past.

That past goes back to the early 1880's when disgruntled ex-samurai, descendants of Japan's great warrior class, formed their nation's first ultranationalist organizations. They were disturbed and aroused by the great social and ideological changes sweeping across their land under the Meiji reforms. Made up largely of men who feared progress and hated all foreigners, these organizations, which eventually included the infamous Black Dragon Society (founded in 1901), became self-appointed guardians of national morality and backed an expansionist, jingoistic foreign policy. They helped push Japan into wars with China and Czarist Russia and aided the military in taking control of the Japanese Government during the 1930's. Their terroristic activities helped stamp out all opposition to Japan's entrance into World War II.

Rightist activity continued after the surrender in 1945, despite two mass suicides of hard-core elements—one atop Atago Hill in Tokyo's Minato ward; another at the Yoyogi military training ground, where the American military housing area of Washington Heights now stands. General MacArthur's Occupation headquarters immediately purged 3,000 more rightist leaders from public life and dissolved their 232 organizations. Although kept under constant surveillance and official disapproval, an estimated 266 rightist groups remained in existence when the Occupation ended, and their activities have continued on a small scale ever since. These organizations trained their recruits in judo, swordsmanship, and boxing, dressed them in uniforms, and schooled them in varying forms of ultranationalist ideology. Some, like the Fatherland Protection Corps, were led by assassins of the early 1930's; another, the Martyr Youth Corps, was founded by Hidezo Toyama, son of a prominent prewar ultranationalist; and a third group, the Seisanto, or Production Party, was a revival of an offshoot of the Black Dragon Society.

The dangerous nature of their dogma soon became obvious, for police uncovered four rightist plots on the life of former Premier Shigeru Yoshida and investigated fifty threats. The first warning that the fanatic right could once again be mustered in more than token strength came in November, 1954. Storm troopers of the Martyr Youth Corps, nattily attired in dark-blue uniforms, caps, and black combat boots, poured into a rally at Hibiya Hall in downtown Tokyo; after an address by Yoshio Kodama, a prominent, prewar terrorist, they formed up in tight, disciplined ranks to parade, 4,000 strong, through the city. Some open activity continued on a small scale over the next five years, but then as the Security Treaty storm rose in intensity, the rightists, fearing that an actual Communist uprising might be in the making, became more active too. By the time the screaming, chanting leftist columns were snake-dancing around the Diet during the thirty days' attempt to block the United States alliance prior to its final ratification, the rightists were turning out regularly. Attired in khaki uniforms and helmets, they appeared on the fringes of the demontrators to attack Zengakuren and Sohyo members with clubs and stones and heckle their speakers with insults and loudspeaker harangues. Zengakuren feared the rightists' physical assaults, and Sohyo viewed them with considerable respect since many of the rightists involved were the toughest kinds of street fighters, some of them thugs from Japan's underworld.

Early in 1961, police estimated that at least 200 rightist organizations with a combined membership of about 300,000 were active again. They ranged in size from a handful of members to Akao's nation-wide establishment, and in character from militarist-fascist groupings with purely nationalistic goals to criminal gangs and goon squads that could be hired whenever those with enough money felt violence necessary. There have been numerous examples of this. Rightists fought against the Communist-influenced, anticompany union in the Miike coal-mine strike, and a rightist was accused of stabbing to death the only striker to die in the picket-line fighting. When Kishi was stabbed, too, in the closing days of the Security Treaty crisis, newspaper reports strongly hinted that his assailant, Taisuke Aramaki, a former member of the prewar ultranationalist Taikakai, was hired to do the job. They alleged that a political rival, angered by Kishi's refusal to back him rather than Hayato Ikeda for the premiership, was behind the plot to punish, but not kill, the outgoing Premier. Aramaki was later reported living in high style while free on bond awaiting trial.

A much more spectacular attack, in this same vein, was made on *Mainichi*, one of Japan's largest daily newspapers. *Mainichi* printed stories in its editions of March 28 and 29, 1960, reporting that a number of prominent but unnamed Liberal-Democrats had sent flowers to the funeral of the wife of a leader of the Matsuba-kai, an ultrarightist group. It hinted that there were well-established connections between these conservative party leaders and the Matsuba-kai. The rightists demanded a retraction, but were refused. The following Saturday night, ten men suddenly burst into *Mainichi's* printing room, threw sand into the rotary presses, and set off a fire-extinguisher bomb, seriously damaging the plant. Later, Hiroaki Watanabe, a Matsuba-kai member, was arrested as the leader of the attack but denied that he or his companions had been hired. He said that he had acted mainly out of personal rage. The incident stirred memories of the attack on the *Asahi Shimbun* by rightist fanatics during the February 26, 1936, incident, one of the flare-ups during that period of military take-over that helped head Japan down the road to war. After the *Mainichi* raid, *Asahi*, fearing similar attack, boarded up all but one of its entrances at night and posted extra guards; but the attack never came.

Takao Kona, editor and publisher of the monthly magazine *Seijikeizai*, was subjected to even more direct pressure from the rightists for printing an exposé in his October, 1960, issue. The story introduced about 100 of the most prominent rightist leaders and gave an account of their activities during labor disputes; it also alleged that there were links between rightists and certain politicians. Seven members of the secretariat of the National Congress of Patriotic Organizations called at Kona's office to demand a retraction, claiming that the article was filled with falsehoods and misunderstandings; they ordered him to meet them at a Ueno Park restaurant in Tokyo the following Saturday afternoon with his reply. And Kona told police afterward that, just to make sure he attended, they sent two men to escort him. "I was ushered into a room and found about thirty or forty men assembled there," he related later. "Among them was Tomeo Sagoya, who was involved in the attack on Prime Minister Osachi Hamaguchi in 1929. He is now an adviser to the notorious rightist group Gokokudan."

Kona said he was questioned intensively for two hours. Some of his interrogators suggested that he kill himself to take responsibility for his story. The rightists finally demanded that he publish in his magazine both a formal apology and a new story about rightists which would be written by them. They released him with a demand that he reply in two or three days; instead, he went to the police.

Of all the new rightist activity, however, the incident that most dramatized the revival of this national affliction was the case of Otoya Yamaguchi, the seventeen-year-old killer of Socialist Chairman Inejiro Asanuma. Yamaguchi, son of a colonel in the Japanese Army, appeared to be a normal youth in his early adolescence; he had not caused his parents any serious trouble, was quiet, neat, and serious-minded, though overly intense. At what stage his intensity deepened into an inflammable rightist fanaticism is difficult to say, but Bin Akao was one of the catalytic agents. According to police investigators, Yamaguchi heard Akao denounce the Reds in a speech and joined his Patriotic Party; in May, 1960, he and two other Patriotic Party members became dissatisfied with Akao's "less radical" methods and broke away to form their own organization, the All-Asia Anti-Communist Youth League. Soon they had a Nazi swastika flag flying from the window of their new headquarters on the Ginza, Japan's busiest thoroughfare, in rooms loaned to them by another rightist. Alongside it were the rising sun of Japan and white banners inscribed with the slogans "Guard the Emperor and Destroy His Enemy" and "Work for the Motherland with Seven Lives."

What went on there until Asanuma was struck down on October 12, is not clear. But police discovered that Yamaguchi and his two co-workers had become intense admirers of Hitler. Yamaguchi was also deeply impressed by studies of a prewar terrorist named Nissho Inoue, who developed a "one man-one kill" principle (each man would have to kill at least one person) for his followers. He later told police that during this period he was also filled with a deep sense of danger for the future of Japan after watching the chaos of the anti-Security Treaty riots.

It was against this background that his plan to kill was formed. Yamaguchi considered four men besides Asanuma as possible victims: Communist Party Chairman Sanzo Nozaka; Chairman Takeshi Kobayashi of the Japanese Teachers Union; Liberal-Democrat Ichiro Kono, who played a part in re-establishing diplomatic relations with the Soviet Union; and Liberal-Democrat Tanzan Ishibashi, who after his return to politics, following the illness that ended his brief reign as Premier, became President of the Japanese-Soviet Friendship Society.

Yamaguchi phoned them each several times and visited their neighborhoods to make his plans. During August, two months before the slaying, Yamaguchi is known to have received "spiritual training" at a private school known as "Gakunan Gijuku." Then, a week before the Asanuma attack, he paid homage at Meiji Shrine and composed a poem that seemed to foreshadow an impending action that might cost him his life. "Deep is my love of the motherland," he wrote. "Smiling, I'll start on my journey to the other land."

Despite these seeming preparations, his selection of Asanuma as his victim apparently was dictated at least partly by chance. He told investigators that he was sitting in the front row of the Hibiya auditorium when Asanuma moved to the podium. He heard the master of ceremonies urge Asanuma to hurry "because the time is running out." Then, "I thought it's now or never," he said, and leaped onto the stage. His technique was virtually flawless: Asanuma hardly knew he was under attack until Yamaguchi drove his short sword deep into the Socialist leader's chest. It was a fatal thrust, doctors said later, but Yamaguchi whirled with perfect timing and struck again before the huge Socialist collapsed. There was immediate speculation that others had trained him and ordered the killing, and the strongest suspicion fell on Akao. He and the members of the All-Asia Anti-Communist Youth League were arrested; but since the police were unable to prove sufficient connection with the crime, they were released. Yamaguchi calmly went to jail. Shortly after 8 P.M., November 2, 1960, in the solitary confinement cell of the Juvenile Classification Office in Tokyo, he wrote on the wall in toothpaste: "*Shichi sho ho kuku ten no heika. Banzai!*" ("I serve my country with seven lives. Long live the Emperor!") Then he ripped up a bedsheet, threw the strips over a light fixture, and hanged himself.

This tragic waste of a human life had a far-reaching impact on the nation. Children began playing a game variously called "assassination" or "rightists," in which the coveted hero's role of Yamaguchi went to the one who eliminated all the others in a contest of "jan-ken-pon" (paper-rock-scissors). The one eliminated first played the part of Asanuma. "Asanuma" then would mount a wooden box and begin addressing an imaginary audience. His playmates, assuming the role of rightists, would begin shouting and showering him with scraps of paper, just as rightists often did at Socialist gatherings. A few minutes later, the hero would dash onto the scene, waving an imitation sword, and strike down "Asanuma." Then another group of boys acting as plain-clothes policemen would rush in to pursue and arrest the attacker. Finally, girls, acting as nurses, would administer aid to the fallen Asanuma.

On a more serious level, the Socialists issued loud and angry demands for a complete exposé of those who "financed" the Asanuma slaying and were putting up the funds for the rightist groups. The Autonomy Ministry subsequently revealed that there had been 22 million yen ($61,111) in contributions from prominent conservative sources to rightist organizations between January and June, 1960. This represented a large increase from the past: The Gokokudan, or State Guardians' Corps, for example, reported that it had received 482,000 yen ($1,338) in donations between March and June, 1959, but 1.9 million yen ($5,233) in the first six months of 1960; among its benefactors, Gokokudan listed Yawata Iron and Steel Company, Fuji Iron and Steel, Hitachi Iron and Steel, the Bank of Japan, and the Kochikai, a group of backers of Prime Minister Ikeda. The Liberal-Democratic Party acknowledged donations to the Gokokudan, the Brotherhood Association for Establishment of Peace and Order, and the Emperor System Association. Most of these contributions were in the 2,000–10,000-yen ($5.55–$27.77) category, small enough to be considered token contributions, but contributions, nevertheless, which, added to income from other sources, had made it possible for the rightists to start a comeback. A few of the contributions, while not munificent, reached more significant proportions, including 100,000 yen ($278) in July, 1960—the period immediately after the Treaty crisis—by the Liberal-Democrats to the Brotherhood Association for Establishment of Peace and Order.

There have been other signs, too, of connections between the "respectable" conservative levels of society and the new nationalist-terrorist groups. Most noteworthy was the linking in December, 1961, of a Japanese industrialist with a reported plot to assassinate Prime Minister Ikeda and his sixteen Cabinet members and to bomb the headquarters of the police, the leftist labor federation

Sohyo, and the Japanese Communist Party. The industrialist was Toyosaku Kawanami, President of the Nichinan and Kawanami Industrial Company. He and twelve others who had banded together in a study group called the Society for Japanese History were arrested in a series of raids. Police seized rifles, gas masks, helmets, swords, and work uniforms from their quarters. Perhaps significantly, among those taken into custody was Taku Mikami, a former lieutenant in the Imperial Navy who had been imprisoned for thirteen years three decades earlier for his involvement in the assassination of Prime Minister Inukai, in 1932.

Although in themselves, neither the contributions to rightist groups nor Kawanami's arrest proves conclusively that the conservatives are primarily responsible for increased rightist violence, it is apparent that rightist activities have increased almost in direct proportion to the increase in violent leftist tactics. In the light of Japan's authoritarian past and the refusal of the police to take strong action against the leftists for fear of alienating the people, it would be logical—although certainly not justifiable—for harassed conservatives surreptitiously to back the same tactics of violence against their enemies.

Some sources claim that the contributions reported to the Autonomy Ministry actually were a form of tribute to avoid trouble with the groups involved. Payment of such tribute in other forms is a well-established pattern in Japan. American film-makers, for example, found this out quickly while attempting to shoot street scenes in Japan: For a fee, they could hire gangsters controlling the area in which they wanted to work. The gangsters would keep crowds moving, provide extras, and control traffic; but if the fee was not paid, the Hollywood producers often found their cameras accidentally knocked over or people making funny faces right in the middle of a difficult scene. Tokyo police reported that 22 out of every 100 persons in Japan have been victims of such shakedowns, but very few have reported their troubles to the police. In Tokyo alone, police records show a total of 4,874 gangster-type organizations with this breakdown on membership: 15,456 gamblers; 15,323 racketeers, confidence men, and street-stall keepers; 43,138 hooligans and delinquent youths, and 30,000 other kinds of toughs. Most of these are not ultranationalists or even true criminals; they are largely small-time hooligans who stand around outside pinball parlors to buy up winners' prizes and sell them back to the pinball-hall owner. But police report a definite infiltration of rightist organizations by the better organized gangs, partly because there seems to be an increasing amount of money flowing into rightist coffers. And it could be, too, that there is an increasing demand, there, for hiring strong-armed thugs. More ominous, however, are attempts to unify the hundreds of separate rightist organizations. More than 300 rightist leaders attended a national conference called for that purpose in Tokyo on July 11, 1959. Both the Patriotic Party and the Matsuba-kai have staged subsequent rallies for the same purpose, but so far the pressure for a larger, more unified movement has been hindered by factional rivalries and an inability to agree on leaders.

Bin Akao, of course, envisions himself as the logical choice for the top leadership role. He is certainly the best known and, perhaps, in his distasteful way, the most colorful. He made headlines once by spitting on Foreign Minister Aiichiro Fujiyama and then almost knocking him down. Later he denied that he had shoved Fujiyama. "He was just so frightened by my harangue that his spine melted," Akao stated.

Akao has never been one to allow ideology to stand in the way of opportunity. He acknowledges that as a young man he was a strong Marxist for six or seven years and was jailed in 1923 for denouncing the Emperor, then a leftist target. After he was freed, in 1925, he changed his politics abruptly and the next time he was jailed it was as a rightist—for denouncing a proposed alliance between Japan and the Soviet Union. Akao was active in pre-World War II rightist groups and attempted to pick up where he had left off after the U.S. Occupation ended, in 1952.

He now lives in a dilapidated clapboard house in the entertainment district of Asakusa, surrounded by the noise and gaudy neon signs of jazz joints and cabarets—activities he deplores as signs of Japan's decay. For many years, he was unable to gain even meager recognition for his Patriotic Party. Members of the party appeared every May Day, when, like most rightist groups, they held separate rallies to denounce the traditional leftist-labor celebration of that day. But he did not win widespread attention until he seized upon an opportunity presented by the outbreak of new signs of anti-Semitism, or neo-Nazism, in Europe to publicize his cause.

World attention was focused on the rash of swastikas chalked on walls, synagogues, and public places. Akao's organization, which had never before used the swastika as a symbol, promptly adopted it. Akao plastered swastika signs all over Tokyo until police came and confiscated those he had left. And when West German Chancellor Konrad Adenauer arrived in Japan, on March 28, 1960, members of the Patriotic Party were at Haneda airport to greet him with more swastika signs and banners. They seemed puzzled when German Embassy personnel demanded that the swastikas be removed before the Chancellor arrived. They reluctantly complied; but, since then, in a land that has never known anti-Semitism, Akao has made the swastika the rallying sign of his form of ultranationalism with all it portends of a future of violence and attacks on democratic institutions.

There seems little doubt that the rightists are emerging again, and probably with a certain amount of conservative financial backing, as a counterforce to the rising violence and threat from the left. The rightist resurgence can even be measured statistically, to a certain extent. In 1958, Tokyo Metropolitan police reported only 10 incidents—involving 22 arrests—of rightist violence or interference in the execution of official police duties; in 1959, there were 40 cases and 160 arrests, but there were also 520 rightist demonstrations—2.5 times the number in 1958. In 1960, the Justice Ministry reported 32 cases and 138 arrests, most of them during the anti-Security Treaty campaign, when rightists demonstrated almost daily. Their violence that year included the most serious attacks on public figures in Japan's postwar history—the fatal stabbing of Socialist Chairman Asanuma and the nonfatal stabbings of Socialist Jotar Kawakami and Prime Minister Nobusuke Kishi.

In this manner, the rightists marched onto Japan's political stage and took their place opposite the Communists, Socialists, Democratic Socialists, and the leaders of each in the alignments forming for the final battle over the Security Treaty. Four more groups remain to be similarly moved into position before that drama begins. They are the intellectuals, Zengakuren, the labor unions, and finally the man and the movement that were strong enough to beat off the leftist assault—Nobusuke Kishi and his conservatives. Of all these, the intellectuals have been by far the most difficult for Westerners to understand.

7. The Intellectuals

The United States started World War II in the Pacific.

The United States and South Korea started the Korean War. The United States used germ warfare against the Communist troops.

The United States is warlike and aggressive. Communist nations are seeking peace and social progress.

Rioting is a legal means to express opposition in a democracy.

It is undemocratic for the majority to outvote the minority in the Diet.

Police were guilty of brutality for fighting back when they were attacked by student demonstrators at the Diet; they swung their clubs too hard.

Japan cannot have an anti-espionage law because it would infringe on human liberty.

These are but a few of the beliefs held in whole or in part by the portion of Japanese society that has come to be known as the intellectuals. This vast assortment of writers, critics, social commentators, newsmen, artists, scientists, lawyers, teachers, professors, and editors is one of the most unique—and controversial—groups in Japan. Intellectuals have usually been somewhat controversial in every nation because they often attempt to break with ways of the past. But in Japan, the intellectuals' role has been particularly controversial because they have been deeply involved in politics and have been so successful in disseminating their views to large groups of the population. For example, it is the intellectuals who prevail in the classrooms of Japan, where the minds of the coming generation are being molded; it is the intellectuals who write books and magazine articles for popular as well as high-brow publications; it is the intellectuals who fill the columns of newspapers; and it is the intellectuals who analyze public affairs on radio and television.

Critics both inside and outside the nation have brought many indictments against the Japanese intellectuals. They have accused them of occupying positions of such influence in the universities that those who disagree with them have been afraid to speak out. It has been stated that their concepts underlie the philosophy guiding Japan's left-wing labor movement, that they have roots in the legal professions and the courts, and that their general far-left orientation, which dates back to the earliest days of the Marxist effort in Japan, has created a steady tide that is eroding the foundations of Japan's ties to the Western alliance. Some critics have claimed that the total effect of the intellectuals' activities has been to divide and weaken their nation further, even on some of the most basic tenets of its existence, at a time when it is already deeply disturbed and divided. They cite repeated efforts by intellectuals to do away with any form of armaments, and the intellectuals' objections to police and conservative moves to maintain orderly procedures in the Diet and prevent disorderly demonstrations in the streets.

Whatever the validity of such accusations, there are many understandable reasons for the distinctive viewpoint of the Japanese intellectual. Until 1945, he had lived only under strongly authoritarian governments. Hence all government was bad and was to be resisted when possible. In addition, his first major contact with Western political thought was through Marxism. Japanese scholars were among the first to grasp its meaning and potential impact on the world, and were, perhaps, partly responsible for the wide acceptance of the belief in the near infallibility of this new doctrine. Furthermore, the Communists seem to have done a much better job of communicating with the Japanese intellectual than have exponents of what might be called the modern, democratic state. The image of the United States that emerges from the writings of many Japanese men of letters appears to support this belief. To them, America is a nation of the terribly rich and terribly poor; of people who care for nothing but money and material goods; of sex-crazy young men and lazy women; of a soft, uncultured people with little or no sense of the artistic; a warlike nation, constantly plotting to send Japanese troops outside the borders of Japan to fight other Asians in conflicts that will benefit only the United States.

Against this background, some Japanese actions and beliefs are perhaps a little more understandable. How, for example, did some Japanese come to believe that the United States started World War II in the Pacific?

Both sides, of course, share responsibility for the events that led up to the Japanese attack on Pearl Harbor. America had taken an increasingly strong position against the Japanese and, in the final stages before negotiations broke down, had presented Japan not only with major demands but with a serious economic problem by cutting off Japan's purchases of scrap iron. But it is clear that the Japanese military planned their attack long before this crisis was reached, that they had moved troops into south Indochina ready to invade the Philippines, and—this is perhaps most important—that they struck the first blow.

It took time, of course, for the Japanese intellectual to arrive at his position on this issue; but over the years, his thinking, as expressed in the elite publications, has evolved like this: In the pre-Pearl Harbor negotiations, America would not accept Japan's conditions but, in fact, insisted upon its own, which Japan would not meet. Therefore, since America had taken a position directly opposing Japan and would not change that position, Japan had to attack. Therefore, it was America's opposition that caused the attack, and consequently, it was America who started the war in the Pacific. There is at least one major variation on this argument: The United States deliberately tricked Japan into an attack, thus ensnaring Japan in an elaborate trap that would lead to its annihilation. This closely resembles the theme of defeating one's enemies by cunning and guile that crops up repeatedly in Japanese folk tales; but it does not explain why the United States should deliberately provoke an attack at a time when it was so unprepared that it lost almost its entire Pacific fleet.

The idea that the United States and South Korea started the Korean War is even more widely accepted—or, more accurately, is doubted less—in Japanese intellectual circles. This fabrication long ago became a basic propaganda line in Communist broadcasts to other areas of the world. In Japan, it was used by such front groups as the Japanese Peace Council, Japanese Council Against Atomic and Hydrogen Bombs, and Japan-China Friendship Society. Then it became popular among some Japanese writers, who presented it in magazine articles, and today it can be heard from almost any Japanese student and a surprising number of the more articulate members of society.

Again, none of the advocates of this concept has ever explained why North Korea just happened to have its armies poised and equipped so that they could instantly explode a full-scale counteroffensive that was just barely halted at the southern tip of the Korean peninsula. Since anyone with even a rudimentary knowledge of military matters knows that it takes months to prepare a major offensive, the North Koreans had obviously been preparing for many, many months to launch the invasion themselves.

Arthur Koestler, the Hungarian-born former Communist who wrote *Darkness at Noon*, was shocked by his first brush with the workings of the Japanese intellectual mind. He was in Tokyo in 1959, at the time of the Soviet Government's attack upon Nobel Prize-winning author Boris Pasternak, who, in his book *Doctor Zhivago*, had so magnificently condemned Soviet oppression and demonstrated its failure to conquer the human spirit. Most of the world's literary figures and organizations were boiling with anger at the spectacle of that lonely, gray-haired man being hounded and reviled by the all-powerful Soviet state. Not so the Japanese branch of the international literary group PEN: It only expressed "regret."

Koestler promptly broke an engagement to address the club. He called it a "political organization" and stated in an open letter:

> The Japanese PEN purports to stand for freedom of expression . . . yet when one of the most prominent members of our international

> fraternity was deprived of that right, was hounded and besmirched in a manner rarely paralleled in history, you . . . issued a statement . . . which puts more blame on the defenders of the victim than upon his persecutors.

PEN denied that it had failed to support Pasternak adequately, claiming that the pre-World War II treatment of Japanese writers by the military suggested a softer approach for Pasternak's own sake.

This was not the first time, however, or the last, that the Japanese PEN was to be in hot water. When the government attempted to increase police powers in 1959 to deal with unruly demonstrations, PEN jumped into the ensuing political quarrel to fire off a protest to Prime Minister Kishi against the legislation. Three foreign members residing in Japan—Edward G. Seidensticker, of America; Dr. Ivan Morris, of Britain; and Joseph Roggerdorf, of Germany—filed a written complaint with the club, charging that it had unnecessarily interfered in politics. And when in 1960 the Japanese PEN again protested to the government against the "forced passage" of the Security Treaty in the Diet, the same three foreign members again protested and this time sent a copy of their complaint to PEN International Headquarters in London. The London leaders, after looking over the evidence, admonished the Japanese PEN for "the excessive political inclination" of the Japanese literary world.

If such be danger signals, they have not gone entirely unheeded. American philosopher Sidney Hook charged, in a November, 1958, article printed by the Japanese magazine *Toyo Keizai Shimpo*, that "Japanese university professors have no views of their own. Their views are stereotyped." He accused them of not knowing true democracy, not understanding freedom of thought and expression, and applying different thinking to Western and Communist worlds. "Strangely enough," he wrote, "they get angry and excited when an infringement of freedom is reported from the United States but keep silent when such news comes from the Soviet Union."

Edward Seidensticker, one of the three foreigners who protested the Japanese PEN political activities, and an expert translator of

Japanese works, has come to the conclusion that much of the popular writing adds up to a "hate America" campaign. He has pointed out these typical examples from popular Japanese publications: an account of a Japan Air Lines crash on Oshima Island, in which Americans in some unexplained way are held to be responsible; a piece on the 1952 shooting of a Sapporo police inspector, for which two members of the Communist underground were accused instead of the author's candidate, a right-wing thug who had had dealings with the American Counter-Intelligence Corps; an article picturing American troops who fought in Korea as cowardly and lacking in discipline; and repeated articles openly implying that America and South Korea started the Korean War and then employed germ warfare; that the revised U.S.–Japanese Security Treaty was forced on Japan, will involve it in war, and is a Caucasian plot to mistreat Orientals.

Japanese professors and teachers are the sources of much of this material, and added a loud chorus of complaints after the Diet passed the Security Pact. Hirotatsu Fujiwara, a professor at Meiji University, stated in the April, 1960, issue of *Bungei Shunju* that the new Treaty "is the most humiliating treaty in the history of Japan." Why? Because, he said, "Japan will entrust itself to another nation's strategic system" and "believes such a relationship is based on equal status and expresses its pure and unselfish will for peace." The humiliation, he contended, lies in the fact that the Treaty does not express Japan's will, although it was approved by a majority of the popularly elected members of the Diet, who later won a general election fought largely over the Security Treaty issue. Another professor, Yoshimi Yakeuchi of Tokyo Metropolitan University, a prolific writer for high-brow monthlies, resigned in protest against Diet passage of the Treaty. He explained in a published letter:

> When I became a professor at Tokyo Metropolitan University, I took an oath that as a public servant I would respect and safeguard the Constitution. My belief is that the parliamentary system, one of the fundamental principles of the Constitution, has been a lost cause since May 20 [when the Treaty was passed]. . . . I would break my oath and act against my conscience by remaining. . . .

After the rioting over the Security Treaty reached its peak in the June 15, 1960, student attack on the Diet, President Kichiro Sasaki of Meiji University issued a statement siding, in effect, with the students. He said he did not blame them, would not forbid them to demonstrate, and charged that the police who defended the Diet "swung their clubs merrily" and attacked unarmed students. Still another professor, Renji Koide, said that the police "brutally assaulted innocent student demonstrators," and one overexuberant editorial writer charged that "they swung their clubs too hard." Both Koide and President Sasaki, as well as the editorial writer, failed to mention that the police were repulsing a student attack when they used their clubs.

Although these comments caused considerable consternation in conservative ranks, the statement that stirred the greatest indignation came from Seiji Kaya, President of Tokyo University, long considered Japan's finest educational institution. He said that the students had a right to be angry because "parliamentary democracy" went astray when the "new Security Treaty unilaterally passed the House of Representatives, and the rules of parliamentary democracy were trampled upon." He implied that the rioting was justifiable because the minority Socialists had not agreed with the majority's action, but he ignored the Socialist refusal to participate in the final vote. Kaya's opinion was widely shared by many intellectuals, including some who contended that the entire issue should be submitted to new elections.

Probably no one has ever answered this view better than did Seidensticker in a July 6, 1960, *Yomiuri* column on the concept of parliamentary democracy Kaya was espousing. "What precisely is the 'parliamentary democracy' he is talking about?" Seidensticker asked, then answered:

> I do not know. I do know, however, of certain things which are not rules of parliamentary democracy, and I would have thought them so self-evident as not to need stating. . . . It is not a rule of parliamentary democracy that the minority must approve of every important measure that goes through parliament. It is not a rule of parliamentary democracy that the electorate must be consulted on every important measure.
>
> There is no rule of parliamentary democracy which the Liberal-

> Democratic Party violated by passing the Security Treaty unilaterally, and there is no rule of parliamentary democracy which is violated by not holding elections. It is nonsense to scream about the tyranny of the majority when the majority passes a measure distasteful to the minority.
>
> All the majority is required to do is to let the minority appeal to the electorate from time to time and reverse the acts of the former majority if it succeeds in becoming a majority itself. There is no indication the government intends to deny this right to the Socialists.

Japanese newspapers were deeply involved in the storm that broke after the Treaty passage and were later accused of inciting the violence that swept through Japan for thirty days. Tokyo's huge dailies supported the Socialists, attacked the government for pushing the Security Treaty through the Diet, and expressed great alarm over police being summoned to remove Socialists who had blockaded the House Speaker in his office as a means of preventing a final vote. Little was made of the fact that the police were not summoned until the Socialists had ignored repeated appeals to restore order and that the Speaker had full legal power, although no established precedent, to order in police when needed.

Somehow, in all the turmoil, the popularly accepted view began to emerge: It was unparliamentary and undemocratic for the Liberal-Democrats to use their majority to pass the Treaty when the Socialists did not want it passed, but it was not unparliamentary and undemocratic for the Socialists to try to block the vote by force. It was unparliamentary and undemocratic for the Speaker to summon police, but it was not unparliamentary and undemocratic for the Socialists to lock him in his office and make the summoning of police necessary. And it was unparliamentary and undemocratic for the Liberal-Democrats to pass the Treaty without the Socialists present, although the Liberal-Democrats had both a quorum and a clear majority, but it was not unparliamentary and undemocratic for the Socialists to boycott the session of their own free will, although they were elected to protect their constituents' interests on the floor of the Diet.

Time magazine, in its issue of June 27, 1960, said that the Japanese press was responsible for much of the violence that followed the Diet approval. Its "Press" section stated in part:

> For months, Japan's newspapers willfully and methodically laid the groundwork for crisis with a steady vilification of Premier Nobusuke Kishi and raucous demands that President Eisenhower stay away from Japan. . . . After Kishi pushed the U.S. Security Treaty through Parliament, *Asahi* (Japan's largest daily) called the action "a dictatorship of the majority," provocatively suggested that violence was the only appropriate response. As the street mobs took the cue, increasingly virulent headlines demanded Kishi's resignation, concocted highly imaginative crises: "PARTY LEADERS DESERT KISHI, AND NATION'S DIET SYSTEM IS STANDING AT CROSSROADS OF LIFE AND DEATH."

Time said that the conservative owners of the papers had surrendered their editorial control to "hundreds of young liberal intellectuals in Japanese newsrooms." It continued:

> Espousing no cause but that of full-throated antagonism to the party in power, these leftists not only incite people to riot but often themselves join the rioters. Last week when a part of the mob broke off to charge police guarding the Diet building the sortie was led by a phalanx of screaming, pole-waving newsmen.

This article was later answered by Matsutaro Shoriki, owner of the *Yomiuri Shimbun.* He said that his paper had contended it was right to pass the Treaty but that the majority party mishandled the issue, particularly in pushing the Treaty through only thirty minutes after extending the Diet session fifty days, which would have allowed more time for debate. *Asahi* also published a statement outlining its editorial position on the Treaty issue. It condemned violence in any form and criticized the majority party for pushing the Treaty through so suddenly and for not allowing more debate; it contended that the majority party must pay due heed to the minority and backed the view that the electorate should have been consulted.

Later when Japan's newspaper publishers met for their thirteenth annual convention, in Kyoto, they were in a mood of sober self-reflection over foreign-press criticism. In a speech, Tomoo Hirooka, *Asahi's* managing editor, described the difficulty of covering the anti-Treaty demonstrations. "It was difficult to grasp the truth sometimes because of the activities of left-wing groups," he acknowledged. He cited left-wing charges of police and rightist incitement, which were not borne out after investigation by *Asahi.* Dr. Masamichi Inoki, professor of political science at Kyoto University, told a panel discussion at the meeting: "It is not just the newspapers, but it is the intellectual class in Japan generally that is traditionally opposed to the government." He said that before World War II the governing forces were very strong, leading to the intellectuals' traditional feeling that government should be strongly challenged. "But perhaps we could do with a little more cool and considerate treatment of the news—a little reserve," he said.

Perhaps Japan's unique intellectual climate would not be so serious if it did not strike so deeply into Japanese life. Japanese are among the most literate people in the world; virtually all of them read the nationwide newspapers and one or more popular magazines. It would therefore be most difficult for them to avoid being influenced by the concepts of democracy presented there, and by the insidious campaign to undermine relations with the United States. Millions of others are affected by their labor unions, by the Socialist Party, and even by the courts and schools.

A flaming ideological argument was touched off in the labor movement in 1958 by Professor Itsuro Sakisaka of Kyushu University. He charged that the labor movement was losing sight of its goal of "Socialist revolution." He contended that workers who should be represented by a purely labor-class party, had fallen into grave ideological error by permitting the Socialist Party to include elements such as small businessmen, which made it a "mass" rather than a "class" party, and that it should not be too concerned with parliamentary methods of procedure since these sometimes stood in the way of reaching the ultimate goals. In part, it was this dispute that led to the split of the Socialist Party in 1960. Many of the more conservative elements who wanted a broadly based party joined Suehiro Nishio in setting up the new Democratic Socialist Party. But a similar dispute erupted in January, 1961, when the Socialist Party was attempting to soften its policies because of the censure it incurred by its anti-Security Treaty violence. Saburo Eda, then the acting Chairman, and Tomori Narita, the policy-board Chairman, proclaimed that the Socialists would work for gradual reform of Japanese society "within the framework of the existing capitalist structure." Sohyo, the big, far-left labor federation, which had always virtually dictated Socialist policies, immediately demanded to know how a "Socialist revolution" could be achieved under such a program.

The intellectuals' imprint on Japan's court system is more subtle. Tokyo District Court precipitated a constitutional test of the legality of American bases in Japan by ordering charges dismissed against the Zengakuren students who broke into the American air base at Tachikawa during the demonstrations against its expansion. The decision was based on the "no war" clause of the Constitution, which banned war potential of all types; in the eyes of the court, the base was "war potential," and therefore illegal. Anyone who reads this controversial "Article IX" will agree that the court's ruling was based on sufficient evidence and that a court test was needed. But a side issue, introduced into the arguments on which the decision was based, presented an alarming danger to the future of the Japanese nation, for the ruling actually challenged the right of Japan to maintain the Self-Defense Forces. It claimed, in effect, that they too were "war potential," which would seem to strip Japan of the right to defend itself—a right that would seem to be irrefutably part of the concept of independence and sovereignty; a right that most lawyers would attempt to find grounds to uphold rather than to destroy.

Another Japanese lower court ruled in 1960 that the Constitution contained no provision making rioting a crime; therefore, such violence was constitutional, legal, and democratic. The court ordered charges against a group of the anti-Security Treaty rioters dismissed, but, fortunately, the Japanese Supreme Court, which takes a more mundane view of public issues, reversed both decisions.

Perhaps as a result, former Chief Justice Kotaro Tanaka, who presided during both of these reversals, has publicly proclaimed his concern about the strange pressures and beliefs that have crept into the process of making judicial rulings in Japan. In a speech on July 21, 1960, at the Tokyo Foreign Correspondents Club, he said it was a matter of "public notoriety" that Japanese courts are being obstructed by organized labor unions, leftist parties, and "groups of lawyers led by Communists or their fellow travelers. . . . Their true intention is the destruction of the final fortress of the government to prepare for the Communist revolution." In another passage he emphasized the intellectuals' unusual concept of law by stating: "Many of the Japanese intelligentsia, including professors, teachers, and students, are hostile to law, instinctively thinking law is incompatible with freedom and democracy. Such an anarchistic idea makes a peculiar spiritual climate in our country, which may provide a most favorable condition for the growth of Communism."

Perhaps even more serious is the intellectuals' impact in the classroom and on the textbooks that nourish the minds of Japan's future citizens. As described earlier, a large proportion of those who have spread ideas already presented here are professors and teachers. From the high-school level down, most are members of the Communist-manipulated Japanese Teachers Union, a group, Education Minister Masuo Araki has charged, that is both "lawless" and "working for a Communist revolution." In a speech on October 17, 1960, before a Tokyo metropolitan Parent-Teacher Association Conference, he said, "An estimated 3,000 schoolteachers who are members of the Japanese Communist Party are daily brainwashing their pupils as future bearers of a revolution in Japan." Police confirm that of the 500,000 JTU members about 3,000 are card-carrying Communists. Although this leaves the vast majority in the non-Communist category, the high additional number of far-left Marxists, the organization's over-all class-warfare outlook on world affairs, and its deep involvement in politics certainly does cast great doubt on the quality of teaching and guidance its members provide. The Japanese Teachers Union participated vigorously and violently in the anti-Security Treaty campaign, and it is no secret that teachers egged on the students to displays of violence.

In 1960, a bitter dispute broke out between the JTU and the government over the contents of textbooks. The union contended that the government was forcing textbook writers to delete portions that showed Japan's past in an unfavorable light. Specifically, they claimed, the Education Ministry had ordered passages removed from elementary texts which described peasant uprisings in the feudal ages, and they objected to sections citing the international prestige Japan gained by winning the Sino-Japanese War of 1894–95 and the Russo-Japanese War of 1904–5. They particularly complained about the deletion of a sentence stating that "many lives were lost" in both conflicts. An objection was even raised to the fact that the color of a flag carried by a fire engine in a textbook illustration was white instead of red; the critics suspected this to be a form of censorship for political reasons, although it was later determined that fire engines on night duty, like the one in the picture, carry white flags because they can be seen more easily.

Socialist Kan Kase, at an April 14, 1960, meeting of the Standing Committee for Education of the Diet's lower house, charged that the government was having textbooks revised to place "the main emphasis . . . upon the glorification of the Emperor system while reflections on the evils of feudalism and war are eliminated." Conservative critics countercharged that Japan's intellectuals want to pass off on Japanese students a simplified version of history that divides past leaders into heroes of the people and fascist beasts. Under this interpretation, Japanese history is largely seen as the rise of the proletariat—a Marxian concept, which views the present stage of Japanese development, with its civil liberties, parliamentary government, and free elections, as only a passing stage. Presumably, something called the "socialist state" lies beyond.

Fortunately, there have been a few voices on Japan's intellectual scene that have spoken out sharply and clearly on the major issues of the day, displaying the wisdom and scholarship a nation of Japan's stature is most certainly capable of and so rightly deserves. Dr. Shinzo Koizumi, former President of Keio University and for many years Crown Prince Akihito's tutor, was one of the first to seize upon the historical parallel between the student violence of the anti-Security Treaty demonstrations and the actions of the fanatic militarists who led Japan into World War II. "If we condone in the slightest any violence such as that of our students recently, we will be lighting the match that will utterly destroy Japan as a nation dedicated to democratic government," he stated in a newspaper commentary.

Dr. Koizumi recalled the young army officers who assassinated Makoto Saito, Lord Keeper of the Privy Seal, and Finance Minister Korekiyo Takahashi on February 26, 1936. "The young officers," he continued, "ostensibly were determined to eradicate political corruption and they protested that the worthiness of their objective justified their murderous conduct. Others, incited by the terrorists, added to the turbulent situation by actually currying their favor. With dead certainty they set the stage for the inevitable chaos of World War II. This tragic lesson is something the Japanese people must never forget."

Koizumi said the student rioters of 1960 were "overexcited . . . agitated and inflamed to the point of blind fury . . . expressing their confused political beliefs. The abominable events can never be erased from history nor can anyone ever completely repair the damage done."

He did not question the students' sincerity but warned strongly against approving their actions in any way. He said that university professors, many of whom had been encouraging the students, should instead become a stabilizing influence upon them "at a time when they are being goaded into destroying their own democratic government, ruining the economy of the country, and belittling their own self-respect." And then he concluded: "The exuberance, idealism, and the chivalry of the students deserve much better training, disciplining, and nurturing on the part of their professors than has been forthcoming in the recent past. It will be a long while before the dark shadow recently cast on Japan by our irresponsible students will disappear."

Dr. Masatoshi Matsushita, President of Rikkyo University, wrote another perceptive commentary, shortly after President Eisenhower's visit to Japan was canceled. He took the position that a basic cause of the riots was the uncertainty and insecurity that had resulted from Japan being caught in the middle of the Cold War. He said in part:

> Japan . . . fought against the West and was occupied by the West and particularly by America and became independent with the support of America. America's support of Japan was not emotional. It had a political aim based on the policy of anti-Sovietism.
>
> Japan, in return for its cooperation with this political aim, has received economic prosperity. While the financial circles derived the greatest benefits, all sections of the Japanese nation have shared in a larger or smaller way in this prosperity.
>
> Should Japan adopt an anti-American policy, this enormous gain must be abandoned even if there is no war. Therefore, the business

people and those with common sense consider a separation from America impossible.

On the other hand, Japan is geographically close to the Soviet Union and Communist China. It is not only constantly influenced by them but also extremely sensitive to their power because Japan has neither the ability nor the will to defend itself.

The United States pledges assistance through the Security Treaty, but public sentiment resents protection by a foreign country and is yearning for a more independent way to assure its security.

Therefore, there are many people who think it may be better at this time to leave the United States, which is far away, and get closer to the neighboring and powerful Soviet Union and Communist China.

It is absurd to ignore these two important factors.

But whatever may be said, it is unsafe and unhealthy for a powerless nation to be hostile toward the nearby Soviet Union and Communist China and be surrounded by countries artificially supported by America.

That is where the public feels an indefinable sense of insecurity.

There may be illogical factors in this, but it cannot be laughed away as something without any cause.

Dr. Matsushita claimed that the government scarcely recognized that this feeling of insecurity existed and called those who shared it "Reds." Yet, he said, he was conscious of the same indefinable feeling and believed that all Japan's intellectuals as well as its students, laborers, and white-collar workers were, too. His statement continued:

What is the true nature of this sense of insecurity?

I don't quite understand it myself. It is complicated.

Leaving the Soviet Union aside, there is a mixture of a feeling of affinity and fear for Communist China.

It is like living free of want, due to a stranger's help, but in return one must live at odds with his brother.

It seems there is an instinctive call of the blood, though this is irrational.

Rather than be an enemy to your brother, throw away all this prosperity—such a latent desperate feeling may be hidden in this somewhere.

I consider this feeling illogical and dangerous. I can't support it.

But politics that do not understand this feeling and don't do something about it are also dangerous.

The thinking of the government, ruling party, and business circles is too materialistic. It is the kind of thinking that believes it is enough if the people get work under economic prosperity. It is like a father who pays his son's school tuition and asks, "What more do you want?"

The intellectuals and working people will be further alienated.

If this lack of understanding continues, there is the danger of a flare-up in the "call of the blood," adding up to a racial struggle.

I think the foreign policy of the government, ruling party, and financial circles is basically correct. But the sense of insecurity which I have mentioned above does exist actually, and has actual causes.

It will not do to call it irrational and get angry.

How can this contradiction be solved?

Japan must not leave America. At the same time, it must get close to Communist China, which America dislikes. This is impossible.

Japan's agony lies in the fact that Japan is placed in a position where this is impossible.

I don't have a solution to offer.

The only thing we can do is to recognize the impossible as the impossible and to understand the truth as it is.

The anguish in Dr. Matsushita's words is the anguish of Japan—an anguish imposed by its inescapable position between East and West, by its attempt to digest the conflicting cultures and ideas that go with each. This difficult role seems to have been made more precarious by the intellectuals, the very men who should be lighting the way for their nation along the twisting and precipitous road ahead. Instead, they have obscured many of the pitfalls, have conjured up some that do not even exist, and have failed to recognize many that do. They have dwelt in a strange world of their own, where all too often right is wrong, black is white, democracy is license, violence is legal, law enforcement is brutality, and faith in the concepts of Karl Marx is the hallmark of the "progressive" scholar, indeed of the only people worthy of being considered scholars. Woe betide him who differs with Marx, for he is labeled a "reactionary" and not worthy of being listened to.

Many explanations have been suggested for this situation. Obviously, in part, it reflects a cultural lag; Japanese intellectuals do show much of the same softheadedness toward Communism and its dangers that intellectuals in the Western world did in the 1930's. Others have contended that Japan's intellectuals have fallen behind because their language is not an adequate instrument of precision and logic. There is one theory that vague and indirect speech became a national habit in the days when the shogun's spies were everywhere, for people spoke obliquely to avoid committing themselves on any subject lest they be overheard. Even today, in ordinary conversation, it is considered impolite to speak in too direct and precise a fashion, particularly if the speaker does not know the listener's views. One should always try to please.

Some scholars have even claimed that the nature of their language makes the Japanese reason differently from Westerners. H. Nakamura, a Japanese philosopher, contended that it causes the Japanese to think in a series of progressive equivocations that do not permit closely knit sequences of thought: "The ambiguous character of Japanese patterns of thought and expression naturally tends to prevent the Japanese from thinking with logical coherence or consistency." Japanese scholars and scientists are often prone to speak of "kan," which, very loosely translated, means an intuitive approach to reasoning. They have it, they say, but Westerners do not.

It seems probable that language does play a part in this problem, for thought is most certainly dependent upon language, and language forms are bound to be reflected in reasoning. On the other hand, language is itself a reflection of thought structures, so the converse conclusion might also be substantiated. And without digging too deeply into the Japanese psyche, a much more obvious source of the intellectuals' dilemma suggests itself. It is Marxism and the dull, senseless conformity it has stamped on the Japanese mind. There is no better example of how successful this indoctrination has been than the Japanese student and his Communist organization, Zengakuren. But that is a story of its own—and it very appropriately begins with a demonstration against Prime Minister Kishi when the turbulent year of 1960 was less than three weeks old.

8. Zengakuren

EARLY ON THE MORNING of January 16, 1960, Prime Minister Kishi stepped into a black sedan at his official residence and sped in a convoy over back roads to Tokyo International Airport. Overhead a radio-equipped police helicopter hovered to make certain the route was clear; fifteen policemen mounted on motorcycles led the way; a dozen trucks loaded with policemen brought up the rear, and off to one flank, patrol boats guarded sea approaches to the airport. At the field, the long stream of vehicles sped through cordons of police guards, circled the terminal building, and raced up to the ramp of a waiting Japan Air Lines plane. There Kishi bade a hasty farewell to assembled members of the Tokyo diplomatic corps, quickly boarded the plane, and flew off in a gray, rain-sodden sky for America, where three days later he was to sign the revised U.S.–Japanese Security Treaty.

Why was he forced to sneak out of Tokyo? Because 1,200 baby-faced, banner-waving young men and women who opposed the alliance with the United States were milling outside the airport along the regular entrance route in an attempt to prevent him from leaving. All were from the National Federation of Student Self-Government Associations, commonly known as Zengakuren. Some wept bitterly because they had not been able to throw themselves under the wheels of Kishi's car or into the path of his plane. Others shook clenched fists at his aircraft, rapidly disappearing in the sky to the east. And all vowed that they would yet block Kishi's plans for continuing Japan's alignment with the Western democracies in the Cold War.

They had already made their feelings quite clear. Beginning at 8 P.M. the night before, Zengakuren students had started gathering in the airport terminal. They sang songs, listened to speeches by their leaders, and waved red banners. Their numbers built up while police, caught by surprise, debated what to do. Riot squads, however, began arriving by midnight, and at 1 A.M. they gave the students an ultimatum: Get out or be removed.

"We shall stay here and prevent Kishi from leaving," retorted the Zengakuren leaders. Then they took over the main floor of the terminal, threw up barricades of chairs, tables, and signs, and, while students armed with bamboo poles manned the barriers, locked arms and waited. At the last moment, however, they changed their plans, broke open the doors to the airport coffee shop, and crowded inside.

At 2 A.M. the police attacked. They pulled down the barricades, charged into the massed student ranks. In a bedlam of shouting, splintering timbers and breaking glass, the two forces came together. The officers formed a long double column, pulled the fiercely resisting students out one at a time, and passed them down the line and outside the building. Those recognized as Zengakuren leaders or as students wanted for previous acts of violence were arrested. By 4 A.M. the building was clear, but the coffee shop was in ruins, its loss estimated at 3.23 million yen ($8,980).

What is this organization that could turn such innocent-looking teen-agers into screaming fanatics, and, as it had many times in the past, send them storming through the streets shouting for the death of their Prime Minister or charging into battle with the police?

The student movement in Japan dates back to World War I, when Western liberal and left-wing thought began to permeate the country. Students were among Japan's first radicals, but these early pilgrims of the proletarian movement were harshly dealt with and, under the militarists in the 1930's, were crushed. After World War II, student-government organizations were created in each university to help teach the students democracy, but that aspiration was never realized. An act of the Japanese Government created an issue that made it possible for the Communist movement to weld these groups into a nation-wide federation with entirely different goals from those originally envisioned for the separate organizations. In October, 1947, tuition in government-operated universities and colleges was suddenly increased from 600 to 1,800 yen ($1.66 to $5.00), a 200 per cent jump at a time of such extreme economic distress that it was not at all unusual for monthly wages to range below 10,000 yen ($27.77).

The Communists went into action immediately. Student protest rallies broke out, and the agitation grew until, on June 23, 1948, students struck at twenty-nine universities in the Tokyo area. The next day, student strikes erupted at thirty-three universities elsewhere in the nation; another boycott of classes followed at forty-three more universities the following day, and by June 26, the strikes had spread to 114 state universities of 200,000 students. A nation-wide gathering of students convened September 18; when it adjourned the next day, Zengakuren had been born. From the beginning, it was built around Communist cells already existing in many of the 266 universities and colleges represented, and the record of the organization has been written in blood and violence ever since—as this brief chronology indicates:

In 1949, it joined with the Communist-dominated Japanese Teachers Union in a new campaign against the increase in student tuition.

In 1950, it demonstrated against the Occupation's directives purging members of the Japanese Communist Party's Central Committee and editors of its newspaper *Akahata (Red Flag)* from public life.

On November 12, 1951, Zengakuren students surrounded a car in which Emperor Hirohito was riding near Kyoto University, scattered handbills, and shouted for "peace."

On May 1, 1952, Zengakuren students and labor-union members battled police in a bloody May Day riot against American policy.

In 1956, Zengakuren students fought police trying to complete a survey for the expansion of the runway at America's big air base at Tachikawa. (Some broke into the base area itself, were arrested, and eventually provoked a Supreme Court test of whether such bases violated the no-war clause of Japan's Constitution. The court held that they did not.)

On November 17, 1959, Zengakuren students, led by Socialist Secretary-General Inejiro Asanuma, forcibly invaded the grounds of Japan's Diet in a protest against the U.S.–Japanese Security Treaty.

And from May 20 to June 23, 1960, Zengakuren students rioted, issued threats, and stormed through the streets of Tokyo in the emotional rampage over Diet ratification of the Security Treaty, capping their performance with the June 10 attack on White House Press Secretary James Hagerty and the bloody June 15 riot at the Diet.

This list of Zengakuren disturbances could be expanded almost indefinitely. Yet the student-government program had entirely different goals when first started.

"The idea . . . was to develop leadership and democratic ideals in the students," explained Shuichi Hasegawa, head of the student-affairs section at Tokyo University. "The school considered it a means of student education, but the students didn't. They regarded it as an integral part in the democratization of the campus. They said then, and still say, that the school consists of three equal parts—the authorities, the faculty, and the students—with the students having an equal voice in the operation of the school. . . .

"Most of the students are indifferent," he continued, "so it is the aggressive students who get the top posts. They are very often students from the Communist cells who are organized and come to meetings well prepared with arguments to push their views. The organized groups soon take over. If there is any argument, they are prepared to prolong the meetings until others are tired and ready to give in. There are only about 200 to 400 activists in all among our student body of 9,500, but around 2,500 have taken part in Zengakuren demonstrations."

The words of the students themselves show how far their movement has veered from the original democratic ideals outlined by Hasegawa. "Our belief is that unless we overthrow imperialism, there can be no way of avoiding wars," said twenty-three-old Kentaro Karoji, who was Zengakuren Chairman during the Security Treaty riots. "Capitalism has entered a stage of imperialism," he continued, "and must therefore be overthrown. . . . People talk about the aggravation of the contradictions within the imperialistic camp [meaning that it will eventually fall without outside help], but as long as imperialism exists, there is always danger. Without making progress toward overthrowing imperialism, there is no sense in any talk of how to maintain peace, because such talk is superficial."

Another typical Zengakuren member is Yoshiyuki Enami, twenty-two, an official in the student self-government organization at Tokyo University. He opposes the Security Treaty because he feels it will eventually bring the nuclear arming of Japan and war, but he denies that Zengakuren is linked with the Communists.

"We don't support any special party," he said, "even though the students have always been in the forefront of the agitations led by the Socialists and Communists against the conservative government."

What kind of government does Zengakuren want for Japan then?

"The best government will be the one we set up," he claimed. "We are planning for it now. We can't tell whether Communism is the answer for what Japan needs. It must be looked at once more through a microscope. On the other hand, capitalism is the final class society. It is objectively necessary to change it. We will have roles in that process."

A pretty twenty-year-old girl arrested in the January 16 airport riots was less definite when questioned about Zengakuren's goals. Just released from twenty-one days in prison, she was willing to discuss her views but insisted on remaining anonymous. "I saw danger in the Treaty in view of the direction in which postwar Japan was going," she said. "The Treaty invited war, but I opposed it because it was part of the Liberal-Democrats' reactionary policies. . . . From the viewpoint of the class-war theory, all Liberal-Democratic policies are reactionary." And, she hastened to explain, it is all right to use violence to fight anything that is "reactionary."

Still other Zengakuren members questioned during the period of the anti-Treaty turmoil firmly maintained that Kishi's government did not represent the people, even if his Liberal-Democrats had won a majority of the seats in the Diet at the last election. Said one: "As long as the Liberal-Democrats are in power, it won't make any difference who is Premier. I don't know right now what type government would be best, but I think it should be one representing the interests of the workers. The society of the future must rest in the hands of the workers, who are the producers. As long as man is exploiting man, this is a bad world."

Such remarks indicate the basic Marxist—actually Communist—character of Zengakuren and its policies. Over the years, it has divided ideologically into three groups that differ only in the types of Communism they advocate—the Communist League, Revolutionary Communist League, and the Stalinists, or Russian-line Communists. The first two are the most numerous and control Zengakuren; they are considered "Trotskyites" because they refuse to obey the orders of the Japanese Communist Party, advocate world-wide revolution, and consider war inevitable as long as "imperialistic capitalism" exists in the world. The Stalinists accept the Russian view that "socialism" can be perfected in a single country while coexisting with capitalist states and that, consequently, war is not necessarily inevitable.

As a result of this split, which actually involves the same ideological issues that are in dispute between Moscow and Peiping, Zengakuren's "Trotskyites" have often denounced Communist Parties all over the world as "conservative fence sitters." They refer to the Japanese Communist Party as the "so-called Japanese Communist Party." And to them, Soviet Premier Nikita Khrushchev's peaceful coexistence talk is "humbug." Even the Camp David talks between President Eisenhower and Khrushchev, which were given such wide approval in the Communist press, were "ridiculous," according to Zengakuren.

Because of such ideological differences, an open break between Zengakuren's "Trotskyite" leadership and the Japanese Communist Party, which follows the Moscow line, was only a matter of time. It came on June 1, 1958, when the JCP invited Zengakuren's leaders to talk things over. A violent argument developed. The

Zengakuren leaders demanded the dismissal of the entire JCP Central Committee; when refused, they beat up the JCP participants. The Communist Party, in turn, expelled Kenichi Kayama, then Chairman of Zengakuren and a card-carrying Party member, and two others. Thirteen more Zengakuren members who belonged to the Party were put on probation, and eventually eighty-four Zengakuren members were thrown out of the JCP. They were too radical even for the Communists.

Zengakuren is basically a product of the Communist infiltration of Japanese intellectual and educational thought that began more than four decades ago. The Communist cell at Tokyo University, one of the first organized in Japan, had always played a major role in its activities, and so have those at Waseda, Keio, and other top educational institutions in Tokyo, Kyoto, and Hokkaido. But Communist thinking could not have taken hold, and could not have been sustained, had there not been very deep unrest and dissatisfaction to exploit.

The average Japanese student is born into a life of toil and despair. A high percentage work to help support their families. Their diet of rice, fish, and a few meager vegetables makes them fall easy prey to tuberculosis, malnutrition, and serious intestinal disturbances. They are often inadequately clothed, live in flimsy, badly heated homes, and attend unheated schools in the winter. They are bound by a strict social code and a series of interlocking obligations to their family, friends, employer, and Emperor. If they fail to pass the stringent entrance examinations given by all universities, they are automatically relegated to poor, wage-earning jobs for the rest of their lives. If they pass and eventually graduate, they are virtually assured of employment by the government or by one of Japan's mammoth business enterprises, but at low pay. There they are swallowed in a sea of struggling fellow employees with hope of advancement not on the basis of merit but only on that of age. Marriage, an austere life, children, death, a Buddhist funeral, and a small headstone, where the grandchildren will come to bow their heads, sprinkle water, and leave flowers on holidays—all these lie just a few years ahead.

This pattern was shaken but not destroyed by Japan's defeat in World War II. Many of the accepted symbols were broken or shattered—the divinity of the Emperor, the invincibility of Japanese arms, the legitimacy of the class system, and the authority of parents—as a result of which an ideological vacuum was created. Postwar Japanese youth, surrounded by a new climate of intellectual freedom, certainly wanted something better than his parents had. What he wanted was "peace," "democracy," and "progress"—whatever these things were—because he had heard they were the labels that went with a better life. In short, he was ready for some answers; the quicker and easier they were, the better.

The Marxism already deeply implanted in the Japanese school system, pushed hard by Zengakuren and by teachers motivated by many of the same forces that disturbed the students, was right at hand to give predigested solutions to the world's most perplexing problems. The teachers added to the ferment by freely expressing their personal views on public affairs in the classroom. Thus was created a three-part stew compounded of a grim, often desperate economic and social life, a shattering of old patterns, and political agitation along with lessons. Now drop in two more ingredients —too much time and normal, youthful yearning for adventure— and you have a mixture that makes student demonstrations—and the violence they lead to—possible. For strangely enough, once entrance examinations are past, Japanese university students have a great deal of freedom. Attendance at classes is not required, for some schools would not have enough desks if all students did attend. Even instructors are often absent. So why not demonstrate if there is something worth demonstrating about? It is a stimulating and sometimes exciting way to burn up excess time.

The Japanese understand this underlying pattern; perhaps it explains why they have always taken an overtolerant view of student conduct. They nearly always blame such conduct on an excess of energy and maintain that the students will change later. "They are serious and pure of heart," said Jundo Uehara, an associate professor of Oriental history at Tokyo University. "They are young and have physical stamina. Some are not yet twenty, others a little over. On the whole they are not yet adults. They consider the Socialists, Communists, and Sohyo labor-federation leaders all fools. They have the sense to get at the essence of things afresh.

They want to bring out the heart of problems, lay bare the vital issues."

Many university presidents and other school authorities sided with the students during the anti-Treaty riots, and even their parents have showed little concern about student behavior. This tolerance was also mirrored in the reluctance of the police to fight back even when attacked, although there was never a time when they could not have dispersed Zengakuren's formations quickly and efficiently. With the exception of editorial writers for the English-language *Japan Times* newspaper, which often reflects the views of the Foreign Ministry, almost all Japanese critics, educators, and commentators have found reasons for excusing the students' activities. A notable exception was novelist Fusao Hayashi, an ardent leftist during the 1920's, who later broke with the proletarian movement. In a newspaper commentary, he called Zengakuren's behavior "outrageous" and "unforgivable" and its members "spoiled brats." He charged further:

> They have been playing at revolution in a country where the conditions simply do not exist for revolution. They climbed over the Diet grounds [November 27, 1959] and made a thorough nuisance of themselves. And when warrants of arrest were issued, some of them went scurrying for safety to a university campus and surrounded themselves with barricades of chairs and benches. All of this is just a piece of horse opera.
>
> In Japan today . . . none of the conditions for revolution exists. . . . It is perfectly obvious to everyone that, however much the students brandish red flags, climb into the Diet grounds, and build barricades on university campuses, none of this has anything to do with revolution, but is simply a foolish game being played by a pack of mollycoddled university students. . . . Zengakuren today is an organization engaged merely in a grotesque sport. . . .

He recalled that in his youth student radicals were thrown in jail under the National Security Law.

> During their confinement, they managed to get a lot of reading done. After six months or so in solitary, they learned more than they would have in three full years at the university. They were shocked to discover how ignorant they really were.

> There is no possibility whatever of the present police law being turned into anything like the National Security Law. . . . Zengakuren students will therefore be thrown out into the world without ever having the opportunity to study and learn. Even after they graduate they will be unable to grow out of their leftist ideologies since they will never have studied or learned anything. . . .
>
> Both the conservatives and left-wing political leaders are to be blamed for the fact that these striplings have gotten too big for their boots. The political leaders lack the spirit of "angry old men" and are acting with the proverbial folly of tolerant parents. . . . If a son goes too far, it is kindness on the father's part to give him a good hiding to bring him to his senses.

Such wise and long-overdue counseling has gone unheeded. The result has been that students within Zengakuren have become almost unbelievably foolish and arrogant.

When President Eisenhower's scheduled visit to Japan was becoming a heated issue because of the Security Treaty approval, Zengakuren issued a statement: "If Eisenhower forces his way in in spite of our warnings, he will be forced to tremble before hosts of hostile demonstrators."

Tatsuo Hayama, leader of the Communist League group within Zengakuren, said: "We must stone Eisenhower as the brave Venezuelan students did Nixon in Caracas. We can down tyrants only by violence."

When the trip was canceled, Zengakuren claimed that it was due to "our might." And when only an exchange of ratification documents remained to make the Security Treaty effective, a Zengakuren spokesman warned that "If Premier Kishi dares to try to exchange the documents, we will prevent U.S. Ambassador MacArthur from entering the Foreign Office . . . will stop the exchange by force, if necessary."

The widespread belief in Japan that such activities, including Zengakuren's violence, should be gently dealt with is obviously loaded with serious portent for the future, but it is offset by the fact that Zengakuren actually speaks for only about one-third of the 700,000 university and college students in Japan. At the same time that Zengakuren's legions were storming through the major Japanese cities, representatives of the International Council of

Youth Organizations, claiming to represent nineteen member groups with more than 7 million members reaching down to high-school levels, called on the U.S. Ambassador, Douglas MacArthur II, June 8, 1960, to promise a warm and friendly welcome for President Eisenhower when he arrived in Japan.

"There have been some movements against the President's visit that pretend to represent all of the Japanese people," Eiichi Nakao, the Council's Secretary-General, told newsmen who covered the meeting. "We don't believe this is the case," he said. "We feel that the invitation extended to the President represents the will of a large majority of the people. It is just a small percentage who are taking political advantage of the occasion."

Another factor diminishing the future danger of the Communist indoctrination of Zengakuren members is that thousands of them go along with the student mobs as much for excitement and recognition as from any ideological convictions. As a consequence, although many of them do become lifelong left-wingers, and sometimes professional revolutionaries, most seem to fade gradually into the conservative ranks of Japanese life. Tokyo University, where the student Communist movement is strongest, is also the source of most of Japan's traditionally conservative diplomats, government officials, and highly trained technicians for the largest and most prosperous firms.

The *Weekly Yomiuri* magazine once conducted a study indicating that students do not hold their left-wing beliefs very seriously. Among other things, it showed that most university graduates did not have the slightest desire to work for the small and medium-sized business enterprises they eulogized as the victims of "monopolistic capitalism" during their radical school days. Instead, they wanted a position with Mitsubishi, Sumitomo, Mitsui, or one of the other giant "Zaibatsu" combines.

Still, the long-range dangers should not be overlooked. Japanese university students are an intellectual elite. They have won their status by passing some of the toughest college-entrance examinations in the world, and they are the future leaders of their nation. It can never be worthwhile to fill the heads of future Prime Ministers, Cabinet members, industrial tycoons, engineers, economists, novelists, and artists with nonsense.

Zengakuren's obsession with certain word symbols is a case in point. "Imperialism," "monopolistic capitalism," "reactionary," "class struggle," and "socialism" are terms that crop up in virtually every conversation with a Japanese student. In such conversations, one hears all sorts of sweeping conclusions: Capitalism is evil, oppressive, monopolistic. Imperialism is the final stage of capitalism, and it inevitably generates wars to maintain its position. Socialism is the system of the purest democracy, under which classes disappear, workers get a far greater and fairer share of what they produce, and everyone lives happily ever after.

This may actually be the devil theory of history in which capitalism becomes the cause of all the world's ills. Or, if you prefer, it is the "good guys and the bad guys" of a Western movie in different dress; the good, hard-riding, straight-shooting ones, of course, being the Socialists; the evil, whisky-drinking rustlers, the capitalists. It is almost impossible to find a Japanese student who has dug behind these clichés to measure their neatly packaged conclusions against the obvious evidence in the world around him. After all, Karl Marx wrote his *Das Kapital* in 1867, almost a century ago; although the power of his economic and social thought cannot, and should not, be denied, several generations of scholars in the same field have added to the world's knowledge and have developed weaknesses and flaws in his arguments. Yet it seems doubtful that any of this later knowledge has impressed Japanese students, if it has been passed on to them at all.

An examination of the true nature of capitalism—both its faults and merits—might be a worthwhile project in a Japanese classroom. It would be foolish to deny the suffering and distress it has produced at various stages of history, but it is equally foolish to overlook benefits that have flowed from it, and the fact that in its more sophisticated forms—in the United States, for example—it has produced the most widespread prosperity ever enjoyed by a working class in world history.

The concept that capitalism creates war could stand a closer look in Japan, too. Wars were fought long before there were any capitalistic states, and if another one is fought in the future, it will probably be because of the same basic struggles for power that have caused them in the past, regardless of whether one or both sides are "capitalistic" or "socialistic."

Zengakuren's double standard of political morality—one standard for Western nations, another for Communist nations—was amply illustrated by the Hungarian revolution. Like all the left-wing groups in Japan, it found reasons to excuse the Soviet actions, and when four Hungarian students who had experienced the uprising came to Japan, Zengakuren refused to debate with them. "I can't understand," said Karoly G. Derecsky, spokesman for the group, "why as students and members of an intelligent class they are afraid to speak in a public forum." Another one of the four, Alpar Budjoso, added: "Even students in Soviet Russia and Communist China have had the courage to discuss the Hungarian revolution. It seems strange that Japanese students aren't interested."

Another long-range danger illustrated by Zengakuren is that Japanese students are so easily led—or misled. The fact that only an estimated 2,000 members of Zengakuren are Communists shows the degree to which other students, most of them admittedly Marxists, went along with the mobs during the 1960 riots, regardless of whether they believed in what they were doing. President Nobumoto Ohama of Waseda University stated this at the time, in trying to explain the students' conduct at the June 15, 1960, riot at the Diet: "I believe that the great majority of the students had no intention of charging the Diet," he stated. "In our university the majority are indifferent or are sitting on the fence over the issues earnestly taken up by Zengakuren students.

"Even those who participate in the demonstrations are not so serious in their motives. Judging from my talks with them, they regard it as just another new experience. But once they become a part of the mob, the situation changes. That they get disorganized and become violent may be due to the tactics of the leaders. The only explanation I can give is that they become the slaves of mass psychology. . . . I cannot but conclude that the students do not have much individuality of their own. This lack of individualism is also common among the Japanese in general who have lived, not for themselves, but for the state and their families. They cannot resist the mood of the moment and have a tendency to become unduly emotional."

Perhaps one of the gravest errors has been to take Zengakuren seriously. Its leaders have held press conferences, issued press releases, and have never hesitated to state their opinions on the most complicated questions of world affairs. News media, both Japanese and foreign, have duly reported these statements from immature youths hardly out of their teens. Consequently, Japan has created a situation it may be a long time eradicating, unless the Japanese Government, public, and parents eventually begin treating their radical students like the unruly and foolish children they are. But even if that time should ever arrive, there will still be other organizations even more dangerous that will have to be dealt with. The giant leftist labor federation Sohyo is most certainly one of them.

9. The Labor Movement

THE OUTSKIRTS OF WESTERN Tokyo lay gray and damp in the first light of the day. Somewhere in the distance a rooster crowed and a soba boy's flute wailed momentarily.

Junzo Kume stirred in the warm fluffy futons spread on the straw-mat floor of his four-room house. His wife, Kazuko, sat up and rubbed the sleep from her eyes.

"Ohio gozaimasu," she mumbled as her husband opened his eyes and looked at her.

Their four-year-old son, Toshiichi, rolled over and gazed sleepily at his parents and then at the heavily bundled form of his baby sister, Masako, still sleeping peacefully in her crib.

Soon the house was bustling with activity. A battered brass tea kettle, on the glowing charcoal in the hibachi, spouted a column of steam into the chill room. The sweet, heavy odor of rice cooking came from a pan on one of their two gas burners.

From the street outside, the cracked voice of the neighborhood fishmonger filtered through the window, and Kazuko slipped her bare feet deftly into wooden clogs at the door and rushed out quickly.

Junzo splashed cold water into his face, finished dressing, and then sat down to a breakfast of scalding hot green tea, rice gruel, and a tiny piece of fish. A few moments later, he mounted his old but well-kept bicycle and pedaled slowly through the winding, narrow streets to nearby Mitaka Station. Another day had begun for Junzo Kume, thirty-six years of age and a veteran motorman of the National Railway Corporation.

Aboard the shining new electric commuter he runs between Tokyo Central Station and Kofu in Yamanashi prefecture, Kume watched the placid, green Japanese countryside flash by. Crowds waited impatiently at every village and town, knowing that the train would arrive with the clocklike efficiency that is a matter of great pride to both Junzo and the nation. And when it moved on swiftly after a short pause, Junzo had time to contemplate the hours that lay before him.

His was an onerous and tiring job. Six days a week he had to supervise the new apprentice motormen, make certain the train operated properly, and carry the responsibility for the safety of an average of 3,500 passengers daily. For all this, he received 29,000 yen ($80.54) monthly. At the end of the day, Junzo wearily pedaled his bicycle back through the teeming neighborhoods to his small home. But after relaxing in the nearby community bath and a good hot meal of rice, pickles, fish, and tea, he could survey his surroundings with some satisfaction and the knowledge that his salary covered at least the essentials. In the long evenings, there were other compensations, too. He could set up his phonograph and listen to any of forty classical records he had acquired over the years. Or he could read to Toshiichi from a carefully chosen collection of books, including some newly bought foreign stories translated into Japanese. More often, the family pulled up a circle of zabutons (hard, flat sitting pillows) around the television set, bought ten months ago on an installment plan, and watched programs ranging from Japanese and Kabuki drama, Sumo wrestling, to "I Love Lucy" and other American shows. When Sunday arrived, he bundled the family off for a walk around the Imperial Palace Moat and snapped some photographs for the family album with the curving waterway and ancient battlements in the background. And that night he and his father played "Go," a Japanese game resembling chess.

So the days slip by. Sometimes Junzo reads an occasional easy novel and on rare occasions goes to the movies, unlike most Japanese, who are avid cinema fans. He has security, too. His income tax, 300 yen ($.83) monthly, is withheld from his salary automatically; so, too, is a 500-yen ($1.40) deduction for labor-union dues and 1,400 yen ($3.90) that pays his entire medical bills and 60 per cent of his family's medical costs. This same charge entitles him to purchase food, medicine, cosmetics, underwear, and other items at 20 per cent under normal market prices.

Thus, Junzo's basic wants are provided for. He can look forward to a small increase in pay every year or two, won by him and his co-workers of the Japanese National Railway Workers Union in the noisy, flag-waving demonstrations, rallies, and short work stoppages that make up the typical Japanese strike. And every June and December, he can count on a bonus of one and two months' pay, respectively. But other than this, his life is firmly fixed. His lack of both a high-school and college education, or a higher skill, have relegated him to his present level. When Junzo reaches fifty-five, he will have to step down and accept a final assignment as an assistant master of a small railroad station. No matter how hard he may work, the railroad management will never give him a higher position. His future is preordained, set in the rigid framework of Japanese society, which assigns a place and a status to everyone. Junzo accepts it with the fatalistic "it-cannot-be-helped" philosophy of his people.

Junzo Kume is one of 7 million organized workers in Japan whose living standards have been raised tremendously by one of the most militant labor movements in the world. He is typical of the skilled employee of a stable, well-financed concern—in this case, a government corporation. Unlike Japanese workers of previous generations, he can afford to buy and wear Western business suits, ride a taxi occasionally, take a two-week paid vacation every year, and even accumulate a small bank account. Mild in manner, dedicated to his family and his job, he lives in a not too oppressive poverty that admittedly would be almost bountiful in other areas of Asia. But he is limited in his contacts with the outside world to what he reads in his daily newspaper, sees on television, hears on the radio, and is told by his labor union. Japan's labor movement is, in fact, one of the most important forces in all workers' lives. It has won many economic gains for its members, but it has also involved them deeply in politics and made anti-government agitation a guiding, and seemingly at times a ruling, concern. It is regimented, capable of violence, and paradoxically quite amenable to carrying out a program almost identical with that of the Communist Party although it is not predominantly Communist either in membership or in intent.

Labor's first stirrings began as early as 1897, shortly after the Sino-Japanese War, when Japanese capitalism had reached the first stage of its growth. In the liberal political climate that followed World War I, the labor movement developed rapidly, although still on a small scale, only to fall victim to Communist penetration after 1927 and then to the ruthless suppression of the militarists who seized control of the nation in the 1930's.

After World War II, the American Occupation encouraged labor to organize, feeling that this would direct a fairer share of national wealth into lower levels of the economy and promote democratization by counterbalancing the overwhelming power of organized financial interests. Unions were formed in virtually every major enterprise, and Japan's first labor federation, Sambetsu, or Congress of Industrial Unions, was born. But under the skillful direction of Sanzo Nozaka and his henchmen, Communists soon had a majority of the Sambetsu unions under their control. In 1947, taking advantage of a severe food crisis, Sambetsu marshaled workers for a general strike in an effort to bring down the conservative government, whose bumbling had helped create conditions of near starvation. Only last-minute intervention by General Douglas MacArthur, the Occupation Commander, prevented a crippling tie-up.

Public distaste for the Communist role in this crisis led to the formation of Sohyo, The General Council of Japanese Trade Unions, in July, 1950. Although launched as an anti-Communist organization, it soon donned the familiar leftist-neutralist political dress. Some of its unions refused to load and unload supplies for United Nations forces fighting in Korea, and some of its members were accused of sabotage at plants handling munitions contracts for American troops. They were also involved in the violent, Communist-instigated May Day riot of 1952, when union columns battled police, burned American cars, and threw two American sailors into the Imperial Palace Moat. This increasingly pro-Communist orientation precipitated the formation of still another labor federation in 1954—Zenro, or the National Council of Trade Unions. It drew away the more moderate elements in Sohyo and left that organization with an even more dominant, far-left political character.

In this manner, the current pattern of the Japanese labor movement was set within nine years after the end of World War II. Sambetsu, mortally weakened by Sohyo's birth, tottered along for seven years before its final collapse in 1957. Sohyo, likewise hurt by Zenro's withdrawal, although not nearly as seriously, stabilized its membership at a claimed 3.6 million members organized in fifty-seven vertical-type or industrial unions, and made the Socialist Party its captive political organ. Zenro built its strength slowly to a claimed 1.1 million members and eventually made the Democratic Socialist Party its political arm. Another 2.3 million workers in private unions remained outside the federations but tended to support the Socialist Party politically. Beyond them lay the vast, unorganized labor pool of Japan—some 35.5 million day laborers, cottage-industry workers, and destitute derelicts, who lived from day to day on what they could pick up from occasional jobs.

Of all the labor groupings, Sohyo is clearly the most powerful—and the most political. Its own self-styled sense of mission, which embraces the belief that it is fully entitled to use force to block the government, was clearly demonstrated in 1955 when it prevented the lengthening of runways at the big American air base at Tachikawa, near Tokyo. The improvement was needed to permit modern jet planes to land and take off there—a purpose that ran counter to Sohyo's professed neutralist goals. It was also understandably opposed by farmers who would lose land in the extension, for the government had offered them only a pittance in compensation.

Sohyo had its forces in motion throughout the early morning hours of the day that the first surveys were planned. In trucks and long marching columns, they converged on the tiny village of Sunakawa, bordering the air base, and when the government survey men arrived, blocked their way with a human wall of workers.

Police, who had expected trouble, moved in, too, until two small armies tensely confronted each other. I was there that day and recorded this scene:

> As far as you could see, thousand of workers wearing white headbands, a traditional workman's symbol, had jammed into a narrow road running parallel to the side of the air base where the surveys were to be made. Their huge red banners were implanted along the sides of the road. The police halted about forty yards from the workers' front ranks. Sound trucks moved up to warn the demonstrators to disperse. The laborers responded by locking arms and raising their voices in a union song, swaying from side to side with the rhythm.
>
> The police gave a final warning, then formed into a wedge, and rammed into the workers' front ranks. Twice they hit them in a giant pushing-and-shoving battle, gaining only a few feet each time. Some of the workers went spinning into a small sewer ditch along the road. There was a terrible crush where the blue of the police uniforms merged in an uneven line with the white headbands. Faces of both policemen and workers at this point were contorted in pain, and blood-smeared faces appeared as fists smashed down wherever there was sufficient freedom of movement to swing an arm.
>
> Suddenly, at a shouted command, the police backed away, and almost the entire front rank of the workers was ripped away with them. The startled workers saw these front-line leaders hoisted quickly into the air and passed back over the heads of the police into the rear ranks, where they were taken into custody. Some fought back viciously along the way and took a severe pummeling in return, ending up gasping and bleeding as they were herded into trucks. Time after time the police repeated the tactic, pulling away the workers' front men, then charging into them again while they milled in confusion. Slowly they pushed the workers back more than a half-mile, and the survey parties moved in to drive their first stakes.

Sohyo was soon disorganized and discouraged; but just when it appeared that the workers would be driven completely out of the area, the police backed away. They were displaying the same reluctance to use their full power they were to demonstrate later in the 1960 anti-Security Treaty riots, apparently to avoid popular condemnation as the equivalent of the prewar police. As a consequence, Sohyo was out again in greater strength when the next stage of the survey began several months later. This time it had strong help from Zengakuren. Socialist Diet members were also arrayed ostentatiously in the workers' front ranks, and Communist Chairman Nozaka was on hand to harangue the demonstrators from a sound truck nearby. A dispute that had started over the amount of compensation the Sunakawa villagers should receive for their land had ballooned into a major political clash over "peace," "neutrality," "racial independence," and numerous other stock phrases in the Sohyo lexicon. It ended up in a complete deadlock, and all plans for enlarging the air base were indefinitely postponed.

An even better demonstration of Sohyo's increasingly violent turn of mind developed at the Miike coal mine in northern Kyushu. There a tragic situation had arisen from a slowly evolving technical revolution in Japanese fuels. Oil had replaced coal in many enterprises as a source of power, and a serious economic sickness had settled over the entire coal industry. Miners' families were living in deep poverty, barely staying alive on government and union doles. Their children were in rags, suffering seriously from malnutrition and lack of medical care.

The Mitsui Mining Company, one of Japan's largest, decided that it would have to drastically trim the labor force at all its diggings and adopt more efficient methods of production to survive. This included the dismissal of 1,200 workers at Miike; but when notices were posted, the workers, all members of Tanro, numerically one of Sohyo's strongest unions, struck to shut down the mine. There was no question that they had serious grievances and would be unable to survive unless given major assistance. The work stoppage dragged on for 311 days while the miners' condition grew steadily worse. Out of the struggle came an unusually generous company offer of compensation for those losing their jobs: It averaged 465,000 yen ($1,291) per miner—practically a fortune in Japan. Workers scheduled for discharge at other Mitsui diggings accepted the offer, but only 623—about half of those to be let out—did so at Miike. Sohyo, with the strong backing of the Communist elements in Tanro, said that all the workers must go back to work—or none. Those not fired and wanting to return to their jobs formed a new company-oriented union and tried to re-enter the pits. Members of the old union stopped as many as they could in a series of increasingly violent clashes. Every time a new group attempted to enter or leave, it had to run a gantlet of stones, fists, angry denunciations, and beatings administered by pickets of the original union.

Police poured in from surrounding areas. So did the Communists and—so it was charged, but never proved—funds from Communist China. *Akahata*, the Japanese Communist Party newspaper, circulated freely among the strikers. Rabble-rousing speakers whipped up their emotions and reassured them of the righteousness of their cause. Reinforcements from other leftist unions arrived. Soon there were fights almost every day while the police tried to clear the way for the nonstrikers as they entered and left the pits. The encounters flared at first on land and then erupted into "sea battles" as the company-oriented union tried to sneak workers in by boats to the company docks. The strikers strung a picket line of boats across the approaches and attacked the sea invaders with huge firecrackers, stones, clubs, and explosive charges.

The crisis deepened until police delivered an ultimatum, backed up by a court injunction, that they would forcefully clear the strikers from company property if they did not leave voluntarily. This converted the area into a battlefield: The strikers dug trenches, strung barbed wire, began drilling teams in riot tactics, and armed their men with clubs, spears, and huge timbers for battering rams. The original union was obviously ready for a brutal showdown it could not possibly win. Many Japanese, including the deeply concerned leaders of Sohyo, knew this, since more than eight hundred workers had already been injured and one killed in the fighting.

The crisis stage was reached just as Hayato Ikeda was taking over from Kishi as Premier in the aftermath of the anti-Security Treaty struggles of 1960. Ikeda promptly stepped in and through his able Labor Minister, Hirohide Ishida, produced a face-saving formula that both sides were eager to accept—a compromise keyed to the company-offered compensation and government help in retraining and relocating the discharged workers. It was a long-overdue solution, and it prevented the bloody clash that the Communists had been eager to create and that the government had helped foster by not acting sooner in behalf of the destitute miners.

If life is filled with such violence and turmoil for Japan's organized workers, it is even worse for those who are neither organized nor skilled. They are among the most exploited humans in Asia, unable to quibble about the callous disregard of labor laws and receiving pay sometimes as low as 300 yen ($.83) daily. When the pay is better, it is often keyed to brutally long work periods or extremely rigid piece-work minimums that have to be met.

Employers have always liked to hire from this vast, hungry pool of manpower whenever possible because of the low costs involved. One of their favorite recruiting areas is the Sanya flophouse district of Tokyo, where drug addiction, drunkenness, prostitution, crime, and riots flourish. It is a dismal jungle of clapboard and grimy brick buildings, garbage-filled streets, flies, tiny restaurants, and noisy market places, where prostitutes, clad only in panties and brassieres, wander through the vegetable stands in summertime and men squat on street corners with a jug of shochu, a strong intoxicant, slowly drinking themselves into a state of oblivion. One of the favorite recreations of these people is to drink in groups near a new police station and hurl insults at the officers. This soon leads to rock-throwing and frequently to a full-fledged attack on the station. Police have questioned those arrested in these riots and have been able to discover only one consistent reason for the violence—the participants simply do not like the police and do not want them around.

These hopeless and resentful men of Sanya can be seen gathering before the sun is up on prearranged street corners where hiring agents from big construction companies load their trucks with human cargo. They are taken to the huge building projects or other construction works under way at all times in Tokyo and put to work at the most rigorous forms of manual labor. After dark, they are returned, fourteen to sixteen hours later, exhausted and near collapse.

It is in just such situations as those of the Sanya workers that the need for a strong, independent labor movement in Japan is rooted. Yet the political character the movement has assumed has led to serious questions about the true objectives of the men who head the more powerful unions and the future that lies ahead for their members.

The leaders of the now-defunct Communist-dominated Sambetsu were obviously bent on using the workers for their own political purposes from the very beginning. Zenro's chiefs have so far been reasonably responsible and, in fact, have dealt with economic issues other than political ones. But the top command of the giant Sohyo, despite its anti-Communist origins, began treading a far-left political path soon after its separation from Sambetsu. Under one of its early leaders, Minoru Takano, a small, shrewd, birdlike man, Sohyo marched along in stride with the Communists. Its announced goals included the by now familiar neutralization of Japan—withdrawal of American troops, breakup of the American base system in the Far East, abrogation of the U.S.–Japanese alliance, recognition of Communist China, and increased trade with the Communist world.

This political coloration is partly traceable to the fact that two-thirds of Sohyo's membership consists of government workers, whose livelihood and hopes for more pay are directly linked to the national budget passed each year by the Diet. The strong Marxist thinking imbedded in the labor movement, and its basic concept of class warfare, also has led to political activity. And then, too, the government workers have been infiltrated by both deep-cover Communists and extreme Marxists, who, of course, have exerted what influence they could to promote their own ends. The political nature of Sohyo is expressed through the Japanese Socialist Party; in fact, Sohyo is the Japanese Socialist Party, since the party could not exist without it. The party has never had a nationwide organization and has very poor fund-raising capabilities. It has to depend on Sohyo, which has both. If Sohyo disapproves of what the Socialist leaders do, there is an immediate scramble to get their views coordinated again. This is not to say there are not differences. Sohyo and the party both have their conservative and radical elements, which are constantly in conflict; but once Sohyo sets a course, the party immediately sails in the same direction. Even after Takano was supplanted as Secretary-General by tough, muscular Akira Iwai in an upheaval against Sohyo's Communist-tinged left wing, and after Kaoru Ohta, a very able leader, became Chairman, the federation remained as deeply involved in far-left politics as before. Iwai considers himself an anti-Communist and has denounced the Communists on many occasions, yet he was in charge of Sohyo throughout the violent demonstrations of late 1959 and the spring of 1960, when a distinctly Communist pattern emerged. Many months before the Security Treaty crisis erupted, I interviewed Iwai at Sohyo headquarters and asked whether he felt there were many Communists in the organization.

"Communists!" he snorted. "We may have a few, but not among our leaders." He obviously did not like the question, particularly from an American newsman. He paced back and forth, anxious to complete the interview and return to his own work.

Iwai looked every inch a tough, resourceful labor chief. His face had grown fleshy around the jowls, and there was a noticeable thickening of the waist and hips, but there was obvious power in the sloping shoulders and barrel chest, developed by long hours of labor as a railroad worker. In one corner of the room was a showcase filled with trophies and gifts from Communist China, presented over the years to Sohyo delegations that had taken advantage of China's expense-paid tours for any mildly influential Japanese who wanted to get a peek at the new giant stirring behind the bamboo curtain. The rest of the room was almost bare, relieved only by Iwai's desk, a scroll, and a ring of chairs about a low table, where callers were served green tea.

"The Communists don't play any important role in Sohyo," Iwai snorted again with an air of dismissing the subject. Then, he launched into a more popular Sohyo issue, the increasing power of Japanese "monopoly capital."

"Our capitalists are out to dominate all of Asia again," he claimed, "and America is helping them." Iwai spoke bitterly of what he considered the increasing trend toward a new strongly capitalistic state in Japan, its rearmament, the plight of Japanese workers, and the danger of Japan's becoming involved in a future nuclear war. And he spoke with enthusiasm of the need for all Japanese to band together in a political movement to halt this drift, adopt a neutral role in world affairs that would lead to "peace," and create a "workers'" government that would ensure Japan's "racial independence." He said the severance of military ties with America and the removal of American bases were absolute necessities.

Unfortunately, Iwai's claimed aversion to Communists has failed to find full expression in Sohyo policies. In fact, Sohyo has seemed to become more and more enmeshed in the Communist program as it casts about for issues and tactics that will bring the Socialist Party victory at the polls. After each defeat at the polls, it has tended to move further to the left, apparently believing that the path to greater popularity lies in that direction. This drift went so far that former Socialist Chairman Asanuma said on one occasion, "It seems the only way we can take over the government is by revolution," and the remark caused hardly a flicker of surprise in an organization whose membership was still overwhelmingly non-Communist.

Haruo Wada, Secretary-General of Zenro, has described Sohyo's Communist inclinations in this manner: "At first Sohyo said, 'We will oppose the Communist Party.' Then it became, 'We will form a common front with the Communist Party.' This changed to, 'There may be occasion for Sohyo to engage in joint struggles with the Communist Party.' Then came the stand, 'There is nothing wrong in joint struggles with the Communist Party.' Finally, Chairman Ohta and Secretary-General Iwai made the statement, 'We will, in principle, engage in joint struggles with the Communist Party.' "

Omer Becu, General Secretary of the International Confederation of Free Trade Unions (ICFTU), openly accused Sohyo of working with the Communists when he visited Tokyo in October, 1960. After a brief study of the situation, he challenged Sohyo to break with the Reds and criticized it for spearheading the mass demonstrations against the Security Treaty. "The advice we have given and shall always give is to leave political issues to political parties and concentrate on the economic and social interests of the workers," he said. He attacked Sohyo for maintaining contacts with both the ICFTU and the Communist-oriented World Federation of Trade Unions (WFTU). His organization might decline any future invitations to Sohyo conventions, Becu stated, if WFTU officials were also to be present. "We have had our experiences with Communists," he added, "and do not like to sit on the same platform with them."

Iwai and other Sohyo officials attempted to convince Becu that the Japanese labor movement was subject to unique problems that made political activity necessary. Their argument was that there is so much unemployment in Japan, and so many workers living at mere subsistence levels, that any reduction in the number of jobs is a matter of life and death to thousands. They claimed that the summoning of police to almost all labor disturbances gave such disputes a political character. As for the accusation of Communist influence, they said that Sohyo wanted to create a Socialist state by parliamentary methods, not by violent revolution. Only about 50,000 of Sohyo's 3.6 million members were extreme leftists or Communists, they concluded.

Such protestations from Sohyo cannot negate the fact that it casts a far different image by its actions than it realizes. And this image, projecting a shadow over the future of the entire labor movement in Japan, raises the possibility that Sohyo's leaders have drifted toward the Communist camp more from the desire to maintain or seek political power than from efforts to improve the welfare of their members.

This, at best, is a most dangerous game and would obviate any conclusion that Japan's labor movement is off to a good start. True, there are many strong unions, and Sohyo and Zenro are both so powerful that Japan's big employers cannot manipulate them for their own purposes. In addition, workers in other fields are being organized slowly, and wage levels are being forced upward. But the charges of overemphasis on politics and Communist influence are not empty accusations. Despite Sohyo's claims to the contrary, a great deal of its political agitation could be cast aside and supplanted by a more vigorous concentration on economic objectives. Likewise, no matter how much Sohyo protests, it obviously does have its card-carrying and hidden Communist members, who, although not numerically strong, are aided and abetted by a very vocal and extreme left wing that is quite willing to carry out many of their plans for them. Iwai and Ohta may claim that Sohyo wants to change the character of Japan's government only by parliamentary means, but their union's violent tactics indicate that they do not mean what they say.

Zenro has demonstrated that nothing in Japan's labor movement need necessarily involve it deeply in politics or make it resort to violence. Zenro, like Sohyo, is somewhat political because the Democratic Socialist Party is its political mouthpiece, but it stayed completely out of the Security Treaty riots and has never been accused of using other than parliamentary methods.

Japan's postwar labor movement has developed in what appears to be a cyclical pattern: first, the formation of a labor federation; then Communist penetration; next, revolt against the Communists and the establishment of a new federation, which, in turn, becomes the target for new Communist infiltration. Thus, Japan has had Sambetsu, followed by Sohyo, followed by Zenro. Whether or not this pattern will repeat itself, and bring down Sohyo as it did Sambetsu, remains to be seen, but it is not in sight for the present.

Standing high above this unhappy spectacle of Sohyo's deep involvement with the violent left is the most important issue of all—Japan's desperate need for a healthy, free labor movement. I have seen its exploited workers toiling for a pittance far into the night on construction projects; I have seen them collapse with exhaustion onto seats of Japan's Yamate Line trains, and I have seen their homes, where they freeze in the winter, swelter in the summer, and somehow manage to stay alive on rice, fish, a few pickles, and green tea.

Japan's labor movement need not be a political eunuch. There is no reason why it should not promote worthwhile social goals through candidates who stand for such progress. But if it is to survive and grow as a strong, independent force in Japanese life, rather than eventually be crushed because it has become the handmaiden of a foreign power, it will have to do some serious soul-searching. Most certainly, it needs a much more diligent and responsible approach to improving the welfare of its members than its leaders have demonstrated so far. And if those leaders need some hints on how to rise to the demands of their jobs, they might well take a closer look at the career of one of their bitterest enemies—Nobusuke Kishi. It is doubtful if any other man in recent Japanese history has come closer to true statesmanship. He broke with his authoritarian past and laid out a course for the future growth of democracy and prosperity in his nation.

10. Kishi and the Conservatives

One cold winter evening soon after the war, a gaunt, slightly stooped man clad in heavy workshoes and an ill-fitting soldier's uniform walked slowly to the back entrance of the Prime Minister's official residence.

"I would like to see Mr. Sato," he told the maid at the door. "Mr. Eisaku Sato, Chief Cabinet Secretary. Tell him his brother is here."

Moments later an immaculately groomed man burst into the waiting room. "Nobusuke!" he shouted. "Nobusuke! At last."

Nobusuke Kishi had had a varied history. Once a fervent rightist and nationalist, he had been suspected of Class A war crimes, served as Commerce and Industry Minister for Japan's wartime Premier Hideki Tojo, advocated Japan's Greater East Asia Co-Prosperity Sphere, and directed the industrial development of the Japanese puppet state Manchukuo. And now he had just been released from grim Sugamo—the prison where Tojo and his companions who had led Japan into war had been hanged, where hundreds of others had been incarcerated.

It was Christmas Eve, 1948, and a joyous reunion awaited him. At a party at Sato's home, friends kept bursting into the room to welcome him back. Kishi gorged himself on sushi—raw fish wrapped in rice and seaweed; while smoking cigars, he talked incessantly of the three years and three months he had spent behind bars before being released without having been charged or tried. When he answered a phone call, his face split into a grin, for he recognized the well-modulated voice of an old friend, business tycoon Aiichiro Fujiyama. But suddenly tears welled into his eyes; in a voice strained with gratitude he mumbled good-by. "He offered me the chairmanship of several of his companies," he said.

If ever a man had cause to think back over his life, it was Nobusuke Kishi as he lay alone with his thoughts that night—a broken man in the burned and ravaged capital of his vanquished nation. Virtually everything he had espoused and believed in was gone—most of the empire, the seemingly invincible Imperial Army and Navy, the strict class structure of Japanese society. Instead, there were strange new ways and new methods he did not understand, a foreign-written Constitution, Japanese girls boldly walking the streets arm in arm with American soldiers, youths who did not respect their elders. The entire nation was filled with a free-wheeling, impudent air.

It was a time for memories: recollections of the rice fields of his native Choshu, green as emeralds in the summer sun; of the sagging, dilapidated building where he went to grade school; of the stern visage of his mother, who kept repeating, "Never forget you are a samurai!"; and of the stately halls of Tokyo Imperial University, where he graduated near the top of his class in law. There was, very likely, a nostalgic memory of a proud Nobusuke Kishi standing at the door of his quarters in Manchukuo, gazing at the belching smokestacks on the horizon—an industrial complex he helped to create. And there must have been disturbing recollections of a violent argument with tough, bespectacled Tojo; of an endless column of young men, rifles shouldered, marching toward death in the jungles of the South Pacific; of burning cities, of his own home collapsing in flames, and of the high-pitched, child-like voice of the Emperor that hot August 15, 1945, telling his people it had all been in vain. And most assuredly there were thoughts of the high-nosed foreign soldiers, GI's they called them, who arrested him, pushed him on a truck, and hauled him off to prison.

If Kishi could have gazed into the future as readily as his mind roamed the past, he would have viewed a kaleidoscope of even greater import, leading toward a climax in which he stood as a lone figure against a background of burning trucks, of surging, screaming leftist mobs, and of Japan's gray-stoned besieged Diet building. For it was a strange role that awaited him, one completely alien to his authoritarian past. He was to be cast as the lead in a drama of seething passions in which he would—at least in the eyes of many foreign critics—stand up for the principles of majority rule, nonviolence, and continued close association with the Western democracies. And before he had spoken his last line and stepped down, an embittered, seemingly hated man in his own nation, he was to emerge as a statesman of far above-average stature on the international scene, a man who had the courage to fight for something larger than himself and his past, and win.

In appearance, Kishi does not remotely resemble any stereotype of an outstanding leader. He exudes energy, a dynamism and youthfulness belying his more than threescore years, and the startling homeliness of the man is soon forgotten in a face-to-face meeting. Kishi speaks slowly and distinctly, smokes continuously; crow's-feet, at the corners of his brown eyes, crinkle with humor when he makes a good verbal thrust. He does not use many gestures: Now and then an arm sweeps through the air to emphasize a point; more often, one hand is occupied only in flicking ashes off his ever-present cigarette. But as he looks searchingly into your eyes for a reaction to what he has said, his own suggest that he understands much of the conversation even when working through an interpreter. There is a continual crossing and uncrossing of legs, a slightly nervous jiggling of the suspended foot, and at times long pauses while he gazes out the window and ponders an answer.

Kishi was well known in capitals of the world even before the violent explosion that climaxed his nearly three-and-one-half-year Administration. After he became Premier, on February 28, 1957, his long-striding figure in striped pants, morning coat, and top hat crossed Asia, the United States, and parts of Latin America to urge nuclear disarmament and an end to nuclear tests. He made two sallies into Southeast Asia and one into Australia and New Zealand, attempting to lay the basis for future trade by overcoming with his "personal diplomacy" the smoldering legacy of hate left by Japan's wartime activities in those areas. He kept hawking a Southeast Asia Development Plan that he wanted America to finance and Japan to profit by, a plan that would, in effect, have created by peaceful means the East Asia Co-Prosperity Sphere Japan failed to forge by war. And he successfully carried to the inner sanctums of the U.S. State Department his quest for removal of American ground forces from Japan, for more trade with America, and for more equality in their alliance.

There was little to hint at a role of world-wide scope in the young Kishi. He was born on November 13, 1896, at the southern Honshu village of Hakkenya in Yamaguchi prefecture, near the beautiful, winding Inland Sea. He was the second son of Hidesuke and Moyo Sato, who had ten children—seven girls and three boys. Yamaguchi, formerly known as Choshu, provided a gentle but realistic environment for his quick eager mind; it had rolling hills, endless paddy fields, short, swift rivers that swept to the sea, and a long history of great warriors who tempered their fighting spirit with a deep practicality.

Kishi remembers his father as a gentle, scholarly man, for many years a minor government official who later became a brewer. The father was born Hidesuke Kishi, changed his name to Sato when he married the eldest daughter of the aristocratic Sato family, and so ensured continuance of that family's name in the absence of a male heir. This "adoption" procedure, not uncommon in the Orient, was later applied to Nobusuke when he married his cousin, Yoshiko, at the age of twenty-two. In this way he regained the name of Kishi. "My father and mother were poles apart in character," Kishi recalls. "Among our relatives she was spoken of as a woman of 'remarkable spirit.' The rearing of the children was always the job of our strong-minded mother." Yet Kishi was a frail, sickly child. His friends nicknamed him "Darkie" because of his swarthy complexion, but they also respected his quick fists. Proud and tough-minded, he was addicted to picking fights with older pupils, a characteristic that cropped up repeatedly in later relations with his superiors.

But those years passed swiftly, for Nobusuke developed an early mental discipline and craving for knowledge. "I studied diligently," he once told some young students. "There were ten children in my family, so we passed our books around until they were ready to fall apart. I always studied my lessons one or two hours before leaving for school and before retiring."

By the time he reached middle school, he was known as a top student who liked to smoke, drink rice wine, and entertain girls. His fragile health, however, forced him to abandon ambitions for an army or navy career in favor of government work. He sailed through First Higher School in Tokyo, studying German law, and in 1917 entered Tokyo Imperial University, which accepted only the brightest young men in the nation. Kishi's mind was soon fired by the heavily nationalistic emphasis of Japanese education, and particularly by rightist leader Ikki Kita, later executed by the dreaded Kempeitai police for sparking the February 26, 1936, soldiers' uprising. Kita's writings on the Emperor caused Kishi to take pen in hand and enthusiastically state in a student paper:

"The glory of the national structure in the genuine sense of the term can be given the fullest value only when the Emperor is with the people and among the people. It is a matter of urgent necessity that the peerage be abolished and the Imperial Household Department be reorganized." This call for eliminating Japan's privileged nobility and cracking down on the protocol-minded bureaucrats who surrounded the Emperor did not sit too well with the school authorities, but there were no serious repercussions.

Kishi entered government service and rose rapidly in the Ministry of Commerce and Industry, acquiring a marked skill in examining and spotting flaws in important documents. It was not long, however, before he was in hot water, staging what he called "my first rebellion against higher officials"; for he led a successful fight against a proposed 10 per cent salary reduction and almost had to resign. In 1935, as Director of the Ministry's Industrial Affairs Bureau, he helped form the cartels and trusts that mobilized Japanese industry for the coming war. And in October, 1936, he was appointed Vice-Director of the Industrial Department of the government of Manchukuo, the subempire the Japanese military had carved out of Manchuria and north China.

There he took a firm stand with the military.

"I know industry better than anyone else here," he told General Seishiro Itagaki, then Chief of Staff of the Kwantung Army. "If anyone interferes with my work, I will quit. If you want a 'yes' man, you should get someone else."

General Itagaki gave him a free hand and ordered him to formulate and push a five-year industrialization program.

As a result, Manchukuo boomed: Railroads spread across its rolling plains; mines were sunk; new factories began to pump smoke into the gray, endless skies; new buildings appeared, and the streets were filled with the tramp of marching troops. It was almost entirely a Japanese Army show, and Kishi was proud to be a part of it. When ordered home in October, 1939, to become Vice-Minister of Commerce and Industry, he said: "The industrial world of Manchukuo is my creation. It is my creation, and I shall always be proud of it. I shall never forget it as long as I live."

Back in Tokyo, Kishi was soon fighting with his superiors again. He clashed with Commerce Minister Ichizo Kobayashi over a plan for putting Japan's economy on an even more warlike footing than before. He favored it, Kobayashi did not, and Kishi had to resign.

By now war clouds were dark and heavy over the Pacific. Tojo came to power on October 18, 1941, named Kishi his Commerce Minister, and less than two months later sent the first wave of planes screaming down on Pearl Harbor.

Kishi has never sidestepped responsibility for participating in that decision. "The Imperial Headquarters Liaison Council made the initial decision," he explains. "It was then approved by the Cabinet and confirmed at a conference with the Emperor. I don't wish to defend myself. All the state ministers were responsible for assisting the Emperor in making a decision. So I think I should not say I was against the war."

Japan's great gamble paid off for a time with victory after victory, but by the spring of 1944 the Americans were sweeping back across the Pacific, savagely attacking the Japanese fleet and Japanese shipping. A massive battle was shaping up for the strategic island of Saipan, within B-29 bomber range of the Japanese homeland. Tojo rushed in reinforcements and proudly announced, "Let's see them take it now!" Kishi thought the preparations inadequate and said so.

"Tojo and I did not see eye to eye on the future development of the war situation," he said. " 'Saipan is Japan's lifeline,' I told him. 'If it is taken, surrender. It would be the silliest thing in the world to keep on fighting after that.'

"Tojo shouted at me, 'Don't poke your nose into affairs of the Supreme Command.' But I persisted and argued that when such an important issue as the nation's survival is involved, anyone's opinion should be listened to."

Tojo would not listen, and Saipan fell. Kishi renewed his argument, suggesting that it was time for all members of the Cabinet but Tojo to resign. But the Prime Minister thundered back: "No! Only you resign!"

"I called that a silly idea," Kishi said. "Then Tojo began begging me to resign." Kishi told him huffily: "I was appointed personally by the Emperor. My sense of responsibility is to him. It doesn't allow me to resign meaninglessly when there is no sign the tide of war will turn in our favor." The fight finally brought the fall of the entire Cabinet, and Kuniaki Koiso took over as Premier.

The Kempeitai (military police) began to shadow private citizen Kishi after that. He rented an office in the *Mainichi* newspaper building and conducted his personal affairs quietly. In the spring of 1945, during the fire bombing of Tokyo, Kishi's home in the Shinjuku area burned down, and he moved back to Yamaguchi. There his health broke; when the surrender came, he was in the hospital.

"When I heard the Emperor's voice, I was at a loss what to do," Kishi related later. "Should I live on or kill myself? I thought there would be military trials. I decided I had to live on to clarify the situation under which Japan plunged into war."

A short time later ex-Commerce Minister Kishi was hauled away to prison. "I was arrested on September 12, 1945," he recalls, "less than a month after Japan's surrender. Many other members of the Tojo Cabinet were also arrested. I thought we would all be hanged or shot, and I entered the prison with resignation.

"For the first three months, we were held at Omori and Yokohama prisons before being moved to Sugamo. The treatment was stern but respectful. Some of the guards even surprised us by saying 'Yes, sir' and 'No, sir' in talking to us. But after we moved to Sugamo the treatment became vengeful. The guards were combat-seasoned men. They would order the Class A war prisoners to scrub the dirty floor with soap and water until it shone. Then they would tell us to do it all over again. Just before I was released the treatment became milder, apparently because new recruits from the States were replacing the older, tougher guards. When I found out I was not to be indicted and hanged, I began to think about the rest of my life as a bonus to be spent wisely. I had long reflections on the past."

Kishi was a humble, softspoken man, deeply critical of his own past, when he left Sugamo, but his friends soon restored his spirit. Fujiyama, who had called him that first night at his brother's residence, made Kishi Chairman of the Toyo Pulp Company, Tokyo Kozai Company, and other firms under his control. After Kishi's name was removed in April, 1952, from the Occupation's list of those banned from public office, Premier Shigeru Yoshida, an old political enemy soon to become a stanch friend, called him in for a talk. A month later, in February, 1953, Kishi was dispatched on an inspection tour of Europe and America. It had every earmark of a prestige trip to groom a promising leader for better things.

Kishi's political career soared like a rocket. Within four years he became Prime Minister, replacing Tanzan Ishibashi, who fell ill and stepped down only two months after having taken over from Ichiro Hatoyama, the successor of Yoshida.

I particularly remember Kishi in November, 1955, two years before he became Prime Minister, when he was helping weld the separate Liberals and Democrats into a united conservative party, which he would help manage as its Secretary-General. I found him in his office at the Tokyo Grand Hotel busily answering the phone. He waved me to a chair and grinned as he hung up.

"That was Yoshida," he explained through an interpreter. "He's coming in." He meant that Yoshida was joining the move to merge the parties.

Kishi was crackling with suppressed energy and sense of purpose. He had many plans and readily outlined them for me.

"We need to replace Japan's multiple election districts with a single-district plan," he explained, for he thought that many Socialists were elected to the Diet only because the existing system of choosing three to five men from one district split the conservative vote and permitted Socialists to ride in with smaller totals. And as he spoke, it became clear that this single-district proposal was the key to virtually everything he hoped to accomplish. In his opinion, it could bring a two-thirds conservative majority to the Diet, which in turn would make possible a minimum rearmament, revision of the Constitution, laws to curb Japan's rowdy left-wing labor movement, and reforms in the school system.

Kishi was obviously enjoying his work. He neither paced the room nor pounded the table; but the fire in his eyes, the animation in his face, the constant lighting and snuffing out of cigarettes at a pace rapid even for him, and the obvious interest in using an American newsman to get his ideas across to the American public told their own story. Many times later he displayed this same relish for the day-to-day intrigues of political life, the excitement of public affairs, the obvious quest for power, the warmth of basking in the spotlight of public attention.

Kishi's Administration lasted from February 28, 1957, to July 19, 1960—three years and five months of gradually increasing political turbulence. There were fights in the Diet over his attempts to end the multiple-district system, to amend the Constitution, to increase police powers, and to revise the Security Treaty. When he finally stepped aside after a month of rioting over the alliance with the United States, former Finance Minister Hayato Ikeda was elected Prime Minister with Kishi's blessing. Then, while the angry din of the last big anti-Treaty demonstration sounded faintly in the distance, Taisuke Aramaki, a former member of the prewar nationalist organization Taikakai, slipped up behind Kishi during a victory celebration at the Prime Minister's official residence and stabbed him six times in the left hip and thigh. Kishi was carried out, dripping blood, painfully though not critically wounded, and a chapter in Japanese political development had come to a close. Without question, he had carved out a significant place for himself in his nation's history, and the contributions he made toward preserving Japan's shaky democracy and its ties with the West may long engross students of the Japanese scene.

Most certainly anyone who digs very deeply will find that Kishi had an un-Oriental flair for political showmanship. He once stopped traffic on Tokyo's bustling Ginza by unexpectedly dropping a 1,000-yen ($2.77) donation into fourteen-year-old Noriko Goto's Community Chest collection box. While in America in 1957, he appeared at a New York Yankee baseball game, jauntily wearing a Yankee baseball cap, and in Japan he launched the American custom of having the nation's chief executive throw out the first ball. But he didn't settle for a feeble toss from the stands; he marched to the pitcher's mound and winged it right over the plate.

The newspaper *Yomiuri* took him to task editorially for such grandstand antics, and during the 1957 political campaign it fired this blast:

> Premier Kishi rode through the streets of Fukuoka under showers of confetti in an open car the other day. He had a huge red emblem across his breast and stood up waving his arms. Some citizens dashed out, thinking it must be a parade of their favorite baseball team which had just won the Japanese Pacific League pennant. . . . It is too flippant for a prime minister to act like a baseball player. . . . We are fed up with such antics. . . .

If Kishi was a showman, he was also a fighter. Not only had he wrangled with nearly all his superiors over the years, but he had also carried on a battle of words with the Japanese press right up to his final days in office. When the newspaper *Asahi* criticized him for using a big U.S.-built sedan instead of a Japanese car on a weekend excursion to Hakone, he fired back in a signed magazine article: "I went to Hakone in my own private car, a Chrysler. . . . I cannot afford a new car for my private use. I would like to say that it is not necessary to sell a still usable car just to buy a new car of Japanese make. . . ."

When other papers criticized him for spending a lot of time on the golf course, a gibe not unfamiliar to Americans during President Eisenhower's Administration, Kishi retorted that he played golf for his health. "And whenever I do, newspapers report it," he said. "They give the impression that I am always playing golf in disregard of affairs of state. Golf plays a great role in my life. When I visited Washington last June [1957], President Eisenhower enjoyed playing golf with me. We had a shower together, and he sent me back to the Japanese Embassy in his car. . . ."

Kishi's biggest clash with the press came early in the anti-Security Treaty campaign, when virtually all the articulate elements of Japan seemed aligned against him. En route to sign the new treaty in Washington on January 19, 1960, he stopped off at the home of relatives in Honolulu. There he removed his shoes, loosened his tie, sipped a highball, smoked, and spoke bitterly of his treatment by Japanese newspapers, apparently not realizing that a reporter who understood Japanese was in the room making notes. And the account in the *Honolulu Star-Bulletin*, which Kishi objected to but never denied, quoted him as stating:

> Japanese newspapers have a lot to do with misguiding their readers—especially students. Unlike your reliable *New York Times* and other good newspapers, you can't—or mustn't—rely on the Japanese press. . . . The newspapers are always knocking me and my government's efforts to do a good job. On the other hand, these same papers give glowing accounts of the Reds and their activities. However, the general public knows better. Else how could I continue to win elections? They vote for me in spite of the press.

Despite these problems with the domestic press, Kishi displayed an amazing aptitude for dealing with the foreign press. He was the first Japanese Premier who attempted to cultivate foreign newsmen as an aid to his political career. He met with them frequently before becoming Prime Minister, accepted invitations to press parties, and often held private meetings with foreign press groups.

Unlike most men who are aggressive and ambitious, Kishi also has a keen, impish, and sometimes sarcastic sense of humor. When Japan's curvaceous Akiko Kojima won the Miss Universe title, the Prime Minister, examining a news photo of her in a bathing suit, quipped: "She looks like an atomic bomb." On one occasion, he ruffled American diplomats by describing negotiations with the U.S. Embassy in Tokyo as "Kakka Soyo," or "like scratching itchy feet with your shoes on." He angered Japan's left wing when he stated that he had not read Soviet Premier Nikita Khrushchev's latest demand for Japanese neutrality because "I didn't have my glasses handy."

Kishi's unusual qualities include a capacity for taking himself lightly. Two months after becoming Premier, he decided, tongue in cheek, that "my outstanding accomplishment so far has been to cut the age of Japan's Prime Minister by ten years," an allusion to the fact that at sixty he had replaced a series of Premiers who had all been over seventy. On another occasion, after watching himself in a newsreel, he turned to a companion and asked, "Am I really that ugly?" And he once noted, as a smile plucked the corners of his mouth, that "a friend of mine told me I am too roundabout in the way I speak. He told me not to laugh too much when appearing on television, since this ruins my dignity."

Such maturity has always been one of Kishi's greatest sources of strength. When Ishibashi defeated him in 1956 for the Liberal-Democratic Party presidency by a slim seven votes, a job that meant the Premiership too, Kishi wholeheartedly participated in the victory celebration for his opponent. Likewise, during the height of the 1960 Security Treaty riots, which plumbed depths of bitterness and personal denunciation seldom seen elsewhere in the world, he was still able to sit beside Socialist Chairman Inejiro Asanuma during television debates and exchange pleasantries—a most unusual circumstance in a nation where face means as much as it does in Japan.

Despite his proclivity for picking quarrels with superiors, Kishi has always had a rare ability to work with people. When he first went to America in 1926 as a thirty-year-old government official to set up a Japanese fair exhibit, objections were raised to his moving into Philadelphia's Fairmont Park area. He solved this quickly; as he recalled it, "I invited my neighbors to dinner and talked them out of their hostility."

"He's the kindest man I've ever known," one of his former aides told me months after Kishi had lost power, and there was little to gain from such remarks. "He's that way with everybody he really knows." Eisaku Sato describes his brother as "honest, single-minded, and frank. He is a man of simple character. He has that simplicity that makes him pursue his objective with a single-minded determination."

Many Japanese, however, have an entirely different image of Kishi.

Critic Kiyoshi Nagai once offered this appraisal of Kishi's success: "As the occasion demands, he can lift his voice to fascism, sing in the stanzas of democracy, or return to extol the reactionary course. Versatility is indeed the sole merit of Nobusuke Kishi."

Japanese newspapers and magazines have virtually charged him with outright dishonesty. When he built a hilltop villa at the hot-springs resort of Atami, they reported that it cost an estimated 10 million yen ($27,777) and asked how this was possible on a Prime Minister's annual salary of 619,800 yen ($1,721) and an allowance of 1.2 million yen ($3,380). A similar storm was raised over reports that Kishi had spent $35,000 in Malayan currency ($11,500) for a forty-carat Ceylon cat's-eye and other gems in a Singapore jewelry store during his 1957 trip through Southeast Asia. Kishi denied making any such elaborate purchases but has never fully answered the Atami villa charges.

One of the gravest errors that can be made in assessing Kishi's personality is to assume that he is a great exponent of the modern liberal society. There is considerable evidence that his inclinations are much more authoritarian, for he has advocated far-reaching changes in the democratic state erected by the American Occupation. "The present Constitution reads like a translation from English," he once stated. "If we merely revise it, it will sound half-Japanese and half-English. It should be rewritten."

On basic human rights he has stated: "I honestly believe that the basic principles of the Constitution based on justice and democracy are very fine and must be retained. But there is overemphasis on human rights . . . which must be made compatible with security, order, and the benefit of the community. . . . For example, many believe it is now unconstitutional to restrict espionage because of the overemphasis on individual rights."

On defense: "We must remove the clause [Article IX of the Constitution] banning war and war potential. Any independent power must have the right to defend itself. And it is necessary to stipulate the people's duty to defend their fatherland. It is not fair to say this will lead to conscription. In a real emergency, however, an independent power ought to be able to draft its people."

On the Emperor: "The Emperor now is very unsatisfactorily defined as a symbol of state. He should be named the monarch and have some power, although not his prewar prerogatives [such as the right to declare war and make peace]. He should not have a veto like the American President, but should have the power to approve high-ranking ministers, the right to decorate and award medals, and to pardon prisoners. He should stay out of politics."

On government: "At present the lower house of the Diet has too much authority. The upper house, which is supposed to curb the lower house, has become even more radical."

In one sense, his was a voice of sanity, an effort to pull Japan back from the many patterns of license its new freedoms had created. At the same time, the consistency of his efforts to move toward more authority in government raised questions as to just how far his desires might have carried him had he remained in power. The bitter battle he waged and lost over increasing police powers is a case in point. Kishi said that new authority was needed to control violent street demonstrations. But many Japanese quickly pointed out that the legislation contained provisions that seemed to go far beyond the bounds of democratic procedure —including the right to arrest upon mere suspicion and without a warrant. An equally bitter fight over proposed efficiency reports for Japan's Communist-influenced schoolteachers likewise raised the fear that Kishi wanted to re-establish government authority over what was taught in Japanese classrooms.

Such a pattern made Kishi, in the eyes of many Japanese, a symbol of reaction and made it possible for left-wing propagandists to picture him as a man who wanted to turn the clock back. Yet for all his efforts to curb at least some of Japan's admittedly abused freedoms, it can be argued that there is an equal consistency and balanced maturity in the role he advocated for Japan. "Japan must never again go to extremes, left or right," he stated over and over again. On other occasions, he emphasized that "there can be no bright future for Japan without stability and order in national life. There must be guarantees and hopes for an improved standard of living, as there must be order and moderation in every aspect of national life."

It took great courage for Kishi to steer such a course, and courage is indeed one of his greatest attributes. His moral fiber was particularly evident during his two trips through Southeast Asia after becoming Premier. He knew he would face embarrassing, cold, and even hostile receptions, especially in Manila and Australia, where the memory of Japan's wartime conduct was still fresh. In Melbourne, for example, he was watched by tense, unsmiling crowds and could not have escaped hearing of an elderly woman who tried unsuccessfully to force her way through the crowd to speak to him. "I must see him," she told officers who restrained her. "He can come and go as he likes, but he is not going to put wreaths on our war memorials. My son was butchered with 366 other Australian boys—all of them prisoners—at Rabaul. It would be hypocritical of Mr. Kishi to try to honor them."

Still, despite the difficulties, Kishi made both trips gestures of apology and atonement for his nation and laid the groundwork for better relations to come.

Perhaps the most outstanding demonstration of Kishi's courage was his conduct during the 1960 rioting. A man who had long cherished and yearned for the office of Premier, he obviously knew that he was committing political suicide by standing up to the mobs. No man could remain in office too long after such a bitter assault on his character and principles; but he refused to give in until the Treaty was secure, demonstrating an apparent belief in something above and beyond his own personal ambitions—a form of selflessness rare in modern Japanese politics, which seem to be based almost entirely on the principle of personal advancement at any cost.

Mobs surrounded his home almost every night for a month. Many times he had to sleep on his office couch because he was held prisoner by students who claimed to be fighting to save their nation's democracy, yet were using one of totalitarianism's most tested methods—mob assault. Yet throughout, Kishi acted with tremendous restraint, and perhaps he saved Japan from considerable bloodshed by refusing to give the orders that would have hurled the full power of the police at his tormentors.

Kishi, therefore, will probably be best remembered as a man who stubbornly stood up to the riotous Japanese demonstrators and kept Asia's most talented and economically powerful nation aligned with those nations of the world which still subscribe to the dignity of the human individual. But perhaps the accomplishment for which his entire nation owes him the most is that of presiding over the explosive expansion of trade with America. This feat has already created revolutionary changes in Japan—changes that are being felt in every Japanese home and may someday even alter the emotional patterns of Japanese thinking by broadening the outlook of its people. Whether he was entirely responsible for creating this new pattern of commerce or not, Nobusuke Kishi nurtured it during its birth, adolescence, and at least its early maturity. His detractors will never be able to rob him of a major share of the credit.

Kishi's rise and fall in post-World War II Japanese politics offer a fertile field for speculating on the processes of making Premiers in Japan. Such leaders do not rise to the top from the pure force of their personality, ambitions, or abilities, particularly in a society as rigid as Japan's. They must emerge from a social context that supports them, aids them financially, and guides them to the seat of power. In one sense, Kishi developed out of the entire conservative tradition of Japan. He inherited the mantle of the prewar Seiyukai and Minseito political parties and the support of thousands of Japanese who vote for conservative candidates at every election, purely out of tradition.

Numerically, Japan's farmers, comprising roughly 40 per cent of the population, are the most prominent among this group. But, without question, Kishi's most powerful backers were the organized commercial, industrial, and banking interests that must of necessity seek out those men who can do the most to keep the lifeblood of trade flowing into and out of Japanese ports. In a nation so devoid of natural resources, and so highly industrialized, all other questions fade into insignificance beside the basic issue of trade. Trite as it may sound, trade is actually a matter of survival in Japan.

Long before Kishi became Premier, he built strong, lasting ties with Japan's great economic interests. His career in the Ministry of Industry and Commerce, from the time he first entered government service, threw him into constant contact with commercial and industrial giants. His being selected to head the industrial expansion program in Manchukuo before the war attests to the fact he had been looked upon with favor. So, too, does his close association with Aiichiro Fujiyama, who gave him a job as director of many of his firms after the war and then in turn became Kishi's Foreign Minister. But perhaps most telling of all were Kishi's frequently overlooked connections with Okinori Kaya, the brilliant architect of Japan's pre-World War II Greater East Asia Co-Prosperity Sphere plan. A powerful financier at that time, Kaya was imprisoned as a Class A war criminal for his role in helping launch the Pacific conflict; after the war, he remained largely in the background but was active in the formation of government policy.

This was brought home to me one day in the spring of 1957. Kishi was about to take off on his first trip to America as Prime Minister; and Kazushige Hirasawa, Kishi's advance agent and editor of Tokyo's English-language *Japan Times,* was already in America arranging final details of the visit. At that point, Kaya called the Associated Press office to say he would like very much to talk to an American newsman. A Japanese staff member and I met Kaya in his quiet, well-appointed office in the Nishi-Ginza district of Tokyo, overlooking a bustling street crammed with people and automobiles. A portly, affable man, he played the gracious host for a few minutes, ordered the inevitable cup of tea, and then turned quickly to a discussion of Japan's economic problems. "Japan is a highly industrialized nation," he explained unnecessarily. "It must have raw materials and markets. Southeast Asia is rich in resources, but is wallowing in poverty and threatened by Communism."

His remarks that day were, in substance, the first presentation of what later came to be known as Kishi's Southeast Asia Development Program, a grandiose scheme very boldly proposing that the United States lend the nations of Southeast Asia $200–$400 million a year with which to purchase Japanese machinery to develop their natural resources. Japan, in turn, would absorb much of the raw materials produced and then resell the finished products to these same nations. Everyone would end up happy, prosperous, and in a stronger position to resist the siren call of Communism. America's gain presumably was to be the stabilization of a shaky corner of the world, which would bolster its anti-Communist defenses in Asia.

This reworking of the old "Workshop of Asia" role for Japan and reincarnation of Kaya's Co-Prosperity Sphere in different dress was not too surprising. The idea had been mulled over unofficially before. But it was a most startling experience to read news dispatches from America a few days later quoting Hirasawa as saying precisely the same thing in speeches given there. And almost simultaneously Kishi himself began outlining the same plan and disclosing that he would take it up in Washington during his visit. Here obviously was an official government program that could be traced back at least to Kaya, whose commercial influence remained unimpaired by his war-criminal record. And the program had probably been planned by Japanese industrial and commercial interests before it was publicly presented.

This, in effect, was a demonstration of the ability of organized business interests to influence the policies of the government. Since such interests are immediately affected by any fluctuation in trade, it is of course inevitable that they should exert pressure on the government, just as business interests do in other nations. But in Japan these forces are the most powerful of all those in the conservative camp; they are the real makers and breakers of Premiers when they choose to be, for they control the available investment capital of Japan and therefore the fates of thousands of enterprises and the jobs of millions of workers. Their influence in government is such that in a period of crisis it presumably could be extended to decisions affecting the use of the police or even the armed forces. Compared to them, the power that could be mustered by the Socialists, barring open revolution backed by a wide segment of the population, seems almost insignificant.

It has been said that the reason Yoshida was toppled from power in 1954 was that Japan's business interests had decided it was the only way to restore calm to Japan's turbulent political scene. It was not that they or the majority of the people disagreed with his policies. Likewise, Kishi did not want to leave office and undoubtedly could have mustered sufficient votes to block his own ouster. But the business interests that backed him withdrew their support to bring an end to the 1960 riots, which they felt were damaging both Japan's international prestige and its foreign trade. At the same time, they also knew that they needed the Security Treaty—which Kishi had just finished shepherding through to completion—upon which the continued expansion of

Japan's billion-dollar annual exports to America depended. So they not only moved to safeguard their markets by getting rid of Kishi, but retained him long enough to protect their access to the American market by getting the Treaty approved. No realistic Japanese industrialist—and trade is one thing about which Japanese can be realistic—could afford to be against the Treaty. Japan's economic survival was rooted in its provisions for "economic co-operation" between the two nations. To the industrialists, the prospect of increased trade with Communist nations, dangled as a counteroffer by the Socialists, was a shibboleth by comparison and probably will remain so for many years to come. From all this emerges the fact that the real power in Japan lies in the commercial, industrial, banking, and business interests, which support the conservatives.

So, in light of this, it was a man and a very powerful movement—Kishi and his conservative backers—who stood directly in the path of leftist ambitions to smash the Security Treaty when the all-out fight over that issue could no longer be postponed. Kishi and the conservatives had long ago taken their position in favor of the Treaty and were now ready for a showdown. The stage had been filled. All the participants were ready and the curtain was about to rise on a struggle for the soul of a nation.

Part Three

THE BATTLE BEGINS

11. The Explosion of May 19-20

MAY 19, 1960, dawned dark and ominous in Tokyo; heavy, rain-filled clouds hung low over the city. It was an appropriately ominous setting, for this was to be a day of violence.

For months, tension had been building over the Security Treaty. It had been under debate in a special Ad Hoc Committee of the lower house of the Diet for more than 100 days. Now only one week remained before the Diet was scheduled to adjourn: The government would have to pass the Treaty immediately, extend the session, or admit a defeat that would almost surely bring the collapse of Prime Minister Kishi's Administration. All the psychological, political, and social forces that had contributed to the mounting crisis were heading for a collision. Japan's pacifism, the tides of change and unrest loosed by the Occupation reforms, the reborn economy that depended on U.S. trade for its continued expansion, the deep-rooted Marxism, the political parties left and right and their leaders, Sohyo, the students, and the intellectuals—all were to play a part in a great emotional storm.

Already thunder and lightning were crashing around Prime Minister Kishi. The Communists, Socialists, Democratic Socialists, and even some ambitious members of his own party wanted him to resign. The impending visit of President Dwight D. Eisenhower would soon provide another target for thunderbolts because, said the Socialists, he would lend support to Kishi and should not come. A third target—and the most important—was the Treaty itself, the controversial symbol of alliance with the United States. The battleground on which they were to meet was the Diet building—its red-carpeted halls and chambers, its expansive grounds, and the black, macadam streets surrounding its peaked gray-stone dome.

Word had already gone out that demonstrations were to be held on this storm-threatened day. The People's Council Against the Security Pact, a 140-organization leftist front directing the assault on the Treaty, had ordered all its forces mobilized by 12:30 P.M. to mount a new campaign against the government in the critical days remaining before the Diet session expired. Buses filled with labor-union members recruited from surrounding communities began rolling into the city at dawn. Some Zengakuren columns were on the move in the early hours, too, and at Sohyo headquarters early arrivals were breaking out their huge red banners for the coming spectacle.

By 8 A.M., 1,000 members of Zengakuren were already squatting in the streets outside the Diet. Inside, the three areas where most of the action would take place—the suite of offices assigned to Speaker Ichiro Kiyose, the Steering Committee and Ad Hoc Committee chambers—were very quiet, and only a few clerks were on hand to prepare for the day's activities. The Steering Committee, under Chairman Seijiro Arafune, had before it a resolution to extend the session fifty days; the Ad Hoc Committee, under Chairman Saeki Ozawa, was about ready for a vote on reporting out the Treaty itself.

The mobs outside the Diet grew hourly. More students poured in along the new Ikebukuro-Shinjuku subway, which had a station near the Diet, and some of Sohyo's marching columns arrived. Soon thousands of students and Sohyo members were rushing up to the hedge and low fence that encircled the grounds and periodically chanting "*Ampo Hantai!*" ("We Oppose the Treaty!") and "*Kishi wa taijin seyo!*" ("Kishi, Resign!"). Police watched grimly from inside the grounds.

At 10:30 A.M., Chairman Arafune convened the Steering Committee and found it still deadlocked over extending the session. At noon, he gave up trying to reach a compromise and reported the impasse to Speaker Kiyose, who was now in his office. The Socialists would not accept any version of an extension resolution.

While Arafune was struggling to reach an agreement with the Socialists, the chamber of the Ad Hoc Committee was slowly filling with representatives and their secretaries. When Chairman Ozawa arrived, more than 400 had jammed into the room; spotting him, Socialist Shichiro Matsumoto asked that the committee be convened immediately. In spite of the noise and confusion, Ozawa called the committee to order, but Matsumoto immediately demanded that the committee take no action on the Treaty until the Steering Committee made a decision on the Diet extension. After forty minutes of discussion, Ozawa called a recess until 2:30 P.M.; as soon as he rose, Representative Saburo Shiikuma, a Liberal-Democrat, slipped into his seat. This was to block a well-known Socialist tactic of occupying the chair of anyone in charge of a parliamentary group in order to contend that the session could not legally be started because the chairman could not occupy his proper post. On one occasion in the past, the Socialists had seated a woman in the House Speaker's chair, and angry Liberal-Democrats had ripped off part of her clothes while trying to remove her.

It had started to rain steadily outside now, and through the open windows of the committee room the angry voice of the mob rose in an ugly, full-throated chant and thousands of feet stomped in cadence. Zengakuren, formed up ten abreast in a giant column, had begun its first snake dance around the Parliament; above the din came the shrill two-beat blast of whistles, picking up the first two counts of a steady four-count rhythm. Then the marchers picked up the same four beats with their meaningless chant, "*Wasshoi! Wasshoi!*," and this gave way to "*Ampo Hantai!*"—again broken up into the same four-stroke cadence with a rising inflection on the first two until the long black column seemed to fall into a moving, rhythmic trance.

When Chairman Ozawa returned, he found the Ad Hoc Committee's room in chaos. Although the committee was not in session, Liberal-Democrats and Socialists were arguing angrily about the Treaty, the former saying that debate would be completed by night, the latter charging that the government was trying to railroad the Treaty through without sufficient discussion—a rather unique position since the Socialists also opposed extending the Diet, which would have provided time for the extra discussion the Socialists professed to want. Ozawa, however, could not force his way through the throng, and he had to wait for forty-five minutes until Liberal-Democrat Shiikuma shouted that committee consideration should be terminated at 5 P.M., and a vote taken. Socialists rose up angrily to crowd around him and so gave Ozawa a chance to slip through to take his seat.

The Socialists, realizing Ozawa was now in a position to reopen the committee meeting at any time, demanded to know what he was going to do. Ozawa ignored them, gazing first at the nails of his right hand, then his left. The shouting and arguing gradually subsided, since it appeared that no action was imminent. Some of the committeemen walked over to the window and gazed at the mounting demonstration outside; others began to read evening newspapers describing the chaos in their committee room.

Meanwhile, Kiyose, faced with the deadlock in the Steering Committee, telephoned Kishi, Socialist Chairman Inejiro Asanuma, and Democratic Socialist Chairman Suehiro Nishio to ask each to have their parties approve the extension of the Diet. Kishi and Nishio agreed, but Asanuma retorted angrily: "The only thing the Socialists will agree to is the abolishment of the bill. If we agreed to extend the session, the Liberal-Democrats would ratify the Treaty." He also warned Kiyose that if the government tried to vote on the Treaty, the Socialists would use force to stop it.

This meant that they would try either to imprison the Speaker in his office or to take over his chair on the Diet floor. Kiyose was prepared for a long stay, once he reached the Speaker's chair, in case the Socialists attempted further delaying tactics—such as a long series of no-confidence motions against him and numerous other government officials. He purchased several dozen rubber bags in which he planned to dispose of his body waste and placed a large order for milk at the Diet cafeteria, to be delivered to him in the Diet chambers at regular intervals. The Socialist Diet members had met earlier and had decided on imprisoning the Speaker by squatting in front of the doors of his office. They were also prepared to use mass tactics to prevent any action in the Ad Hoc Committee.

Shortly after 3 P.M., Chairman Arafune called the Steering Committee back into session. No sooner was he seated than the heavy committee table suddenly heaved upward and toppled on top of him; somebody hit him in the face, then pushed him down when he tried to get up; but while Socialists and Liberal-Democrats fought and shouted at each other, he finally managed to work free. It took him a few moments to realize that several of the Socialists, hidden beneath the table, had suddenly reared up and toppled it on him when he opened the session; but although hurt, stunned, and bleeding from a wound over his right eye, Arafune banged his gavel for order and called for an immediate vote on the extension bill. The Liberal-Democrats, who had a majority, shouted it through.

Now the Diet could be called into session at any time. Kiyose again called Socialist headquarters and asked that negotiators be sent to his office. When the delegation arrived, he said that he wanted the Socialists to agree to bringing the extension resolution onto the floor so the Diet could proceed in an orderly manner. Saburo Eda, later to be Acting Chairman of the Socialist Party, and the two who came with him listened but did not respond. While Kiyose talked to them, the area outside his office was filling up rapidly with angry Socialists and their secretaries. They had just heard of the Steering Committee's action.

Suddenly, there was yelling and shouting outside. Someone banged on the door. Liberal-Democrat Shiikuma and three others rushed in.

"Speaker Kiyose," one of them shouted, "why are you dragging your feet? Open the session now. We cannot wait."

It was now 5 P.M. The din of the mob outside, swollen to about 150,000, filtered into the building as Kiyose listened to the Liberal-Democrats' demand. He did not answer.

"Shut up, stupid," one of the Socialists shouted at the Liberal-Democrat. "Can't you see we're negotiating here?"

"You shut up!" came back the answer. "There's a limit to our patience, too. I'm talking to the Speaker, not you."

Still Kiyose did not answer, and the Socialists rose to leave.

"We cannot negotiate with you any more," Eda said.

Saburo Toita, Kiyose's secretary, and the Liberal-Democrats followed them; he noticed more Socialists and their secretaries in the room outside the Speaker's office and in the larger lobby beyond that. And more Socialists were indeed running down the hall toward the office, for they had just received orders from Asanuma for all available members to assemble either in the Ad Hoc Committee's room or in front of the Speaker's chambers. Actually, more than 350 Socialists—both lower- and upper-house members, their secretaries, and some students and labor-union members who had entered the building—jammed into the lobby outside the Speaker's room, an area twenty feet wide by sixty feet long.

This was the last time Toita was able to get the door open far enough even to look out. The battle was about to begin.

Kiyose summoned Noboru Yoda, chief of the Diet guard detachment, to his office. When the Socialists let him through, Kiyose asked what could be done to restore order. "I can remove the labor-union members, the students, and the secretaries, but no members of the Diet," Yoda replied. Diet guards were not allowed to use any force against Diet members. As Yoda stood at attention before Kiyose, the Socialists outside began to sing the "Internationale."

Toita tried the door again, but as soon as the Socialists saw it ajar, they slammed it shut. Kiyose immediately phoned Kishi to tell him, "I am afraid that I will have to ask the police to clean this up."

Kishi and the other party leaders objected; they said they would rather summon party members to try to free Kiyose. Kiyose said he would think this over and in the meantime would appeal to the Socialists to restore order. But then Kishi wanted to know if, after the House were convened, the Ad Hoc Committee could report out the Treaty itself while the full House was passing the extension.

"No!" Kiyose almost shouted. "No! This time only the extension bill!" It was almost 7 P.M. now, and the shouting and chanting outside the Diet had settled down to a steady, throbbing rumble as the massive rain-soaked columns swung by in the streets to the beat of "*Ampo Hantai! Ampo Hantai!*" and poured down into the center of the city to tie up traffic and demonstrate before the American Embassy.

Outside the Speaker's office, there was more shouting and cursing too. Liberal-Democrats were forcing their way into the already jammed room; although they negotiated an agreement with the Socialists for all secretaries to leave, more Socialists moved in to take their places.

Now the Socialists picked up the chant of the demonstrators: "*Ampo Hantai! Ampo Hantai! Kishi wa taijin seyo!*" Over and over they chanted it and the walls of the lobby threw it back like the roar of thousands.

Inside his office, Kiyose, sitting straight in his chair, closed his eyes, thinking deeply; several minutes later he opened them, picked up his pen, scribbled on a sheet of paper, read it over several times, and then asked Toita to switch on the loudspeaker system. "I am deeply grieved by the situation now prevailing in the Diet," he read. "I appeal to members of the Socialist Party to cooperate, restore order, and safeguard the parliamentary system of this nation."

There was no diminution of the noise outside. Somebody started to bang on the door. Then there were some clicks. Toita tried it: The door had been locked.

Kiyose ordered the loudspeakers turned on again. Eight times he repeated his plea; then, as the din outside continued to mount, he picked up the telephone and called the Prime Minister's office. He spoke very firmly. "Please get in touch with the Metropolitan police and ask them to send 500 policemen immediately," he stated grimly. This time his determination quickly swept aside party objections.

Kiyose pondered a moment, then penned another speech, warning that he would have to act soon to restore order and urging the Socialists to reconsider their actions. It was now 10:22 P.M. Kiyose pushed the warning bell on his desk, a signal that the lower house was about to convene and then broadcast his latest appeal for order five times.

However, it brought a result Kiyose had not expected. His first appeal had been greeted with jeers and jokes by the Socialists, who had been jamming into the Ad Hoc Committee room for several hours in anticipation that a vote was near; but this time the warning that he would soon have to make a decision was taken seriously.

"The battle is at the Speaker's office," someone shouted. "Let's go help there!"

The Socialists stormed out of the room at a dead run. Chairman Ozawa watched the mass exodus for a moment, then suddenly banged his gavel to call the committee to order. "We will now take a roll call on the new Treaty," he shouted.

Since most of the Socialists had gone, the Liberal-Democrats passed it easily, and Ozawa proclaimed: "With this the committee has approved the Treaty." The time was 10:45 P.M., and the Treaty ratification was now ready for House consideration. It was to be several hours before the Socialists fully realized what had happened.

As Ozawa was taking his roll call, a column of ten trucks filled with special riot-trained policemen approached the Diet building from the south side, where the Prime Minister's residence was located. Since the road was filled with demonstrators, Police Colonel Hidehiro Ito, who commanded the detachment, slowed the trucks to less than five miles an hour. Inching through the surly crowd and ignoring shouts of "Kishi's dogs!" and other insults, the black-helmeted officers in gray uniforms cleared the demonstrators away from a gate so that the trucks could enter the Diet grounds.

Meanwhile, labor-union sound trucks excitedly told the rain-soaked demonstrators that Kishi had ordered police into the Diet and was destroying the nation's parliamentary system.

The chief of the Diet guards, Yoda, phoned Kiyose that the 500 policemen were now assembled just outside the building. Kiyose asked that they wait there; with a trembling hand he drafted another appeal. "It is impossible to continue under the present circumstances," he stated in a voice choked with emotion. "It is with a sense of great sorrow that I have been forced to summon police. This is a dark moment in the history of our parliamentary system and the honor of the Japanese race. However, if order is restored within fifteen minutes, I will not take the final step. I sincerely appeal for your cooperation."

Seven times Kiyose broadcast this final appeal. Socialist Representative Hideo Nakamura, one of those squatting in front of the

Speaker's office, said later that he could hear the loudspeakers but could not understand what Kiyose was saying because of the noise in the room. But since many Socialists understood that an ultimatum had been delivered, the noise tapered off and a new tension settled over the room. Many Liberal-Democrats began to gather outside the chamber.

At 10:54 P.M., Kiyose telephoned Yoda to bring the police into the building. Yoda promptly relayed the order to Colonel Ito and the commander of Ito's combat group, Colonel Hajime Kondo, a career policeman. Kondo told his officers to leave their pistols, helmets, and clubs behind, but to put on their white gloves, which were normally reserved for parade formations. (They were told later that this was "to keep from scratching the Socialists" while forcibly removing them from the area around Kiyose's office.) In two long files the officers then moved quickly and quietly down a long corridor in the Diet Building. "When I looked back at them," Yoda said, "they were pale and tense." This was only the third time that police had been ordered into the Diet, each time to restore order.

Yoda led them to the lobby outside the Speaker's suite of rooms. Bedlam confronted them: Singing and shouting, Socialists, members of left-wing labor unions, and students were squatting in solid ranks across the floor; jammed against one side of the chamber, the Liberal-Democrats were shouting back. On one side of the huge room were the doors leading to Kiyose's office and the offices of his secretaries; on the other side, stairs leading to the House floor. Hence, there was no way that the police could get Kiyose to the stairs without first removing the Socialists.

The din ceased abruptly as Kondo's men marched up to within three feet of the Socialists' front rank. Kondo surveyed the situation: The Socialists had put their oldest members in the front, leaving the younger and tougher ones to hold the line closer to the Speaker's door. Some of the Socialists, recognizing Yoda, shouted at him angrily: "Stop, Yoda, or you'll pay for this!"

Four officers reached down, grabbed, and carried one of the Socialists bodily from the room. One by one, the squatters were hauled away, some fighting, kicking, and denouncing Kishi, others only mildly resisting. Liberal-Democrats, their secretaries, and, reportedly, some strong-arm thugs they had brought in for emergency use jammed both sides of the corridor to watch the show.

The work went slowly. After one-half hour only eighteen had been removed, and Yoda was concerned: His orders were to get the Speaker to his chair on the Diet floor before midnight; otherwise, no proceedings could be held after midnight because no prior notice had been given for a session on the 20th. And by 11:30 P.M., more than half of the Socialists were still firmly in place, grouped around the Speaker's door, still full of fight. Yoda then told Colonel Kondo that there was another way to reach the Speaker—through the secretaries' room, which also opened on the lobby; but, he added, at least forty Socialists were occupying the room and had dragged chairs and desks to barricade the door.

The police forced it part way open, anyway. The room was dark; the Socialists inside had turned off the lights, but their tense breathing was audible. When a policeman stuck his head inside, a heavy stick whacked him across the back of the head; as the officer fell to the floor, the Socialists laughed and shouted with delight, then pushed the policeman out, and slammed the door shut. Kondo next renewed his assault on the Socialists who were guarding the Speaker's door, but his men had increasing difficulties. The remaining students and union members were experts at mob tactics; because they linked arms, the officers, who were trying to avoid hurting the demonstrators, often had to pull the weight of ten to disengage one.

Suddenly an opportunity appeared, for at 11:40 P.M. the last remaining group of older Socialists stood up, apparently too tired to fight any longer. Kondo shouted an order. The officers quickly formed a flying wedge, crashed into the Socialists' ranks, and broke through to the Speaker's door. As precious minutes ticked away, the officers began to bang and kick at the locked door while fighting off the screaming Socialists around them. If the Socialists could keep the door closed until midnight, they would technically delay the crisis at least a day—a day that would give them more time for political maneuvering. But more officers poured into the fight and beat back the Socialists. Finally, a panel gave way, the door was battered open, and Diet guards and policemen rushed in; they lifted Kiyose over their heads and carried him, blinking and bewildered, through the screaming, swirling Socialist mob outside. As they reached the House floor, the policemen stepped aside, and the Diet guards carried Kiyose the remaining distance, depositing him unceremoniously in the Speaker's chair. Prime Minister Kishi, Foreign Minister Fujiyama, and most of the Liberal-Democrats were already seated, waiting for him.

Roughed up and hurt in the final power play, Kiyose nevertheless hauled himself up to his full height, took a deep breath, and with a rap of his gavel called up the motion to extend the Diet session fifty days. The time was 11:50 P.M.—ten minutes to spare—as the Liberal-Democrats shouted it through. There were no Socialists on the floor.

Kiyose then asked for a motion to bring the U.S.–Japanese Security Treaty to the floor for a vote. There was no opposition. He banged his gavel for a recess until 12:05 A.M., but he did not leave his chair. Most of the Liberal-Democrats did not leave the floor. The Socialists, confused and disorganized by the swift pace of events, remained off the floor. They were still not there when the final vote approving the Treaty was taken, immediately after the recess ended.

To this day, they say they were tricked and had no idea that the Treaty itself would be voted on. Some say that they did not even realize the Treaty had been cleared by the Ad Hoc Committee and was therefore ready for floor action. To this, only a few known facts can be added: The Socialists were not present because of their own decision not to attend; they had full knowledge that a session would be held if the Speaker reached his chair; they were not prevented by the police from attending, as some later contended; and, as they well knew, they did not have the votes to prevent the Treaty's passage, even if they had been present. That is the reason they resorted to physical force in an attempt to block it.

12. The Beast in the Streets

Now the deed had been done. The hated Treaty had been approved by the lower house of the Diet, although by means of questionable procedures and amid scenes of chaos that made a mockery of the parliamentary process. Still, there was little doubt it had the approval of a quorum of the House as required by law, and two paths were now open to its final legislative approval: Either passage by the upper chamber, the House of Councilors, or, failing that, automatic approval after thirty days had elapsed without a negative vote by the Councilors. Then only an exchange of ratification documents would be necessary for it to become law.

Japan's entire left wing, at first stunned that it had been outwitted, then shocked that Speaker Kiyose had dared use police in the Diet, gathered its forces for a final onslaught to block the alliance. If they could force Kishi to resign before the thirty days had elapsed, the lower-house approval would be voided by the fall of his Administration. With blazing fury they began their fight. At last, they convinced themselves, they had a cause that would win widespread public backing. Japan's parliamentary system had been imperiled, they reasoned, by the "tyranny of the majority" and the use of the police in the Diet itself. Democracy was at stake, and so too, in their minds, was peace, for the Treaty meant war. They must save their nation from these evils by mounting the most massive pressure campaign in Japan's modern history, a campaign they hoped would rally most of the nation behind them, force new elections, and sweep the Socialist Party into office on a tide of popular approval.

Almost every day for the next thirty days the mobs formed to march, shout, snake-dance, and besiege not only the Diet but both the official and private residences of Prime Minister Kishi. By noon each day the black-uniformed ranks of Zengakuren were on the move; trucks rolled into the city with labor-union reinforcements; assembly areas came alive with red banners; and loud-speaker cars roamed the city, warning of the grave "crisis" facing the nation unless Kishi resigned. Students and members of the Communist Party gathered at the railroad stations to scream their message of "Japan at the Crossroads" and to pass out handbills—more of which fluttered down from airplanes in the sky. Police, weary from their vigil the previous day and night, moved into position to protect the Diet, the American Embassy, and numerous public buildings.

At first, a carnival atmosphere prevailed as the demonstrators gradually filled the streets surrounding the Diet. Street vendors hawked ice cream, hot dogs, and baked sweet potatoes, and the students laughed, joked, and waited for the orders to begin their march. Foreign newsmen, particularly Americans, who were the most numerous, moved among the demonstrators with complete safety and without signs of hostility. Then whistles would blow, and the great sea of squatting figures would begin to stir. Leaders would come running back to their sections with their orders for the day. Shouted commands and more whistles. Columns formed; banners moved into alignment; then, ten abreast, those in the front rank grasping a pole held horizontally across their waists to keep them in line, the column would begin its slow, sluggish movement around the Diet. Whistles picked up the first two beats of the four-beat rhythm, and the inchoate column gradually found the cadence. Slowly it began to take shape, then it became a long, writhing monster, acting under one will, and finally the chant began that will forever be remembered by those who heard it ringing through the streets of Japan: "*Ampo Hantai! Ampo Hantai! Ampo Hantai! Ampo Hantai!*" It filtered through the windows of the Diet where Japan's deeply worried conservatives could hear it and sent its pulsating beat through the heart of the city with an ominous, strangely hypnotic effect not unlike the sound of distant jungle drums. Now the mob was acting with one voice as well as one will.

Soon the carnival atmosphere dropped away. The mood became ugly. The columns swerved closer and closer to the ranks of the waiting police and their trucks blocking entrances to the Diet. Then there were flare-ups of pushing and shoving, but no great amount of fighting. As darkness settled over the scene, lighted lanterns spread through the demonstrators' ranks, and the monster began to writhe and twist through the city like a great bejeweled dragon.

In the narrow confines of streets leading to and from the American Embassy, the columns came pouring through in a giant river of lights, sometimes thirty abreast. "*Ampo Hantai! Ampo Hantai!*" —the thunder of their protests battered against the white walls of the Chancery building, where a few lights behind the locked, barred, and police-guarded gates shone from second-floor windows as Embassy personnel worked late to report on this latest assault on the Treaty. Despite the pounding din of whistles, chanting, shouts, and commands, each unit as it came abreast of the black-iron Embassy gates would halt and shout chorused slogans against the alliance that meant war. The chanting, twisting stream of lanterns cascaded past the Embassy into the downtown area to merge with other columns of marchers from the Diet already jamming the streets with flags and sweating bodies. The thoroughfare leading to Shimbashi Station always piled up with these human cells. Other tentacles filled the street leading down past the Imperial Palace Moat, the Hibiya intersection, past Yurakucho Station, where some would disperse, and the broad street in front of the *Asahi Shimbun.* In an undulating sea of red banners and blank faces, cadenced by their pulsating chant, they moved on to the Ginza, Tokyo's Broadway, and eventual dissipation somewhere along its concrete confines after drawing the applause of spectators watching from the side lines.

These were days of pageantry and passion in Japan, of an exhilarating sense of conflict and of a national mood that was pitched on a high level of sustained excitement. It was like living in the midst of a cheap, motion-picture melodrama in which a highly impulsive and foolish minority was tearing up everything that had been gained in the postwar years in one great spree of emotional debauchery. Strangely, these agents of destruction kept the demonstrations surprisingly orderly, particularly at first, despite their size and ominous undertones. There were no great flaming bursts of mob terror, no assaults on foreigners, who lived and moved freely throughout the city, and, for a time, only sporadic clashes with police, precipitated almost entirely by Zengakuren. But with the mounting tension, the bitter confrontation of left and right, and the intensifying emotion on both sides, a new and frightening quality did creep into the mobs ruling the streets of Japan. It was both a subtle change in mood and the slow unveiling of a previously unrealized potential.

One aspect of this potential was the terrifying discipline that was so unlike the insane disorders of mobs elsewhere in the world. The huge columns acted only on orders from their section "captains," who shouted instructions through megaphones. They would shout, "Crush the Treaty!" and the thousands would hurl back, "Crush the Treaty!" They shouted, "Hang Kishi!" and the columns responded, "Hang Kishi!" They shouted, "*Ampo Hantai!*" and the cry came rolling back again. The participants acted with one brain and seemed to fall into hypnotic states: Heads rolled back, eyes glazed, arms and legs pumped rhythmically to the chant that filled the city. This robot-like conformity was terrifying, much more terrifying in its own way than the white-hot anger of mobs that loot and burn and then lose their anger and break up, leaving thousands of dazed and aimless behind, wondering where to go and what to do next. For if the Japanese demonstrators could be held within such orderly bounds, what would they do if their orders were suddenly changed and those guiding their tactics decided it was time to get rough. In this sense, the danger of the Japanese mobs never dissipated; it was always there to be tapped whenever the time was right.

Another side of this newly realized potential of the mobs was their obvious power. In sheer numbers alone, they were Gargantuan, many more than the police could hope to cope with if the mobs' masters decided to provoke an actual revolution. Time after time, more than 150,000 demonstrators poured through the city, and once an estimated 300,000 stormed through Tokyo for more than fourteen hours. The figure was probably exaggerated, but to those who watched the mammoth, writhing columns go by, hour after hour, it seemed believable. On several occasions, Sohyo demonstrated that it could partially paralyze the nation by calling for limited general strikes: Sohyo action teams blocked main railroad tracks, kidnaped engineers, kept nearly all public transportation to and from Tokyo frozen for hours, and defied police and public authorities to break their grip. If it chose, Sohyo obviously could have staggered Kishi's already beleaguered Administration with a nation-wide strike.

The opposite side of this was the seeming inability—or, more accurately, refusal—of the government to take any counteraction. Fearing to inflame the mobs even more, and claiming that it did not have sufficient authority to act under existing laws—a very doubtful position—the government attempted to roll with the punch. Police tried only to contain the demonstrations, not to block them, and when faced with outright attacks, gave ground. This strange acquiescence caught most foreigners completely by surprise, and it probably partly accounted for the cancellation of President Eisenhower's visit. It is a good guess that the American Embassy personnel who planned the visit failed to realize that the Japanese Government would demonstrate such complete unwillingness to act in restoring order.

Finally, the most obvious side of the new potential was the emerging Communist pattern. The red banners, the tight regimentation, the slogans, the skillful organization of the demonstrators, and the obvious fact that money was available to pay some of them, to cover the cost of transporting them to Tokyo, and to underwrite the cost of hundreds of thousands of lunches for the marchers—all these fitted neatly into a pattern of increasing Communist influence. The most obvious symptom was the skillful way in which the targets of the demonstrators were being changed. At first, they were only Kishi and the Treaty; then attention began to focus more and more on the coming visit of Eisenhower, who was due to arrive on June 19, the day the Diet's ratification of the Treaty would be automatically completed. More and more anti-American overtones crept into the campaign, and soon it was evident that what had started out largely as an internal Japanese political quarrel was broadening to undermine the role of the United States throughout the world, discredit its President, and picture the United States more and more as an aggressive, militaristic power ready to plunge the world into a nuclear war. The ill-fated U-2 spy-plane flight of Francis Gary Powers over the Soviet Union, the collapse of the Paris Summit Conference, and the cancellation of Eisenhower's trip to Moscow during this same period provided good material for bringing about this change of direction. Now the cry went up against the Eisenhower visit, and there were increasing warnings that he would be attacked by the mobs if he came.

The role of the Communists in the anti-Treaty campaign became plainly evident on June 10, 1960, when James Hagerty, White House Press Secretary, arrived at Tokyo's Haneda Airport to make final preparations for Eisenhower's arrival. U.S. Ambassador Douglas MacArthur informed him at the airport that the two main roads leading from the airport into town were badly jammed with Zengakuren and labor-union demonstrators; he offered Hagerty his choice of flying to the Embassy in a waiting U.S. Marine helicopter—the method MacArthur used to get there—or of traveling by car through the demonstrators. Hagerty, who was not one to knuckle under to any mob, chose the latter; besides, no one—including the Japanese police—really believed that there would be any serious trouble. As the American convoy started out of the airport area, word spread among the demonstrators that Hagerty was about to slip from their grasp by boarding a helicopter. The students and union members, arms locked, burst from their assembly area and came racing down toward the main airport. Like a human sea, they engulfed the approaching cars. A union leader jumped on the hood of the Ambassador's car, then upon the roof, shouting instructions. The demonstrators battered the car with the poles that carried their banners and signs, cracked windows, slashed tires, and rocked the car until it seemed it would turn over. They shouted "Go home, Hagerty!" and then raised their voices in the "Internationale." While the mob swirled and eddied around the car, Hagerty, Ambassador MacArthur, and White House Appointments Secretary Thomas A. Stevens sat calmly inside. Hagerty even snapped pictures of the demonstrators.

Japanese police were caught completely by surprise. They had only a small detachment of officers at the airport since their advance intelligence had indicated that only a peaceful demonstration was planned. They had not counted on the fact that the attackers were from the Japanese Communist Party-controlled wing of Zengakuren and that the union members involved were from Communist unions. The fact, too, that Soviet correspondents were waiting with the demonstrators should have been a further tip-off, for they seldom attended any functions in Tokyo except Communist-type spectacles. Obviously, word had gone out for an assault that would embarrass the United States and further discourage Eisenhower from the trip. In any event, the mob held the car and its occupants prisoners for eighty minutes. Although the police finally got reinforcements to the area, they could hold back the mob only for moments at a time. U.S. Secret Service personnel assigned to the Hagerty party reacted swiftly, skillfully, and bravely; remaining outside the vehicle, they attempted to shield it with their own bodies and, by means of a portable radio guided the Marine helicopter into position over the mob. Finally, as police cleared an area around the car, the helicopter touched down, picked up Hagerty, MacArthur, and Stevens, and flew them to safety, to the U.S. Army area of Hardy Barracks near downtown Tokyo. From there, they were whisked to the Embassy in a waiting car; but while another mob of demonstrators waited outside the Embassy to intercept them, the car slipped in by a back entrance. And moments later, as word spread that their quarry had eluded them, the mobs came storming around from the front of the building to beat on locked back gates.

The Japanese Government was shocked, grieved, and seriously embarrassed by the attack on Hagerty, and so too were thousands of Japanese citizens. They flooded the Embassy with phone calls to express their apologies. Newspapers deplored the sudden vicious and violent turn the demonstrations had taken, and there was obvious concern even in the ranks of the Socialist Party.

As the day of Eisenhower's visit approached without any sign that either the Americans or the Japanese Government would cancel the trip, serious doubts beset the leftist camp. Sohyo began talking of staying away from the airport when the American President arrived, but the Communist Party, Zengakuren, and many Communist unions vowed that they would be there. During this tense period, even further evidence was obtained that the Communists not only were deeply involved in the demonstrations but had taken over the leading role in directing the strategy and planning a mob assault on Eisenhower. I clearly recall a phone call from a liaison representative of the Socialist Party during this crisis period.

"What, in your opinion," he asked, "would be the consequences of an attack on Eisenhower like the one on Hagerty?"

I told him that the Socialist Party was playing with fire if it was contemplating such an attack and that the consequences could be grave both for the Socialist Party and U.S.–Japanese relations.

"But what can we do?" he asked, a note of desperation in his voice. "The Communists have taken control of everything!"

The control he spoke of lay with the organization that had directed the strategy against the Treaty from the time the revision first began. It was known as the People's Council Against the Security Pact. Although it had a total membership of more than 140 organizations, the executive power was vested in a council of thirteen groups, all deeply indoctrinated with Marxist philosophy, of which the principal ones were Sohyo, the most powerful of all, and the Socialist Party. The Communist Party, technically, was only an observer, but its influence was felt from the very beginning, and police confirmed later that it was indeed running the show by the time the assault on Hagerty was staged.

The Communist influence should have been obvious long before. In its latter stages, the anti-Treaty campaign was tailored too precisely to Communist needs to be coincidental; without the participants' intention, it had become almost totally anti-American because everything the demonstrators professed they were out to destroy involved the United States—a pro-American Prime Minister, an alliance with America, the visit of an American President, American bases, and the image of America as a humanitarian, peaceful nation. And if further proof were needed that the demonstrations by now were Communist-controlled, it should have been clear to any rudimentary student of Communist tactics that in the People's Council Against the Security Pact—a name that is revealing in itself—the Communists had finally created the united popular front they had always believed necessary to win control of Japan.

The demonstrations reached their peak of intensity on June 15, only five days after the attack on Hagerty and four days before Eisenhower was due to arrive. In a soaking downpour, the demonstrators swung by the Diet most of the day, and as dusk fell only the hard core of Zengakuren, about 10,000–15,000 students, was left at the Diet. Although police trucks had been rolled up to form a barricade across the front of the main entrance to the Diet grounds, the students stormed into the police ranks, attached ropes to the trucks, and pulled them, one at a time, out into the street where they were set on fire. They tore down the posts framing another entrance to the compound; they broke the signs off their placards and used the remaining staves with their protruding nails as clubs; they tore up the paving and hurled paving blocks at the police. For hours the battle raged. Under strict orders to use only minimum force, the police were compelled to stand stoically in formation while many of their numbers were battered to the ground by barrages of heavy paving stones and the repeated charges of the students. Their bitterness was heightened by taunts that they were "Kishi's dogs," a reminder that the police forces were composed mainly of uneducated farm boys and that the students belonged to a traditionally higher class, the intellectuals. Only when attacked did the officers fight back, and then only with their clubs. In one of the Zengakuren charges into the Diet grounds, one girl fell in the mud and was trampled to death by her own student companions; but the students and Socialists spread the word that she had been strangled by police—a fabrication that was widely believed for many weeks afterward. Deep into the night the fighting continued: Twenty trucks were burned, a two-story building, the annex to the secretariat, and a guardhouse were sacked, and an estimated 1,000 were injured. Finally, while Zengakuren was massing at the front gate for still another attack, the police used tear gas for the first time and were given orders to attack. Out of the Diet grounds they stormed, shouting, "Smash them! Smash them!" It was the only time in the entire campaign that they were given a chance to show what they could do—and they made the most of it. In a wild, bruising assault, the police columns hit the students, shattered their formations, and clubbed down students like matchsticks. Hundreds were left groaning and bleeding in the streets and gutters.

This was the high-water mark of the anti-Treaty riots. Although the police charge broke up the June 15 demonstrations, Eisenhower's trip was canceled by the Japanese Government soon after, probably upon the insistence of the Imperial Palace Household. Zengakuren's columns joyfully snake-danced through Tokyo. Despite more demonstrations before the June 19 deadline had quietly expired and the ratification documents had been exchanged on June 23 at a secretly arranged meeting, the steam had gone out of the campaign. In the final protest march, professors lined up in a cordon between the police and the students at the entrance to the Diet as a precaution against any further violence; second thoughts about the whirlwind they had helped spawn in the classroom had evidently occurred, and there were signs of alarm as well from other sectors of the leftist front. Newspapers which had seemed to incite the demonstrators issued a joint call against any further violence, and the People's Council, too, rejected a Communist call to convert the Treaty effort into an all-out anti-American drive.

While emotions were at their peak, however, one voice from Japan's silent millions spoke up softly but with ringing clarity in a statement equally as important as those issued by Dr. Koizumi and Dr. Matsushita. Mrs. Shizue Kato, a Socialist member of the House of Councilors, disavowed the tortured reasoning of her party by writing a letter to a Japanese newspaper immediately after the June 15 riot:

> Watching the whole battle on television, my heart sank when I thought of the future of our country. It is cheap and off the point to discuss at this time whether the police did too much or whether the government was wrong. It was an extremely dangerous attempt to throw out the government by resorting to violence, planned by a small group of people run by a subversive ideology.

I have been in the Japanese Diet for more than ten years now as a Socialist. I feel deeply ashamed that we have come to the point where the democracy of Japan is being exposed to the danger of destruction by such violent action. . . .

I sat through many party meetings and when wrong decisions were taken I did not raise my voice. Now I wish to pledge myself to fight all out to save Japan from Communism and defend real democracy.

The Communists, with the extremely active support of Red China and the Soviet Union, have tried to destroy the government by forming a powerful popular front. More than that, they have tried to drive the entire people into a furious anti-American struggle just before the arrival of President Eisenhower in this country so that Japan could eventually be isolated from her friends in the free world —especially the United States.

And so the Treaty riots ended, and Mrs. Kato's words hung over their memory like the troubled conscience of her nation. Japan seemed to sense that something had been irretrievably lost. Perhaps it was a certain sense of national dignity that was completely incompatible with the spectacle of thousands resorting to extra-parliamentary methods in an era that was supposed to be ruled by law. Perhaps it was regret over the implied insult to its own people that they could not guarantee the safety of an American President who had been invited to visit their land. And perhaps, too, it was even a sense of shame that a monstrous, deformed ghost had been dragged out of the recesses of the Japanese mind so all the world could see that it still lived when it was supposed to have been exorcised by the new postwar freedoms. It was the ghost of mass violence and the same old follow-the-leader tendency of the Japanese to fall into its clutches.

13. Ikeda Takes Over

HAYATO IKEDA SUCCEEDED the wounded but recuperating Nobusuke Kishi as Premier of Japan on July 19, 1960, during a period of subsiding but continuing crisis over the alliance with the United States. The Security Treaty riots had come and gone, but the threat of the mobs hung over his government. The Japanese Communist Party was pushing hard to keep the demonstrations going by a new series of protests outside U.S. bases, and it preserved the People's Council that had directed the uprising. But the momentum of the campaign had died, and thousands of Japanese drawn in at its emotional peak had had second thoughts about their conduct. Still, it was difficult to foretell the immediate future, and Ikeda was grim and determined as he hurried from formal installation ceremonies at the Imperial Palace to his first Cabinet meeting. There, in deadly seriousness, he assured his ministers that "I'm determined to uphold the parliamentary system."

His actions in ensuing weeks indicated that he meant it. At his first press conference, he firmly rejected neutrality and reaffirmed Japan's adherence to the Western democracies. He deplored Socialist violence and the month of Communist-led demonstrations that had swept Japan to the brink of anarchy. He stated in an interview, "I won't have that kind of social disorder again." He promised vast improvements in Japan's welfare program, a doubling of the national income in ten years, and "epoch-making reforms in the type of education we have today that divides everyone into either friend or foe." He found a face-saving solution to an explosive crisis at the Miike coal mine in Kyushu, where striking, Communist-influenced workers had dug trenches, formed military-type fighting units, strung barbed-wire barricades, and armed themselves with clubs, spears, and stones for an all-out fight against the efforts of police and management to dislodge and discharge them. And Ikeda charmed the press, cajoled the public, and conducted himself with intelligence and dignity—free from any flashes of his fiery temper—in campaigning for the impending general elections. Until a youthful assassin struck down Socialist Chairman Inejiro Asanuma, Ikeda seemed to have turned public sentiment so strongly against the Socialists that they were beginning to back down from their anti-American posture.

Such political skill was completely unexpected, particularly to those who knew Ikeda intimately. Hayato was born on December 3, 1899, in Hiroshima, the youngest of two boys and a girl sired by a wealthy sake merchant; he was a spoiled and willful child, overwhelmingly confident of his own abilities and consumed with a stubborn determination to carry through whatever he had set out to do. Rebellious and adventuresome, he was addicted in his days at Kyoto University to frequenting gay quarters with his friends and picking up the check for everyone.

Ikeda's teachers recall that he was a good student only in mathematics. His schoolmates dubbed him "the human calculating machine," and for years he has startled his associates by his ability to rattle off entire pages of statistics from reports, budgets, plans, and projected works. Those who knew him well said that beneath the brusqueness was a warmer, more human, and almost tender side of his nature; but to strangers and business associates, an impression of irascibility, willfulness, and determination predominated. Ikeda grew into a lean, hard man, tall for a Japanese and muscular at a consistent 150 pounds. He was admired as a heavy drinker who could handle his liquor, as a leader who expended himself endlessly to accomplish whatever job he was assigned, and as one who had his sights set on higher goals in public life.

Then disaster struck. He was in his first government assignment as head of the Utsunomiya Tax Office, seventy miles north of Tokyo, when his skin began to break out in sores and blisters. As the affliction grew steadily worse, he was informed that he had the rare skin disease pemphigus. With his wife, Naoko, the daughter of a peer, he returned to his native Hiroshima to stage an uphill fight to regain his health. While he was hopelessly ill, his colleagues in the Finance Ministry were being promoted, and his wife, exhausted by her efforts to help him, fell sick and died. To the promising young tax expert, life seemed to have taken a tragic turn. Racked with pain and despair, his body swathed in bandages, he donned the white robes of a Buddhist pilgrim and, from temple to temple on the island of Shikoku, hobbled along on the arm of his ancient mother, dragging his sorely afflicted feet, strapped to boards, in the dirt. There seemed to be no hope for a cure; doctors were unable to help him; and for five years he suffered. Then, suddenly, the disease disappeared. Ikeda had weathered the first of two crises that were to have great impact on his life.

The lost years were not without their compensation, however. During the latter days of the fight to regain his health, a young girl, Mitsue, who was a distant relative, came to take care of him. When he was thirty-five and she twenty-one they were married, against the wishes of his family, who felt her beneath his social standing. She bore him three lovely daughters, the first named Naoko after his dead wife, and has earned repeated praise from him for her patience and gentle ways. "I owe much to my wife for what I am today," he readily acknowledges.

Ikeda's tormenting illness ultimately proved to be a boon in disguise. He spent World War II as Chief of the Kumamoto Tax Supervision Bureau, an insignificant post; but after the war, many of his colleagues who had won high promotions while he was fighting to recover his health were purged from public life by the Occupation, clearing the way for his rapid advancement. In 1946, he became Director of the Finance Ministry's Revenue Bureau, then Vice-Minister of Finance in 1947, and finally Finance Minister in 1949 under Premier Shigeru Yoshida. In this capacity, Ikeda quickly won the praise of all the Occupation leaders for his vigorous conduct of the necessary retrenchment program ordered by the Americans. But the job eventually led, in 1951, to the second major crisis in his life. Questioned in the Diet over the plight of the poor under the severe deflationary measures he was carrying out for the government, he stated: "Let them eat barley if they don't have rice." And when his interrogators complained that small businesses were being ruined in the economic rollback, Ikeda retorted, "It cannot be helped if a few small or middle-class enterprises should collapse for the sake of the national economy."

Because of such frank talk, a no-confidence vote was passed in the lower house, and Ikeda had to resign. He shut himself off from all but his closest friends, brooding and angry. But while in seclusion he formed a new friendship with a Buddhist priest, Daiki Tachibana, who helped him search his soul for answers to his personality problems. When, for example, Ikeda visited Daiki at the Daitoku-ji temple, the priest showed him the kizaemon-chawan, a teacup considered one of Japan's most precious art objects. He explained that the famous Japanese military leader Hideyoshi Toyotomi (1536–98) had possessed a similar cup; but when a page dropped and broke it, Hideyoshi ordered the servant beheaded. However, the ceremonial tea master, Bosai Hosokawa, pleaded successfully for the boy's life and set about repairing the vessel by cementing the pieces together with gold leaf. "Having lost the war," Daiki stated, "Japan is now like the broken cup. It is up to you, Ikeda-san, to rebuild the country by putting the pieces together with gold leaf."

These appeals for a more serene approach to life and a return to more lasting values in remaking Japanese society seemed to help Ikeda seek greater self-control and eventually the seat of power in the government. He returned to public life a revitalized man, became a deep admirer and fast friend of Yoshida, the Premier who did so much to launch the postwar recovery of Japan, and was named Secretary-General of Yoshida's Liberal Party in 1954. After the Liberals merged with the Democrats in 1955, Ikeda helped engineer Tanzan Ishibashi's short-lived victory over Kishi in winning the new party's presidency and the nation's Premiership in 1956. Because Kishi immediately recognized the stature of this able opponent, he brought him into his own Cabinet as Minister of Finance after illness had forced Ishibashi from office early in

1957. When Kishi, in turn, was forced to step down in 1960, Ikeda was obviously the logical successor and the man certain to win out despite a series of maneuvers by other leaders of the Liberal-Democrats to gain the coveted seat of power.

What kind of a man is this former Kyoto University playboy, this spoiled son of a wealthy father, this "human calculating machine" with the statistical brain and dynamic ways? Some indication can be found in the type of denunciation he has elicited from friend and foe over the years; he has been called arrogant, self-centered, brusque, frank, tactless, tough, indifferent to public suffering, rude, rough, honest, ruthless, dictatorial, aggressive, willful, uncompromising, and strong-willed. The consistent quality that seems to emerge from all this is strength—a refusal to let others deflect him from his course, a determination to keep his eye on worthwhile goals and to destroy whatever obstacles lie in the way. This may not be a formula for political success in a country as suspicious of strong leaders as Japan is today, but it is a formula for progress as long as it can be made to work. And combined with Ikeda's new suave public manners, it may last for some time before the iron will beneath the pleasant exterior becomes obvious.

The more thoughtful side of Ikeda's nature, and the depths of his concern over Japan's future, have been amply revealed since he came to power. From the moment he mounted the podium to accept the Liberal-Democratic Party presidency, on July 14, 1960, he set out to awaken the public to the serious threat to democracy posed by the recent anti-Treaty riots. The scene was charged with expectancy that day, and a hush fell over the delegates jamming Tokyo's Hibiya Hall. Ikeda ruffled the papers on the stand. He gazed out over the sea of faces, his own face composed. "The nation is facing a grave political situation," he began in his rasping, gravelly voice. Across the nation millions were listening and watching on radio and television as he told them of the callous bid for power behind the Socialist offensive and of the role of the Communists in trying to create chaos. If the people were yearning for a new firmness and clarity of purpose in government, they were not disappointed that day or in the weeks that followed.

"The emphasis will be on the establishment of a true democracy and instillation in the minds of our people of the need to maintain and respect social order," he told an American-Japanese Society luncheon. "I believe that by doing so we can not only regain trust in Japan by the United States . . . but also gain the respect of the Communist countries. . . . In Japan today, the political ideal cherished by our people is a democracy based on human dignity and freedom."

After his election, he kept repeating that one of Japan's most serious tasks was to regain the international prestige it had lost during the anti-Security Treaty riots. He told a newspaper interviewer, "The government considers this Treaty necessary to the maintenance of Japan's security and consequently will faithfully discharge its duties and obligations under the Treaty." And with considerable insight he told another American newsman: "Japan's problem as a democracy is that its two main parties just do not have any meeting of minds on major issues. In your country the two parties find plenty to argue about . . . but on basic problems of economics, foreign affairs, and how your society should function they do not disagree. . . . I'm afraid we won't get very far until the Socialist Party abandons its claim to fighting the class war. . . ."

Ikeda's popularity grew rapidly. He won wide approval by appointing Mrs. Masa Nakayama as Welfare Minister—Japan's first woman Cabinet member—and by announcing that he had no intention of trying to pass a new electoral-district law, revise the Constitution, or increase police powers at this time. All were conservative goals that Kishi had failed to achieve. Not even the Socialists objected when Ikeda formed a thirty-six-member Foreign Affairs Council to seek the views of civic and journalistic leaders on key issues, and there were smiles throughout his faction-ridden party when he invited all Liberal-Democratic Diet members to a luncheon and announced: "The Ikeda curry and rice restaurant will be open every Tuesday and Friday and will charge 300 yen [$.83] a dish." He promised to build new highways and ports, reclaim land, build homes, and develop water resources. And he even showed up unannounced at a local newsreel theater and talked of riding the subway to give the general public a sense of identification with him.

These early days of his Administration were busy ones for Ikeda. He arose at 6:30 A.M. daily, read or scanned eight newspapers while still in bed, listened to a 7 A.M. news broadcast, bathed, and strolled through his spacious garden. This was his quietest and most pleasant hour. "I feel refreshed when I look at interesting stones," he once confided to a friend. While he ate breakfast, the first of thirty or forty visitors arrived at 8 A.M. He saw them at home in the morning, except when there was a Cabinet meeting, and went to the office in the afternoon. At night, there was an endless sequence of meetings, consultations, and gatherings of his own hand-picked group of advisers. But once in a while, Ikeda slipped away to a Japanese baseball game and sat behind the catcher "to see what the pitcher is throwing." And not infrequently there was an unusual visit to brighten his day, such as the delegation from the Tokyo fish market that appeared at his official residence shortly after his election and piled a congratulatory gift of sea bream and succulent Ise Bay lobsters at his feet. It was often after midnight before Ikeda could get to bed.

Still, in spite of the long hours, this was the honeymoon period of his Administration, and Japanese political life was relatively peaceful. The serenity did not last long, however, for Ikeda soon found himself deeply embroiled in a political crisis bearing striking similarities to the upheaval of 1960 that had swept Kishi from office. Just as in the case of the Treaty revision, which had brought on Kishi's great period of trial, legislation initially advocated by the Socialists precipitated Ikeda's first major trouble. It was a measure cracking down on acts of political terrorism, such as the right-wing stabbings that culminated in the assassination of Socialist Chairman Inejiro Asanuma. But the bill, in the form in which it finally reached the floor of the House, also contained a provision banning demonstrations in the immediate vicinity of the Diet and the Prime Minister's residence, sites of most of the 1960 violence. The Socialists, shifting course just as they had after the Liberal-Democrats took them up on their demands for a revision of the "unequal" Security Treaty of 1951, decided that the prohibition of demonstrations in these two areas was an infringement on freedoms guaranteed by the Constitution. What they did not openly say was that the legislation also presented another opportunity for attacking Japan's conservative government. And doubtless it also occurred to the Socialists that the bill would deprive them of their main weapon for frightening the Diet and public officials into submitting to their will.

The new crisis mounted rapidly, and on June 3, 1961, a violent fight erupted in the Diet. When the time arrived to call the bill up for a vote in the House, the Socialists resorted to tactics almost identical with those used against the Treaty. While more than 40,000 members of Sohyo and Zengakuren demonstrated in a march past the Diet, the Socialists and their secretaries again tried to hold Speaker Kiyose prisoner in his office. This time Diet guards freed him quickly, but Kiyose had to call the session to order from a chair on the floor of the House, since his own chair was occupied and guarded by Socialists. Fist fights broke out, shirts were torn, and clothing ripped as the fighting swirled around the chamber; but in the midst of the commotion both the Democratic Socialists, who supported the legislation, and Liberal-Democrats were canvassed and the results reported to Kiyose by a hidden microphone. He declared the bill passed over violent Socialist objections that the vote was illegal.

In the following days, new violent demonstrations erupted, aimed at preventing a vote in the House of Councilors that would make the passage final. On June 6, more than 600 persons were injured in wild clashes between police and leftist protest marchers in Tokyo, Osaka, and Kyoto. The next day Ikeda, faced with a revolt among upper-house members of his own party, retreated by agreeing to shelve the bill temporarily—at least until after he had completed a trip to the United States and Canada, scheduled for later in the month. It was a major setback for the new Prime Minister, and it demonstrated only too clearly that the same cancerous, divisive forces that precipitated the Security Treaty crisis were still eating away at the soul of Japan.

The eruption of 1961, following so closely the pattern of the eruption of 1960, seemed to leave little doubt that more of the same could be expected in the future.

Part Four

CONFLICT ON THE PERIPHERY

14. The Military-Intelligence Front

THE BATTLE FOR CONTROL of Japan took many shapes and forms other than those that culminated in the riots of 1960 and 1961. While the struggle was being waged on the political and ideological fronts in the years preceding those crises, there were also expressions of the same basic East-West conflict in at least two other major spheres of activity. One was in the realm of military intelligence, the silent war of espionage that surrounds Japan, and it appeared most visibly in the constant search for information along the tense Cold War frontier between Japan and the Communist mainland of Asia. The other sphere was Okinawa and, to a lesser extent, the other islands of Japan's lost empire.

If we begin with the military-intelligence operations in and around Japan, we can easily understand that espionage is a direct result of the Communist and anti-Communist military confrontations in the Far East. From Siberia in the north to Vietnam in the south, the Communists have massed formidable forces, most of them facing the West Pacific they would like to control and set up as a buffer against incursions from the Western world. And from the northern anchor of Japan—strategic Japan—the anti-Communists have countered Red deployment with an outpost line extending south to the Philippines. It bristles with ground troops in South Korea, Nationalist China's Taiwan, and South Vietnam; it is heavily defended by air and naval power and a radar net. Obviously, with such alignments of troops, each side must keep a close check on the intentions, capabilities, and potentials of the other.

The Soviet Union has in the Far East an estimated 400,000-man army, a 4,000-plane air force, and a navy that reportedly includes 6 cruisers and 110 submarines, some of them perhaps capable of firing missiles. There is a major Soviet base at Vladivostok and others along the lower Kamchatka Peninsula and in southern Siberia. China is reported to have a ground force of 2.5–3 million men, an air force of 3,000 planes, and a 170,000-ton navy that includes more than 20 long-range, modern subs. North Korea has a 350,000–400,000 man army, 800 combat planes, and a small navy of torpedo boats and minesweepers. And in North Vietnam there is a tough, guerilla-trained army of more than 300,000.

Arrayed against these are the following: Republic of (South) Korea—a 580,000-man army, a substantial air force, the U.S. First Cavalry and Seventh Infantry Divisions, a Turkish brigade, elements of the U.S. Fifth Air Force, and one Matador-missile unit; Japan—an estimated 170,000-man ground force, which probably numbers less than 160,000 because of recruitment difficulties, a navy of 140,000 tons, including destroyers, 5 submarines in the planning stage, a helicopter carrier, and an expanding air force of perhaps 500 planes, backed up by 250 U.S. aircraft; Nationalist China—560,000 men under arms, most of them in the army, a tiny navy of destroyers and some smaller craft, and a 300–500-plane air force; Okinawa—9 American air squadrons, 2 regiments of a marine division, an airborne regiment, some special guerrilla-trained troops, 2 Nike Hercules antiaircraft-missile battalions, and some Mace-missile units; the Philippines—a 50,000-man army, navy, and air force, and 2 U.S. air squadrons. Backing up all of this is the very powerful U.S. Seventh Fleet, which includes destroyers, up to 3 aircraft carriers, cruisers, and submarines, some of which are probably nuclear subs. Strategic Air Command bombers on Guam and U.S. naval and ground strength in Hawaii help to bolster the perimeter.

Keeping a close watch over the Communists is an endless and difficult task, requiring the use of every intelligence weapon available, particularly since China, North Korea, and North Vietnam are areas shut off from even the normal observation of American diplomatic representatives. The methods used to maintain this watch are of course secret, but over the years an interesting pattern has emerged. An integral part of this pattern is the long and dangerous history of so-called "weather flights" made by American aircraft from fields in Japan. From November 6, 1951, to June 16, 1959, there have been twelve clashes between American "weather" planes and Communist aircraft in the general vicinity of Japan. Sixty-four American airmen lost their lives in these air battles, seven U.S. planes were shot down, and losses on the Communist side were also heavy. This would be a most unusual toll except for the fact that the U.S. planes were always making their "weather" observations immediately off the Communist coasts and probably were not sampling weather at all. More likely, they were taking radar fixes on Communist installations, making photographs, and, in general, learning as much as they could—certainly a necessary and worthwhile military function, but one that has been poorly disguised for many years.

The Communists do much the same thing, but they usually do not come quite so close to Japanese shores. Russian jets fly down the coasts of both the Pacific and the Sea of Japan as far south as Tokyo Bay. During one period, they were becoming so common that Japanese newspapers dubbed them the "Tokyo Express." Russian ships also make regular runs through the Sea of Japan to make radar checks along the Japanese coast that might reveal new installations.

A related but much more secret operation than the "weather" flights was carried out by mysterious black jets—so the Japanese called them—that the United States kept in Japan for several years. They first attracted public attention on September 24, 1959, when one of the graceful black planes arched silently down from the sky to make an emergency landing on a glider field near Fujisawa. Many Japanese gathered quickly to examine the strange craft; they noted its long, gull-like wings, its flamed-out jet engine, and the lack of any national markings. Moments later, carloads of American soldiers arrived and chased the onlookers away.

For months Japanese newspapers and magazines were filled with attempts to guess what the plane really was and what it was doing in Japan. They described the jet in detail, speculated that its tremendous wingspread would permit it to reach great altitudes—far out of range of normal antiaircraft weapons and interceptor planes—and then to shut off its power and sail for long periods like a glider. They said that the black paint was to absorb radar waves and prevent detection; that its powerful engine and tremendous fuel storage would obviously give it great range; that the lack of national identification indicated it was in a hush-hush category; and that it was equipped with high-altitude cameras. The plane was, they concluded, ideally suited for observation flights over other countries. The commentators were obviously being filled in by well-informed sources, for the plane was a U-2, the same type of spy craft that was shot down over the Soviet Union seven months later, on May 1, 1960, and touched off the international uproar that canceled President Eisenhower's trip to Moscow and wrecked the 1960 Paris Summit Conference.

The plane that landed at Fujisawa was one of three U-2's secretly stationed in Japan by the U.S. Central Intelligence Agency, but it was many, many months before the U.S. Embassy in Tokyo reluctantly confirmed it. To still the clamor in the Japanese press, the Embassy finally issued a formal announcement acknowledging the Fujisawa plane's identity; but it claimed that all three U-2's in Japan were being used solely for weather reconnaissance and research. They were assigned to the National Aeronautics and Space Administration, the Embassy said, which accounted for the lack of normal national markings that regular U.S. Air Force planes bear. It specifically denied that the jets had been sent on spying missions over Communist territory. Japan's Socialists refused to accept such a transparently poor explanation and assumed what they could not prove—that the planes were being used for clandestine purposes. They repeatedly charged that the "black jet" incident was another reason for not renewing the U.S.–Japanese Security Treaty; that it showed the United States could carry out spying flights from bases in Japan without Japanese consent, and, therefore, that the Treaty should be abrogated. Eventually, the criticism forced the U.S. Government to crate up the planes and ship them out of the country.

Whether the U-2's in Japan actually were used on spying missions over Communist Asia is a question that cannot be answered with factual proof. But obviously they must have been—else they would not have been in Japan in the first place. From Japan, they could easily conduct missions over an area of the Communist world the Western powers needed to keep under constant check; besides, that is the type of mission for which they were specifically designed and used elsewhere in the world.

A much more subtle, but perhaps not so productive, operation than either the "weather" flights or U-2 activities has been carried out by both sides beneath the surface of the ocean. Communist submarine forces in the Pacific provide one of the biggest military headaches the West faces. There have been reports of their probing U.S. mid-Pacific defenses, and numerous unidentified submarines have been reported off South America. Some of these undoubtedly are Communist craft, both on training missions and information-gathering cruises. The U.S. Seventh Fleet also makes frequent contact with them while patrolling the West Pacific. The usual practice is to drop a small grenade to "ping" the craft and let its commander know that it has been found.

The quality of Russian and Chinese submarines has been poor, but in recent years both have improved greatly. Admiral Arleigh A. Burke, before he retired in 1961 as Chief of U.S. Naval Operations, told the House Armed Services Committee that the Soviets probably even have nuclear-powered submarines and submarines capable of firing missiles. In 1961, the Swedish Navy yearbook, *Marinkalendern*, listed two Soviet atomic submarines as presumably ready for service and three believed to be under construction. Swedish sources have reported that the Soviet Union has test-fired guided missiles from submarines, the best known of which are the Comet I, with a range of only 100 miles, and the Comet II, with a range of about 600 miles. None of these more modern craft has ever been reported in the Pacific, but they very likely will appear later since it has been Soviet policy to replace older vessels with newer types as they become available. When the nuclear submarines do appear, it will multiply demands on U.S. antisubmarine forces as much as five to ten times, because nuclear submarines are much faster, can stay submerged much longer, and thus make detection more difficult.

The United States has never dropped any hints whether or not it uses submarines to gain information about enemy activity. It can be assumed that they keep a close watch on the movements of Communist naval units so that their whereabouts will always be known and that they make close-in observation-runs along Communist coasts. But there is also speculation of a different kind that centers around former Japanese islands now under U.S. Navy control, particularly the Bonins, a chain arching south from central Honshu into the Pacific, as well as Saipan and Tinian in the Mariana grouping further south. Japan had a submarine base at Chichi Jima in the Bonins during World War II, and there have been reports of an American submarine base in that area now, a possibility that has not been diminished by the tight security the Navy maintains over the islands. All the Japanese have been removed, and the U.S. refuses to allow them to return. Not even accredited American correspondents can get in. Communist China has charged numerous times in the past that this cloak of secrecy, which extends over Japan's former mandated islands—the American-controlled Marianas, Marshalls, and Carolines—has been used to hide a spy school for Nationalist Chinese agents in or near Saipan and Tinian. Whether true or not, it is no secret that the Nationalists do have a very efficient intelligence system on the Chinese mainland; they have often been able to report major events that are under way in China proper long before official announcements have been made. How these agents get their information is another question. The submarine, of course, would be ideal for such purposes.

The matter of Communist espionage within Japan is an equally closely guarded secret, but there is no doubt that it goes on. Some agents come and go from Hokkaido, the northernmost Japanese island, which is less than ten miles from Soviet-held Kunashiri, the southernmost of the Kurile Islands. Hokkaido is even closer to the small Soviet-controlled Habomai and Shikotan islands across the Nemuro Straits. There Japanese fishermen tell stories of lights flashing off their coasts at night and of strange boats that come and go in the darkness. Other agents slip into Japan from Korea, and some very likely still make it from China proper. The case of the People's Fleet, the disguised fishing smacks that operated between

China and Japan, has already been cited. The ease with which Communists have gone "underground"—that is, disappeared from public view—at various times also indicates that there still are established channels for getting in and out of the country, despite Japan's efficient police, immigration service, and coast guard.

One of the most rudimentary forms of intelligence activity the Communists carry out is keeping American bases under surveillance. Since there is no espionage law in Japan, it is legal, and not much can be done about it; thus, a fairly accurate story of the U-2's in Japan was pieced together and fed to Japanese publications long before official disclosures even acknowledged that there was such a plane in Japan. Similarly, the Japanese spotted RB-57's, another special reconnaissance plane, at American bases in both Japan and Okinawa; and within a few days after the Soviet Union announced that it had shot down a U.S. RB-47 over the Barents Sea on July 1, 1960—only two months after the downing of the U-2 over the Soviet Union—these same sources came up with reports that this third type of U.S. reconnaissance plane had been seen at Yokota Air Base in Japan. So-called "aviation experts" informed the Japanese press quite correctly that at least one or two of these planes had been there on an irregular basis since 1957. They reported that they usually took off on missions only in the evening.

One of the interesting facts about such reports is that they sometimes seem to be "plants" designed to elicit some form of American or Japanese Government reaction that in itself might reveal information. In fact, some seem to appear on a rhythmic cycle; among them are false reports of American nuclear submarines putting into the American naval base at Yokosuka. If true, such an event would stir widespread, adverse reactions among the Japanese people, who have been, and remain, very sensitive to the dangers of nuclear radiation. But by eliciting a denial, those behind such reports may also gain some indication of whether or not there are any such submarines with the U.S. Seventh Fleet or in waters near Japan. And then too, it is always possible that a new type of submarine was sighted pulling into Yokosuka and that an exaggerated report was released, along with the time and a description, in hope of learning from the denial what type it actually was.

There is activity on the much more dangerous "cloak and dagger" level too; but unlike some of the more obvious probings for information, this type of intelligence and counterintelligence does not show on the surface very often. A notable exception is the still unsolved case of Master Sergeant Emmett E. Dugan of Crafton, Pennsylvania, whose body was found floating in Tokyo Bay on March 12, 1958. He had been assigned to an intelligence unit at Camp Zama, a U.S. Army base near Tokyo, and the Army described his duties as "investigative." Japanese newspapers, however, quoting unnamed Japanese sources, said that he had been assigned to gathering information on Communist China. His record did show that he had completed a Chinese-language course at the Army language school in Monterey, California, the preceding July.

Dugan's wife, Maud, was the last to see him alive. She said that on the evening of February 4, 1958, he handed her his life-insurance policies and said, "If I don't return, you will need these." He told her to return to their Yokohama home, then disappeared, and not until five weeks later was his body found. After a medical examination, the U.S. Army issued a statement saying:

> Dugan's lungs were free of water, indicating he did not die as a result of drowning. He did not die from natural causes. There was no evidence of bodily injury sufficient to cause death. There was no trace of chemicals found in his body. . . . Chemicals could have been present in the body, but with decomposition, chemical traces could have been dispelled. In addition, there are numerous drugs known to be untraceable.

The most celebrated case of Communist espionage in Japan during recent years has been that of Yuri Alexandrovich Rastvorov, Russia's top agent in the Far East until he defected in 1954. Rastvorov's activities in Japan and eventual decision to seek asylum in the United States have already been well documented, but the essentials are worth repeating. From the Russian Embassy, in the Azabu district of Tokyo, Rastvorov operated a network of agents that penetrated business firms, the Japanese police force, newspapers, and Japanese employees of two U.S. Army installations. It even included three men in the Japanese Foreign Ministry, one of whom later committed suicide. From 1951 until the end of the

Korean War, their primary mission was to gain as much information as possible about American troops in Korea, Japan, and throughout the Far East—their losses, equipment, plans, and morale. This was not too difficult to do. Tokyo cabarets were filled with soldiers on leave from the front; and if some of Rastvorov's men just happened to be on hand to buy them a few drinks, it was often possible to loosen tongues that told more than they intended to.

Rastvorov's activities were under close surveillance from 1952 on by both the Japanese police and American counterintelligence agents working together. It was known that he controlled the two bank accounts the Russians maintained in Tokyo and signed the daily radio reports to Moscow, beamed from the Embassy via its very tall flagstaff, which also serves as a radio-transmitter antenna. He played tennis frequently at the exclusive Tokyo Lawn Tennis Club and had made friends with an American girl, a civilian employee of the armed forces, who gave him English lessons. When Stalin died and Georgi Malenkov's new regime took over in Russia, the American Counter-Intelligence Corps (CIC) learned through the American girl, who had agreed to help them, that Rastvorov was greatly concerned. Since a new team was taking over in Russia, he didn't know exactly where he stood; then when his boss, Lavrenti P. Beria, First Deputy Premier of the Soviet Union and chief of its intelligence activities, was executed along with six of his deputies, Rastvorov became deeply worried. Shortly after this, he was ordered home, and he told the girl he feared that he would be killed when he got there. Upon instructions from the CIC, she sought and gained his agreement to defect, although he knew this would imperil the lives of his wife and daughter in Russia. He dropped from sight, with American assistance, and did not reappear until seven months later in the United States.

Since the Rastvorov case, there have been no major disclosures of how the Communist intelligence apparatus operates in Japan. It is known that it still centers around the Soviet Embassy and its staff, which always includes numerous officials highly trained in intelligence work. There is also considerable liaison between the Russians and other Communist diplomatic missions in Tokyo, particularly the Poles, and to a lesser extent with the Japanese Communist Party. But beyond this, Japanese police and the American CIC, which likes to pretend it does not even exist, have been very reticent about hinting at what they know of Communist intelligence activities in Japan. This leaves unanswered the large question of what levels of Japanese society and types of Japanese organizations the Communists have been able to penetrate since Rastvorov's network was uprooted. It can be assumed, as a matter of course, that there are agents working with the Japanese Government, in various strategic industries, and among Japanese employees at American bases. Such top listening posts as the Tokyo Foreign Correspondents Club obviously are kept under close surveillance, as are businessmen's groups and American officers' and enlisted men's clubs.

Another likely target for penetration is the Japanese Self-Defense Forces, not so much for information-gathering purposes as for carrying out the long-range goal of subverting them in the same way that the labor movement, the intellectuals, and the schools have been made more amenable to Communist causes over the years. This is an issue of utmost importance; indeed, the very future of constitutional government in Japan may depend on it, for eventually there will have to be some kind of showdown between the left and right, at which time the balance of power will lie with the loyalty of the armed forces.

The Self-Defense Forces are a unique organization of quasi-legal status under the Constitution, which states in its controversial Article IX: ". . . the Japanese people forever renounce war as a sovereign right of the nation . . . land, sea, and air forces, as well as other war potential, will never be maintained." This has been circumvented by calling them Self-Defense Forces, implying that they are for defensive purposes only, a position made legal by the Japanese Supreme Court in its 1960 ruling upholding American bases in Japan. It held that no nation could be denied the right to defend itself.

The defense forces were created on August 10, 1950, as a 75,000-man Police Reserve by order of Douglas MacArthur, the U.S. Occupation Commander. He said that they were needed to secure the home front because American troops in Japan had been hastily marshaled and sent into the Korean War less than two months before. On May 27, 1952, the Police Reserve was expanded to 110,000 men, and its name was changed to National Safety Force; on October 1, 1954, it officially became the National Self-Defense Forces, a name it seems destined to retain for many years.

For several years after it was launched, the Ground Self-Defense Force consisted of six divisions and four mixed brigades, about 13,000 and 6,000 men, respectively, in each. But under a five-year program announced in 1960, they were ordered gradually to reorganize into thirteen small divisions, each totaling approximately 7,000–9,000 men, to provide greater ease of expansion later without having to create new divisional headquarters. The smaller divisions could all absorb several thousand more men without disturbing their command structure. The Maritime Self-Defense Force, as the 140,000-ton navy is called, consists mainly of destroyers and destroyer escorts, as well as other smaller vessels, many of them former American craft. The potential for expansion, and for obtaining much larger ships, is great; Japan has the world's most productive shipbuilding industry and a long naval tradition that could easily provide qualified command personnel. The Air Self-Defense Force has mainly F-86 Sabrejets, which are being steadily replaced with F-104 Starfighters. Even more modern planes are certain to come later.

The efforts Communist agents have expended on softening up these fledgling forces have had one big factor in their favor—a serious morale problem imposed on members of all three services by lack of public acceptance. Soldiers are often sneered at on the streets as "foreign mercenaries" because they wear American uniforms and generally use American equipment. Former Imperial Army officers have ridiculed what they consider to be a lack of discipline and the modern tactics that rule out *Banzai* charges as wasteful of trained manpower. Some World War II officers also feel that the training methods are soft because enlisted men cannot be slapped or physically manhandled as they were before the war. But the public rejection of the Self-Defense Forces goes far beyond such groups. It is rooted in Japan's pacifism and a widespread belief that Japan does not need an army, navy, or air force. The theory is that since no one is threatening Japan, the money spent on defense is wasted. There is the feeling, too, that the presence of troops can lead to involvement in war, probably through some machinations of the United States. This concept has been widely disseminated by teachers, and it is passed on by the students to their families. Communists and Socialists have strongly supported it, and the Socialists have incorporated it in their platform in the form of a pledge to convert the defense forces into a coast guard and labor battalions. The labor battalions, they promise, will work on public-welfare projects.

The impact on individual servicemen has been serious. One has reported this story to illustrate how military life separated him from his former friends: As an employee of a chicken farmer, he had to rise at 4 A.M. every day and work until after dark, for which he received 1,500 yen ($4.17) a month, plus room and board. So he joined the Ground Self-Defense Force, where he could sleep until 6 A.M., normally be free after 5 P.M., receive good food, clothing, and medical care, plus 7,000 yen ($19.44) a month in salary. He was overjoyed with the prospect of his new life; but the night before he was to report for duty, one of his former high-school classmates, at a farewell party, shook hands sadly and said, "You'll be our enemy tomorrow."

On another occasion, in May, 1959, two Kyoto high schools refused to participate in the Japan Athletic Festival after they learned that policemen and Self-Defense Forces personnel were also entered. "We couldn't afford to have our students associating with them," the school's formal withdrawal notice stated. On still another occasion, a National Defense Academy student described in a magazine article how much he hated to encounter his former school friends, although he was a cadet in the Japanese equivalent of West Point, Annapolis, Sandhurst, or St. Cyr. "It is most painful," he explained. "Before they say anything, I become suspicious that they hate me."

One of the obvious results of such public sentiment has been the extreme difficulty of obtaining adequate financing for the defense program. Less than 2 per cent of Japan's income goes for defense purposes, compared to 20 per cent or more elsewhere in the world; consequently, Japan's ground, sea, and air troops have had to make out largely with World War II and Korean War equipment obtained from the United States. This is slowly being rectified, but in an age of missiles and nuclear warfare Japan's defenses would be in woeful shape if it were not for America's protective umbrella that helps shield the islands. Japan's very prosperous economy has, in fact, had almost a free ride at the expense of the American taxpayer as far as the normal burdens of defense are concerned, and this is not a situation that is likely to change very soon, not at least until there is more general agreement within the country on the necessity for providing such defense.

In the meantime, there is still the unanswered question of how well the Japanese troops would perform if called upon by their government either to help put down civil disturbances, such as the recent anti-Treaty riots, or to engage in actual combat. During the Treaty disturbances, Self-Defense Force commanders resisted, behind the scenes, suggestions that troops be called out to restore order. At the same time, leftists were saying that if soldiers were used they would desert and "side with the people" in any full uprising aimed at overthrowing the government.

Actually, all indications are that the troops would have obeyed orders and carried out whatever assignment they were given, although their commanders were anxious to avoid this if possible because of the added public censure that might result. American military advisers who have watched the Japanese troops maneuver and have assisted in their training rate them highly; although they are small in numbers and not too well equipped, they are tough, of very courageous stock (as any American soldier who fought in the Pacific in World War II can testify), and well-trained physically, despite the claims of former Imperial officers. Their discipline, too, has been good, although not severe, and they have a grounding in modern methods of warfare.

Whether this reasonably good beginning has been undermined seriously either by the divided ideological climate of Japan or by actual Communist efforts is a question only the future can answer. The same forces, however, bearing down on the remnants of Japan's lost empire, have had much more visible and immediate results in Okinawa and the Ryukyu Islands. The fight there, in broad application, is basically the same as the conflict that has rent Japan for the past decade. But there is a difference. It has the added disturbing quality of harboring a ghost of days of past grandeur, which still tug hard at the heart of all Japanese.

15. The Lost Territories

JAPAN'S EMPIRE ONCE extended over a sixth of the world. From deep within Asia to the middle of the Pacific, it embraced Manchuria, part of China, Korea, South Sakhalin, Taiwan, the Pescadores, and the Kurile, Bonin, Ryukyu, Mariana, Marshall, and Caroline islands. Now virtually all is gone, lost in a disastrous war. China took Manchuria and its own occupied provinces; Korea became independent, although divided into two nations; the Russians moved into South Sakhalin and the Kuriles under terms of the Yalta agreement; and Nationalist China retained Taiwan and the Pescadores, after losing the mainland to the Chinese Communists. The remainder of Japan's Pacific island holdings were turned over to the United States—the Marianas, Marshalls, and Carolines under a United Nations trusteeship; the Ryukyus and Bonins under terms of the San Francisco Peace Treaty, with the added stipulation that Japan would retain "residual sovereignty" there. This means that the United States will return them when it feels they are no longer needed for military purposes.

Today, the memory of those lost territories haunts the new and prosperous but overcrowded Japan, which hungers for more resources and land to use in feeding its burgeoning population. The Japanese have argued in vain with the Russians that at least the southern half of the Kuriles historically belonged to Japan; but they have received only a vague promise—that the Russians will return the tiny Habomai and Shikotan islets off the tip of eastern Hokkaido when Japan signs a full World War II peace treaty that acknowledges Soviet claims to the other former Japanese lands it occupies.

Japan's attempts to regain at least administrative control of the Ryukyus and Bonins have also been equally ineffective in repeated negotiations with the United States, although conducted in a much friendlier atmosphere than those with the Russians. But perhaps because the U.S. intention to stay seemed less definite, perhaps because of the strange and unprecedented doctrine of "residual sovereignty," and perhaps because it did return the Amami Oshima portion of the Ryukyus, the United States has been the main target of the "reversion" movement. It is a popular issue on which all political parties agree. They all want the lost islands back, indeed feel they are quite rightfully Japan's. The resulting agitation has been strong and insistent and has involved in part, at least in the case of the Ryukyus, much the same pattern of subversion from the far left that has cropped up in so many other popular movements in Japan. Its very popularity has, in fact, provided the emotional content needed to make it an excellent arena in which those forces seeking first to neutralize Japan and then to move it toward the Communist world could attack the American military posture in the Pacific. Sohyo and the Japanese Communist and Socialist parties have all been deeply involved.

Okinawa, largest and most important of the Ryukyus and site of a $1-billion American military base, has been the storm center of this trouble. Spread out like a misplaced gerrymander midway between Japan and Formosa, with the other islands of the Ryukyu chain extending south toward that Nationalist Chinese stronghold, it is an ancient and troubled island seventy-five miles in length and varying from two to ten miles in width. Historically, it has been tragically poor because of the highest population pressure in the world per arable unit of land; for generations, its undernourished and docile people existed under their own kings but paid tribute to China. When, in 1875, Japan claimed and occupied the Ryukyu Islands, it did little to improve the welfare of the people, treated them as inferiors, laughed at the strange Okinawan names, and disdained intermarriage as a step down socially. But over the years the Okinawans became a reasonably well-integrated portion of the Japanese empire and proudly assumed that they were a part of the Yamato "race," although distinctly darker and smaller in stature than the Japanese. Today, Okinawa is remembered mainly as the scene of the last and most savage battle of World War II, in which 11,260 Americans and 90,000 Japanese were killed and 33,308 Americans wounded. Virtually the entire southern half of the island was laid waste; its civilian population was seriously displaced and left near starvation; and its harbors and fields were littered with the debris of war.

Now all of that is changed. Okinawa is a strange land of contrasts—broad American-built four-lane highways sweeping through a countryside dotted with the grim, unpainted homes of Okinawan farmers, modern American cars intermingled with hand-pushed carts; grimy, filthy buildings still scarred by the World War II fighting next to new ferro-concrete and concrete-block structures; and exquisitely beautiful Japanese inns only a short distance from honky-tonk bars and cabarets filled with prostitutes catering to the American troops. It is a land of swift and extensive change, particularly in the capital city of Naha, and at the same time it is still an island of troubled people. They are no longer hungry; their fears, engendered by a Caucasian administration, have gradually given way under a new prosperity, but they are largely rootless and still seeking stability by some strong link to the past that the American Occupation seems to be rapidly destroying. Okinawa is just now emerging from its own version of the little Cold War that still grips Japan, in which forces on the far left, financed and egged on from the outside, tried hard to make the islands untenable for the United States. They lost, however, and now have steadily diminishing opportunities for subversion. But the passage through this period of turmoil has been difficult, and Okinawa's basic troubles are still partly rooted there.

America's problems in Okinawa began at the end of World War II. At that time there was a native population of only about 500,000, but soon 200,000 more Okinawans scattered throughout the Japanese Empire were brought home. These, in addition to a natural increase of 20,000 persons annually, soon boosted the population to 850,000 on an island that cannot adequately feed half that number. If the United States had the same population density, it would have about 2.75 billion persons.

America's original purpose in retaining Okinawa was to hold it for military reasons until the security of the Far East seemed assured. Until 1949, therefore, the island seemed of little value, but then three events occurred that changed the character of the U.S. tenure completely. First, the Chinese Communists won control of the Chinese mainland, producing an abrupt shift in the balance of Far Eastern power; second, a year later, the Communists launched the Korean War; and, third, a giant typhoon descended upon Okinawa and well-nigh flattened the island. Clearly, a decision had to be made—to build a permanent advance base on Okinawa, taking full advantage of its strategic location within 600 miles of Japan, Korea, China, and Formosa. Thus, Okinawa became a link in the world-wide chain of bases the United States was forging to contain Communism. And a Caucasian society that had virtually every modern advantage known to man moved in to build a billion-dollar base in the midst of an Oriental society that had so little it recognized virtually only one form of wealth—land upon which food could be grown. The results could hardly be expected to be serene.

Statistics tell the grim story of the United States' foolish mistakes in the years that followed. Of Okinawa's 296,206 acres, only 80,000 were arable. The American military at once took over 40,700—16,000 of them arable—and disclosed plans to take over another 12,000, of which 3,000 were arable. In all, 250,000 Okinawans were displaced and 60,000 more were threatened with displacement. This meant that 38 per cent of the Okinawan people either lost, or were threatened with losing, the only insurance against starvation they and their ancestors had ever known—their scarce and precious land. To make matters worse, the compensation provided for the confiscated lands was computed by the Japan Hypothic Bank, using an outmoded and unfair Oriental formula, and amounted to practically nothing—as little as $20 a year for a tiny tract of land that might not be worth any more than that elsewhere in the world but could still feed an Okinawan and his family. A final touch was added when a U.S. Congressional subcommittee, headed by Representative Melvin Price of Illinois, recommended that the United States buy outright—that is, take title to—the land it had been renting on Okinawa.

A more complete formula for political turmoil could hardly have been devised. The cumulative uproar came close to panic, both in Japan, where there was increasing fear that the Americans were now intending to stay permanently, and in Okinawa itself, where farmers loved their soil with the universal passion of the peasant. It was a situation ready made for Kamejiro Senaga, gaunt, bushy-haired Communist chief of the Okinawan People's Party (OPP), and other extreme leftists in the Socialist Masses Party. They sent delegations to Japan to plead for reversion and to tell of the "American violation of our human rights."

All sorts of crimes were attributed to the United States. "It is terrible, my sisters," cried one Okinawan lady, member of a touring speakers' group, in Tokyo's Hibiya Park. "All our women are being forced into prostitution." Another speaker charged that American soldiers "burned out the farmers of Ie Shima," the island near Okinawa where World War II columnist Ernie Pyle was killed. (What actually happened was that U.S. guards at a firing range were ordered to burn off some heavy brush that was a fire hazard. The fire got out of hand and burned over nearly two acres of crops, for which compensation was promptly paid.) Senaga himself railed at "the U.S. rule of the saber," "American oppression of Okinawa," and "American colonialism." These were days when the big lie could be used with telling effect, for when Senaga toured the Ryukyus, one of his backers, a school superintendent, even went so far as to claim in a speech that "American soldiers are promoted for every ten Okinawans they kill."

The agitation grew steadily stronger and was played up in both Japanese and Okinawan newspapers. The U.S. Occupation was soon to realize just how far its relations with the Okinawan people had deteriorated: On July 27, 1956, a long column of students from the University of the Ryukyus, led by 150 students just returned from Japan, surged down the main street of Okinawa's capital city of Naha. "Go home, Yankee! Go home, Yankee!" they chanted over and over again. Later they changed this to "Tear down the flag!" and "Reversion to Japan!"

Then in December, 1956, Senaga was elected Mayor of Naha, and the Occupation authorities realized that they were in serious difficulties. It was the worst crisis in human relations that the American military had encountered in the postwar period, for Senaga was indeed a skillful and dangerous opponent, who could be counted upon to do everything in his power to subvert the American position. A small, thin man with glittering black eyes and an oversized mustache, he had a history as an agitator going back to well before World War II when he was jailed by Imperial Japan for speaking against the Emperor. After the war he was convicted by the U.S. Civil Administration of the Ryukyus of inducing perjury, and aiding and abetting the concealment of a criminal. While serving eighteen months in jail, he organized and staged demonstrations by the prisoners, who until then had been quite docile. He almost died of stomach ulcers in prison, but was saved by U.S. doctors and American blood plasma. When he was released, he twisted the facts by telling the crowd of Okinawans awaiting him that "I now have your blood in my veins."

As a speaker and organizer, he appeared to have no equal either in Okinawa or Japan. Obviously extremely intelligent, he lived in a spick-and-span hut up a dirty, winding street several miles from the heart of downtown Naha. There I talked to him one day in the small tatami room that served as the headquarters of his Okinawan People's Party. A Japanese flag was hung on one wall, inscribed in Oriental characters with such slogans as "Death to the American Imperialists!" "Reversion to Japan!" and "No More Hiroshimas!" He spoke ambiguously of his objectives: He claimed that he only wanted Okinawa returned to Japan, said that he was a "humanist" (a term that crops up frequently in the Orient and seems to have no relationship to the humanist philosophy that goes back to the Greeks of the fifth century B.C.), and maintained that he had no deep-seated enmity toward the United States. His actions later disproved these assertions.

Senaga held a peculiar charm for the Okinawan people; though basically conservative, they admired him as a man who had the courage to say things most of them felt about the U.S. Occupation. Consequently, when he ran for Mayor of Naha, he was promptly elected. In retaliation, the United States cut off $1 million in funds for a modest but well-conceived economic-aid program. Senaga responded with one of the most effective and vitriolic campaigns ever launched against the United States in the Orient. He made repeated headlines in Japan and kept the Ryukyu Islands Legislature and Naha City Council in a state of ferment over the popular reversion issue—a condition of unrest that was exactly what he wanted. He was unaware, however, that his movements and activities were under close surveillance both in Japan and Okinawa. His frequent trips to the Japanese Communist Party headquarters in Tokyo, his seemingly inexhaustible supply of funds for agitation purposes, and his membership in the Communist Party were either observed or established beyond a reasonable doubt. Finally, after all economic progress had come to a standstill in the restless island, General James Moore, then U.S. High Commissioner for the Ryukyus, removed Senaga by issuing a decree proclaiming that no man who had been convicted of a felony could hold the office of Mayor of Naha. New elections were called, but, much to the chagrin of the United States, Senaga's hand-picked lieutenant, Seiichi Kaneshi, won the Mayor's post. In City Council elections two months later, seven of nine OPP-backed candidates, and three independents who would vote with them, were elected.

With three successive election defeats behind them and the errors of the land program deeply underscored, the American command finally took some sound corrective measures. Actually, its record up to this time would have been reasonably good if it had not committed the inexcusable mistakes of taking land from peasants without paying adequate compensation, of unnecessarily pushing a plan to take title to the land under long-term, lump-sum payment leases, and of not dealing more skillfully with the Oriental personality. On the credit side, however, there were these accomplishments: The United States sponsored and helped finance the University of the Ryukyus; built more than 4,000 new and excellent typhoon-proof, reinforced concrete-block schoolrooms; virtually forced the Naha city government to adopt a city plan and begin erecting a much more modern city to replace the one wrecked by Typhoon "Gloria" in 1949; provided funds for draining, cleaning, and lining with concrete a malodorous canal system running through the city; made tremendous strides toward wiping out malaria in the islands; built hundreds of miles of new modern highways; more than tripled rice, sugar cane, and other agricultural production; raised incomes; took steps to rehabilitate the Ryukyuan fishing industry; opened new and fertile lands for settlement in the jungles of the southern Ryukyus; and provided jobs for 50,000 Okinawans, either directly on military posts or indirectly through Okinawan construction companies given military contracts.

But since this obviously was not enough in view of the three election disasters, three major corrective actions were finally taken. First, a new mutually acceptable land-rental formula was agreed upon, offering either yearly or single lump-sum payments under doubled rates that jumped total payments from $3 million to $6 million annually. Next, a special island script, known as B yen, was abandoned, and American dollars were made the accepted medium of exchange. This opened up a new $8-million line of credit with banks in the United States—money desperately needed for loans in one of the most credit-hungry areas of the world. It greatly stimulated investments in new enterprises. Finally, a free-trade zone was proclaimed in Okinawa, whereby "anyone desiring to import goods for storage, display, repackaging, processing, finishing, and other operations . . . and subsequent re-export . . . will be exempt from all . . . taxes, import, and export licensing."

Since the steam had been taken out of the land issue and a new prosperity was seeping through the islands, Senaga's grip on the people began to loosen. Kaneshi, who had been Senaga's puppet as Mayor of Naha, finally deserted his former chief and agreed to cooperate with the American authorities. In return, municipal rehabilitation funds that had been frozen since Senaga's election were released. American officials, too, lost some of their pompousness and began to rub shoulders with Okinawan leaders; some new light industries began to appear; and on November 13, 1960, the island's newly formed Liberal-Democratic Party, a counterpart of the conservatives in Japan, won a major victory—twenty-two of twenty-nine seats in the Ryukyuan Legislature. This is the popularly elected body which theoretically governs the islands under a Ryukyuan chief executive appointed by the American High

Commissioner, who, in turn, holds a final veto power over the Legislature's acts. The Socialist Masses Party, which had shown an increasing willingness to turn against Senaga's OPP, won five seats and the OPP and Independents one each.

There was a distinct improvement in the political climate after the land problem was resolved, but subversion continued under the surface. There were several obvious channels it could use. The most clearly discernible was the small nest of Communists and violent radicals who surrounded Senaga; intelligence reports indicated that they numbered fewer than one hundred and that the true hard core of dedicated revolutionaries was probably only about thirty-five. But their numerical strength was not the measure of their effectiveness, as they had already proved in exploiting every previous opportunity that had presented itself. Both Sohyo and the Japanese Communist Party helped them in preparing and coordinating propaganda attacks, in organizing speaking tours in Japan, and in the all-important matter of obtaining sufficient operating funds. Okinawa's teachers were another good possibility; banded together in the Okinawa Teachers Association, they were strongly under the influence of the Communist-dominated Japanese Teachers Union and consistently worked against most American policies. Another likely channel was the schools. A portion of the student body at the University of the Ryukyus showed the effects of persistent agitation by Okinawan students who had gone to Japan and received training from both Zengakuren and the Japanese Communist Party in organizing demonstrations and setting up a student movement. And, finally, there were Okinawa's numerous labor unions, most of them made up of thoroughly provincial people, who reacted favorably to the exploitation of such themes as "Reversion to Japan," Orientals versus Caucasians, and rich versus poor. Many of the unions took on some of the militant trappings of Sohyo and adopted mass-strike tactics that amounted to pure physical coercion. One favorite method of gaining their ends was to hold an employer prisoner in his office until he accepted the union's demands; in many cases, the employers were Americans who had started enterprises in Okinawa.

But despite these leftist efforts, it was not until President Eisenhower came to Okinawa, in June, 1960, that the full impact of the covert work became apparent. Eisenhower was on the Far Eastern tour he undertook shortly after the now-famous U-2 flight over the Soviet Union and the wrecked Summit Conference at Paris that followed. Orders apparently had gone out from Moscow to all Communist Parties to do everything possible to embarrass the American chief executive and destroy his image as a man of peace. The anti-Treaty riots in Japan were at their peak, and just before Eisenhower's arrival in Okinawa—while he was still in the Philippines—the news was flashed that the Japanese Government had canceled his visit there. It was in this setting of heightened Cold War passions that the President's car headed into Naha. Formations of workers and students began pushing, catcalling, and shoving through the otherwise friendly crowds along the way. The demonstrators, 5,000 strong, waved anti-American placards, shouted "Go Home! Go Home!" and broke through police lines. Then they snake-danced to chants demanding that Okinawa be returned to Japan. The performance became so rowdy that the President's tour through the city was cut short, and while he returned to the airport, American marines went into action to restore order. This was a much stronger demonstration than Okinawa's far left had ever been able to muster before. Organized and carried out by the Council for Reversion to Japan, a front of twenty-one groups dominated by Senaga's People's Party, it showed that much more had been going on under Okinawa's new, exterior calm than had been popularly believed.

Still, despite a continuing danger, the future of the far left in Okinawa seems bleak. Barring the unforeseen, it can go only one way—downhill. The ancient shell of poverty seems to be cracking under the impact of dollar pump-priming and American nudging toward new ways of life. And as poverty recedes and the mother image of Japan blurs with time, those on the far left will have more and more difficulty raising the popular backing they must have to carry out their plans. There is still the possibility that they could hurt the American military forces by a mass strike of organized employees during a period of crisis. A strike of dockworkers, for example, could be particularly troublesome at the wrong moment, but it is doubtful that such efforts could do any serious damage. The former shrill wail for "Reversion to Japan" has subsided considerably as Okinawa's fortunes have become more and more entwined with the American program. Senaga, in failing health, has been left without a major issue to exploit.

There has been no problem of subversion in the Bonin, Mariana, Marshall, or Caroline islands comparable to that in Okinawa. In fact, the situation in the Bonins has been much the opposite. There, a small group of 178 civilians of curious origin want American citizenship; they are descendants of the island's earliest settlers, most of them claiming kinship to Nathaniel Savory, a Massachusetts sailor who arrived in the Bonins in 1830. At that time the Bonins were unclaimed and uninhabited, although their existence was known. A Spanish navigator, Don Ruy López de Villalobos, is said to have sighted the islands for the first time in 1543; a Japanese, Sadayori Ogasawara, visited the Bonins in 1593, and America's Commodore Matthew Perry called at Chichi Jima, largest of the group, in 1853, while on his historic trip to the Orient that resulted in the reopening of Japan to Western commerce. Perry recommended that the United States acquire the islands since it badly needed Far Eastern coaling stations for its ships; but his recommendation was disregarded, and Japan claimed the chain in 1876. It based its action on Ogasawara's visit, and to this day Japan calls them the Ogasawara Islands. The term "Bonin" came into common use as a corruption of a Japanese word meaning uninhabited.

Besides Nathaniel Savory, a Dane, some British, and some Hawaiians settled in the islands in the 1830's, and over the years their descendants mixed with other settlers of Malayan, Japanese, Polynesian, Negro, and Caucasian stock. This little inbred community, bearing such names as Washington, Webb, Robinson, and Gilley, remained distinct from the Japanese immigrants, most of whom, they claim, moved into the Bonins in the 1930's. During World War II, the Japanese moved most of the civilians out, and after the war the United States removed all remaining Japanese. Only the 178 so-called descendants of the original colonizers have been allowed to return. Although they have twice petitioned for American citizenship, technically they remain Japanese citizens. The 7,711 other Japanese Bonin Islanders are still in Japan, a very disgruntled group that periodically presses the government to ask the United States to give them back their homes. The U.S. Government has remained firmly opposed, although it has agreed to pay compensation.

There have been some indications of abnormal curiosity in Japan about what goes on in the Bonins. Some Buddhist and Shinto religious organizations have been particularly persistent in demanding a chance to enter Iwo Jima and reclaim remains of the Japanese soldiers who died in Iwo's caves during the World War II fight for the island. Most of these caves were sealed by bulldozers as the battle progressed. The American authorities did permit Japanese religious services on the island and the erection of a monument to the Japanese who fought so bravely there, but they have sternly refused to let other Japanese visit the island, particularly the caves, some of which are located near a sector of Iwo where activities are classified.

Restrictions against Japanese entry are even more stringent in the U.S. Trust Territories—Japan's former mandated Marshall, Caroline, and Mariana islands. While entry to the Ryukyus has been permitted freely for any Japanese group with a legitimate purpose, and religious services were allowed on Iwo, there has been a total shutdown on Japanese visits to the Trust Territories. Stretched over 3 million square miles of the Pacific, these more than 2,000 islands, archipelagoes, and atolls are held under an American tenure that seems to be going nowhere in particular. Tourists are not allowed, and there has been little effort to develop the islands economically. Their only use has been military, including nuclear testing at Eniwetok and Bikini, and whatever other activities go on behind the navy's tight security screen. Although administration of the islands was turned over to the U.S. Department of the Interior on July 1, 1962, the navy retains control of security arrangements, for the islands remain strategically important from a naval point of view during the present East-West tensions. What their ultimate disposition should be is an open question.

A United Nations committee report to the Trusteeship Council in June, 1961, clearly shows that the United States has made few if any plans concerning their future. The committee said that the United States had done little to encourage economic development, failed to revive island industries the Japanese had started, allowed school buildings to deteriorate, and failed to place any of the native personnel in administrative posts. Actually, the United States has built 164 schools there since 1947 and put virtually all school-age children in classrooms; but the size of its budget for the area—only $6.5 million annually—reveals the lack of any future planning.

In the Cold War, the Japanese home islands and the Ryukyus have already been storm centers of activities that have, as their ultimate objective, the removal of United States' military power from the Far East and the eventual absorption of Japan into the Communist bloc. The Bonins and Trust Territories, kept behind a tight military-security screen, have not been involved, but since they fall within the same geographical and political pattern of conflict that has enveloped Japan proper, they are certain to be dragged into the East-West tug of war sooner or later. They, too, are pawns in the struggle, and Japan's understandable yearning for their return offers the same emotional possibilities for exploitation that the leftists have manipulated so skillfully in the past. Rising nationalism in Japan will keep demands alive that both the Bonins and Ryukyus be returned, and there is no reason to assume that the Trust Territories will not someday be subject to the same type of prodding.

Part Five

JAPAN'S TOMORROW

16. A House Divided

ON A HILL in front of Japan's Diet stands a memorial to the late Yukio Ozaki (1858–1954), Japan's greatest parliamentary leader. It was dedicated on February 26, 1960, a scant three months before the ideological explosion that could have destroyed Japanese democracy. It is perhaps fitting that the figure of this great man, who as Mayor of Tokyo gave America the cherry trees that now line the Tidal Basin in Washington, D.C., should look down over the streets where such chaos reigned for thirty days. His life and his words foreshadowed that crisis and perhaps others that will follow. An unrelenting fighter for human freedom, he thoroughly understood the disciplines, limitations, and responsibilities of self-government and saw long ago that the Japanese were not properly prepared to shoulder them. He once stated that the Japanese did not understand the meaning of the word democracy. "To them, it means license and anarchy," he said. "A bloody civil war may be needed to teach them the worth of the individual."

The riots of May and June, 1960, were not a civil war, and it would be foolish to predict that an internal conflict of such proportions can be foreseen in the years ahead. But the riots were a bloody and shocking civil uprising, and all the forces that made them possible still exist today. All that is needed to start pressures building toward a similar explosion is a new issue that can engender enough anger to enable those with the political know-how to step in and manipulate it to suit their purposes.

As long as this condition exists, Japan will remain far less than a whole nation; it will be incapable of taking its place alongside the other major powers of the world, where it rightly belongs. Because of the present ideological confusion over some of the most basic tenets of its existence—its right to maintain internal order, to defend itself against external attack, to enact and enforce its laws in an orderly manner—Japan is a case of arrested development, half man and half child, incapable of making governmental decisions and carrying them out, particularly in a period of crisis. It can never be sure that an invitation for a foreign guest to visit Japan will not be rejected by riotous mobs, whether that guest be capitalist or Communist. It must forever bear the shame of knowing that pictures of its national Diet members fighting like angry schoolchildren were printed throughout the world. Its public officials must walk in fear of assassination if they dare to follow an unpopular course. Its word in international circles must remain that of a weakened and divided nation that cannot speak with one voice. This is a particularly lamentable situation when one pauses to reflect that these conditions exist in a nation whose economic and scientific accomplishments might otherwise destine it to become the fourth-ranking power in the world—yes, even conceivably the third, if Germany remains divided and China's Communist revolution fails.

What is behind the terrible dissension that has so weakened Japan's nationhood that it remains a house divided against itself? Why did the students and labor unions riot and push Japan so close to that civil war the great liberal Ozaki warned will someday be fought?

The answer is particularly elusive because the normal causes of revolution simply did not exist at that time and still do not exist in Japan. Its elections are reasonably honest, and it is prosperous. Some of the prosperity, although admittedly not nearly enough, is filtering down to the lower levels of society. There are more opportunities for entertainment, advancement in employment, good nourishment, and a stable life than ever before in Japan's history.

Its people and institutions have as much or more freedom than citizens of most democracies.

Still, in spite of these advantages, there is serious unrest in Japan, particularly on the most articulate and intelligent levels of society. Some of the sources of this have already been pointed out: Japan's pacifism; its great, understandable fear of war; its vulnerable economic position; the false image of democracy propagated by the schools and the intellectuals; and the skillful leftist propaganda employed to exploit all of this. But even all these ingredients do not explain the great outpouring of emotion that took place during the riots. To anyone who watched those swaying, chanting columns day after day, it soon became apparent that much more than ordinary unrest or opposition to the Security Treaty was being acted out in the streets of Japan. Obviously, the great mass of the participants had little or no idea of what the Treaty was all about, but a great disgorging of emotions was taking place that had almost a touch of the psychotic in it. Some ocean of inner feeling that had been dammed up for a long time had broken loose and was gushing forth in torrents. Japan, without knowing why, had ripped aside the surface of its social fabric and left a portion of its psyche naked in the public glare.

Dr. Hitoshi Alba, a Tokyo psychologist, who is a member of the International House of Japan, conducted depth interviews with twenty demonstrators and found that with only two exceptions they had no good reason for their antigovernment actions, that they demonstrated for the emotional satisfaction demonstrating gave them. A group of twenty is, of course, far too small a sampling to tell much, but it does suggest the possibility that many demonstrators were in the streets to fulfill some emotional need not necessarily even related to the Treaty.

Finding the source of these emotions is another problem, but there might be a clue in the very revealing analysis of the Security Treaty crisis written by Dr. Masatoshi Matsushita, President of Rikkyo University, in which he spoke of the "call of the blood" between Japan and China. Although his article said much more than he intended, it purported to describe the terrible conflict within the Japanese mind fanned by the necessity for remaining allied with the United States, while having to reject China, to which Japan felt closely bound by tradition, culture, geography, and, as the author put it, "blood" or race. What did he really mean by "call of the blood"? Even if the phrase is as meaningless as I think, there yet remains the weight of centuries of association with China, of common racial and cultural backgrounds, which was suddenly disrupted by events that threw Japan into a close relationship with aliens of a different race and way of life. Not even Dr. Matsushita's formidable education could dispel the emotional distress that this about-face produced in him and, therefore, his analysis.

Let's try another approach—the student demonstrators. They claimed that they were defending democracy, trying to prevent an alliance that meant war. Actually, what they were doing was attacking a decision that had resulted from the democratic process, a majority decision, admittedly made under most unusual circumstances, but approved by a majority of the lawmakers the Japanese people had chosen in free elections. In attacking this decision, they were not acting at all like defenders of democracy. Dr. Shinzo Koizumi, former President of Keio University, has already pointed out the similarity of their conduct to that of the militarists in the 1930's. There seemed to be a great impulse among them to be heroes, not individual but collective heroes, like the young officers in those years preceding World War II. In short, they were fighting against democratic governmental procedures imposed upon them after the war and were responding with methods rooted in Japan's totalitarian past. By their actions, they were at once rejecting the new and supporting the old and familiar. And is this not in essence the nature of the two diametrically opposed forces that disturb Dr. Matsushita? His education and reason tell him that it is best and right for Japan to be associated with the United States in their new Pacific alliance, but since he cannot overcome the strangeness and newness of it, he reveals the misgivings that stem from the emotional ties of the past.

Let's hunt for still another parallel. In 1860, after Commodore Perry's opening of Japan and the long negotiations conducted by the United States' first consul in Japan, Townsend Harris, a treaty of amity and commerce was signed by the two nations. From the moment Perry's ships appeared and for the next several decades, there was serious unrest in Japan over the changes that were being pressed upon the nation. The opening of Japanese ports was bitterly opposed in some quarters; the 1860 treaty was objected to by many groups, and by 1880 some of the ex-samurai were so upset by the great changes sweeping over their land that they formed Japan's first ultranationalist organizations and went all out to restore some of the "values" of the past. So, too, in 1960, when it came time for an independent and sovereign Japan (not the virtually helpless Japan that entered into the original Security Treaty of 1951) to ratify a new alliance with the United States, there was an intense reaction. True, those who launched the anti-Treaty campaign claimed they were upholding parliamentary government and democracy and protecting Japan from a resurgence of the militaristic fascism of its past. But, as we have already pointed out in the case of the students, the demonstrators, regardless of terminology, were employing totalitarian methods from the past, not those of a constitutional democracy. In fact, the emotional storm that ensued was, in effect, a measure of the lack of acceptance of the parliamentary process by thousands of citizens of Japan.

A West German psychologist, Dr. Ingeborg Wendt, has suggested that the riots were at least partly motivated by a psychological revolt against the excessive Westernization that had descended on Japan so rapidly. This is exactly what we have been saying here, that the rioters' targets were a process, decision, and alliance that represented largely what was new in Japan's postwar society, and that that which was new was Western. It seems to me that Dr. Wendt is entirely correct in her approach, and if so, then the source of much of the unrest and pressure that was let off in the 1960 riots is rooted more deeply in psychological strains than in ideological differences—that is, in essence, it represented a revolt against too many things that were new, unfamiliar, and foreign and that were leading Japan down strange new paths that had little relationship to its past. This was true of the new economic ties with the United States, which, as we pointed out earlier, had torn Japan from its traditional trade moorings in Asia and made it possible for Japan to become an ally of the United States and the West. It is also true of the alliance with the United States, which is antithetical to Japan's tradition of proud, independent action—or, at least, to alliances with other Asian nations that Japan had dictated itself.

In this sense, then, the root of Japan's troubles becomes its too rapid thrust into the twentieth century of the Western world. Japan is suffering from indigestion caused by an enforced gorging of Western ideas and concepts. It has had far more pushed down its throat than it has had time to absorb, digest, and adapt to its own special purposes. In the past, Japan has shown an amazing capacity to learn from the West and then embody those ideas in a Japanese framework; but this time there has been too much to absorb in too short a time.

Now let us add one more easily discernible factor to the picture of psychological unrest in Japan—the probable reason why so many people who had no particular interest in the issues were drawn into the riots. The newspapers blossomed with statements of protest against the Kishi Government from people in all walks of life, and these same people poured into the streets, along with the organized demonstrators, to play their part in building up the pressure. It was a form of mass hysteria, of course, but what was behind it? It seems reasonably obvious that the submergence of the Japanese individual is largely to blame. A habit of conformity has historically imprisoned the Japanese with interlocking obligations toward those with whom he is most closely associated. He is supposed to conform to a set pattern and accept group decisions; he who does not conform is rude, and if he dares follow an independent course he is shockingly un-Japanese. In such a strait jacket, the ego of the individual, the desire for self-expression and for recognition, is almost totally suppressed. But when a popular movement such as the anti-Treaty riots develops, there is a magnificent opportunity to perform in front of other people, draw their applause, and gain their approval—something everyone wants in any society. During the demonstrations one could sense that some of the older people pictured themselves in historical roles: Old men stomping along proudly and belligerently, many of them carrying staves in their hands, no doubt saw themselves as reincarnations of samurai of old, en route to a great battle to defend their lord. Here was a socially acceptable way to play the warrior and simultaneously win applause, for they were acting out a dramatic role as deeply rooted in Japan's past as the cowboy is in America's own folklore.

We conclude, therefore, that Japan's internal divisions, however ideological, are rooted in the psychological unrest that stems mainly from Japan's overrapid Westernization and the suppression of the individual. This casts grave doubts on the future of the U.S.–Japanese alliance—a partnership that holds such tremendous promise of lasting value for both nations.

For one thing, it is all too clear that in revolting against the new and the Western, the rioters and those who sided with them—including the majority of the intellectual and articulate members of Japanese society—were not only reacting in an old and familiar pattern, but were also expressing, in effect, a desire to return to the ways of the past. It can be said that, in one sense, the Japanese were demonstrating a desire for a much more authoritarian type of society than they now have.

Such a psychological dilemma bodes ill for the future of Japanese democracy. It could very easily make the Japanese willing victims of a new totalitarianism, as long as that government employed the language and forms of democracy, which remain the symbols to which lip service must be paid. The new totalitarianism would be particularly attractive if it could also incorporate a new type of "Japanism," some new nationalistic trappings that would reflect the masochistic delight Japan has always taken in thinking that it is uniquely different, that the rest of the world misunderstands it, and that it is psychologically isolated from all other nations.

Communism, of course, is such a wolf in sheep's clothing that meets part of the requirements of this formula. It masquerades as a democracy while enforcing a rigid totalitarianism, and it is even conceivable that Communism could be given some special twists that would appeal to the Japanese mind. But at this stage of Japan's postwar development, a Communist take-over does not seem possible. Even the deep undermining of so many levels of Japanese society does not seem to promise enough power for a coup from the far left. Still, the danger from that side must be considered.

The fact that the revolutionary far left in Japan represents only a minority provides no reason to rule out a successful power grab from that direction. Revolutions have historically been carried out by minorities, and at some future period of great internal crisis, particularly if it were a time of economic distress, the Communists could conceivably take over in Japan. Then would arise the great specter of a close alliance or union with Communist China that would upset the entire balance of power in the world today. Japan's industrial genius combined with China's manpower and resources would indeed be a formidable giant in the world of tomorrow. Then add to this the rice-rich areas of Southeast Asia, which such a combine could easily gobble up, and there are the makings of a monster as powerful as either the Soviet Union or the West today. In bringing about such a union, the "call of the blood" would indeed be strong; the old divisions of Oriental against Caucasian might very well come to the fore and create a realignment of alliances that could put a Communist Japan-China combine in opposition to the largely Caucasian Communist world. Would this mean that in such an event the Soviet Union and the United States would become allies? History has played stranger tricks in the past.

But for the moment, as we said, a Communist take-over does not seem possible and the reasons are clear. Since Japan's industrial machinery is tightly controlled by its financiers, not only is it a source of real power but it lies entirely within the conservative camp. The police and the armed forces, too, two other centers of power, at least for the present, also belong to the conservatives. Even in the matter of leadership, the conservatives seem in a far stronger position than the Socialists, whose leadership has been very shortsighted and inept.

In such a situation, then, with the weight of power heavily in favor of the conservatives, what is the likely effect of the explosive ideological and psychological pressures that motivate the left and divide Japan into two warring camps? If the conservatives continue to act as they have in the most recent, leftist-fomented assaults on the government, they are apt to keep backing away from a showdown, hoping to ride out the storm. This, perhaps, is a wise course, for it is a play for time—the great unexploited weapon of history. Time and more time is what Japan needs to work out its internal problems, to ease the burdens of its working people, and to relieve the psychological pressures of over-Westernization. It must have time to assimilate the new Western ideas and to give them a Japanese twist or two that will make them more acceptable to the Japanese mind. It must have time to satisfy the yearnings of its people for more social justice than they have had before. And it must have time to bring about agreement among its people that the Japanese Government has the right to maintain internal order and defend itself against external attack—principles that are now disputed by Socialist beliefs that rioting is a legal form of expressing opposition and that any form of self-defense forces is unconstitutional.

The difficulty is that history seldom gives a nation so much time. And Japan, therefore, under tremendous pressure from both East and West because of its highly strategic position, is much more likely to move from crisis to crisis, which may eventually force the conservative right in Japan to strike back with great force. And when and if this happens, it is apt to sweep away with it much of the democracy and freedom that the Japanese people both casually accept and abuse today. The new government that emerged would almost certainly be much more authoritarian than at present, much closer to what Japan has known in the past, for the conservative right is no more dedicated to democracy than is the radical left.

In such a situation, the alliance with the United States might or might not survive. Even now its future looks dark, for it cannot forever rest on the military bases the United States maintains in Japan. Their days are numbered. It is highly doubtful the bases can be continued—or that it is even desirable that they be continued—beyond the ten-year minimum period of the Security Treaty, which expires in 1970. Then, when the close contact with the United States has been broken for the first time since the end of World War II, Japan will be on her own and have to face up to the realities of nationhood, particularly the unification and defense of her divided population.

All these tests lie ahead for the talented, proud, and long-suffering people of Japan.

Index